MW01249295

Distributors to the trade
in the United States
and Canada:
Watson-Guptill
Publications
1515 Broadway
New York, N.Y. 10036

Distributed throughout
the rest of the world by:
Hearst Publications
International
105 Madison Avenue
New York, N.Y. 10016

Publisher:
Madison Square Press
10 East 23rd Street
New York, N.Y. 10010

Printed in Japan

ISBN 0-8230-5767-4   ISSN   0-942604-12-1

ADLA: 4 CREDITS

DESIGN AND ART DIRECTION	Joan D. Libera
BOOK COMMITTEE	Joan D. Libera Dennis Atkinson Lauren Davidson Trice Walley Karen Ross
PROJECT COORDINATION	Joan D. Libera Dennis Atkinson
PRODUCTION COORDINATION	Dennis Atkinson
TYPOGRAPHY	Andresen Typographics
PHOTOGRAPHY	Roger Marshutz
CONTRIBUTORS	Libera and Associates Andresen Typographics

ADLA:88

Art Directors Club
Los Angeles

The 41st Competition

TABLE OF CONTENTS

PRESIDENT'S LETTER   9

VICE PRESIDENT'S LETTER   11

JUDGES   16

■ AWARDS   25

■ ADVERTISING   59

■ DESIGN   163

■ EDITORIAL   219

■ ENTERTAINMENT   233

▥ INDEX   257

▲ *Library of Congress Selections*

The Show Annual is a chronicle of work judged the best out of more than 4,000 entries which comprised our 1987 competition. It is a reference and record, but more than that, it is an inspiration. . . a springboard for ideas for students and professionals alike.

We celebrated the culmination of the 1987 competition as we have never done before, with both an exhibit and banquet on the night of November 13th. At the same time, we initiated the Art Directors Club of Los Angeles' Lifetime Achievement Award which was presented by Saul Bass to Jack Roberts. It was truly a memorable evening and a milestone in Club history.

It was a personal milestone as well, signaling the conclusion of my first year as Club President; a year which brought into sharper focus, the vitality of the creative community here. It is gratifying to acknowledge that the ADLA competition is truly international in scope.

An interesting aspect of our show is the attention given it by the Library of Congress. Each year, selections are made from the winning entries for their permanent collection. We are only one of two organizations thus honored. In addition, ADLA is participating in the 1988 UK/LA exposition through special invitation—our Show exhibit will be displayed along with the best graphic design of Britain.

Congratulations to those of you who have won this year's accolades. To the judges, who traveled from New York, San Francisco and points in between, thank you for your time and input. And special thanks to those who comprised the Show, Banquet and Book Committees, spending countless volunteer hours to make our competition a success. The result is here in your hands.

Dan Lennon
President

As Creative Director for my own design studio, I am always flattered and excited to be recognized for our work. I can't think of anyone that doesn't get the same charge from the receipt of an award or having work published in a respected annual or journal. As Vice President and chairperson for the 1987 ADLA competition, I have had the happy experience of announcing some of the winners in the show and presenting their awards. This year also marked the beginning of "Best of Show" awards for each general category (Entertainment, Editorial, Advertising and Design) in the competition. It was an honor to present the Entertainment awards as well.

In any judging process, choices between good and excellent are difficult. These decisions are not always purely objective either. In our search for and selection of judges, we choose individuals that are known and respected, not only for their competence and expertise, but also for a sense of style and innovation. I hope that this individual style is reflected in the selections that appear in this year's annual.

Each year, we will continue to have different judges, some established, some brightly shining new stars, each possessing a unique and recognizable personality to their work. In my opinion, it is this variety that makes our judging process (and the resulting exhibition and annual) exciting.

I am also proud that the ADLA annual continues to grow as a "mirror" of national trends, styles and professional achievements. I hope that the exhibition and annual continue in this direction.

I want to thank all of you who entered this year's show for your support. I also want to thank everyone involved with the preparation and successful running of the Judging Weekend and Exhibition.

Good luck with our judges in the 1988 competition. I hope to see you up on the stage next year.

Jeff Spear
Vice President

Gary Valenti
David Ken Tanimoto
Banquet Chairmen

On the evening of November 13, 1987, 400 advertising and design professionals gathered at the Sheraton Grande Hotel to begin the evening by viewing the show exhibit spotlighting the 367 winning entries to be included in this year's ADLA: 4 Show Annual.

At the Awards Banquet Saul Bass took the podium to announce the first ADLA Medal for Lifetime Achievement, honoring Jack Roberts for his contributions to the industry. Carson-Roberts was Los Angeles' largest advertising agency when it merged with O&M in 1971. Mikio Osaki, a past employee at Carson-Roberts, shared slides of Jack's work and escapades.

Toni Hollander and Max Goodrich awarded the First Annual George Rice and Sons Scholarship to Nancy Ogami. She was selected from 55 finalists attending the California State University at Long Beach.

The viewing and presentation of Awards to the top entries in each category followed. There were 51 awards in the four categories: Advertising, Graphic Design, Editorial and Entertainment; four entries were awarded best of show.

Our thanks to those who attended for their continued support, to the hard-working banquet committee, under the direction of Gary Valenti, for their successful efforts, and to the Van Noy Design Group for making the Show possible.

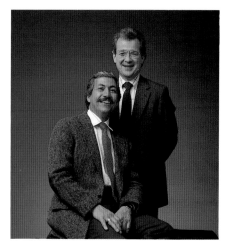

The Van Noy Group
Sam Beeson
Joe Huizar
Show Committee

VOLUNTEERS

Glenda Alcott	Terry Irwin
Sam Beeson	Bill Kent
Michael Bernstein	Steve Kimura
Mike Burke	Sachi Kuwahara
Irene Chen	Carolyn LaLiberte
Joanne Cheng	Dan Lennon
Joe D'Anna	Al Levey
Gerry Diaz	Roger Marshutz
Virgil Elsner	Jim Marrin
Nan Faessler	Marcia Mosko
Brian Fennessey	Mary McCormick
Tim Finkas	Gayle Miller
Kathy Fitzpatrick	Victoria Miller
Robin Garland	Jonah Nadler
Katherine Go	Lisa Levin Pogue
Pauline Green	Booker Rinder
Laura Gruenther	Judy Seckler
Eric Handell	Rhonda Senduka
Lauren Harger	Laurel Shoemaker
Mark Harmel	Karen Sketch
Dana Herkelath	Jeffrey Spear
Leah Hoffmitz	Gary Valenti
Toni Hollander	Jim Van Noy
Joe Huizar	Petrula Vrontikis
John Kawa	Amy Way
Tamara Keith	Hedi Yamada

Leah Hoffmitz
Judging
Chairperson

VOLUNTEERS

Glenda Alcott	Dana Herkelath
Mike Armijio	Leah Hoffmitz
Ruth Berman	Mark Harmel
Karen Birch	Terry Irwin
Linda Bowen	Bill Kent
Lynn Bradley	Tamara Keith
Doug Brotherton	Steve Kimura
Ann Burdick	Sachi Kuwahara
Eugene Cheltenham	Carolyn LaLiberte
Yee Ping Cho	Dan Lennon
Mandy Crespin	Al Levey
Kurt Devinny	Roger Marshutz
Lloyd Der	Jim Marrin
Richard Docter	Marcia Mosko
James Duffin	Mary McCormick
Anne Eichelberger	Victoria Miller
Sue Eck	Jonah Nadler
Bruce Ecker	Lisa Levin Pogue
Marc Eisenman	Booker Rinder
Ted Engelbart	Judy Seckler
Christine Ferguson	Rhonda Senduka
Dina Foug	Laurel Shoemaker
Jan Gartenberg	Karen Sketch
Ilan Geva	Jeffrey Spear
Mark Gilmore	Gary Valenti
Robin Garland	Jim Van Noy
Pauline Green	Petrula Vrontikis
Laura Gruenther	Amy Way
Eric Handell	Hedi Yamada

The 41st Annual ADLA Show was judged on August 22–23, 1987. This year's judging was an impressive, grueling and exhilarating event. The process is spaced over a two day period. Entries are catalogued and organized for viewing, by category. Editorial and Entertainment, our two newest categories, took up one day, while the Advertising and Design categories, because of the quantity of entries and numerous subcategories, took up two days—one for video and slides, the other for print. Scores for the 4,005 entries were tallied and entered into a computer to determine the finalists in each group, and award winners were selected from the finalists by our judges.

The judging ran smoothly thanks to the help of many volunteers. ADLA VP Show Chairman, Jeff Spear, along with the show committee members, worked to make sure that nothing was overlooked, and that every detail and deadline was met.

Joan D. Libera
Art Direction

BOOK COMMITTEE
Dennis Atkinson
Lauren Davidson
Joan D. Libera
Karen Ross
Trice Walley

This year's book, ADLA: 4, is the third full-color, hard bound volume of the Art Directors Club annual competition. A dedicated team of designers worked to compile this year's annual. Using the format established for ADLA: 2, the team streamlined the process to make the system even more efficient.

The ADLA wishes to thank everyone who participated in the making of ADLA: 4, from the art directors and designers who entered the competition to the judges who selected the work, and especially those people listed here.

KEITH BELLOWS
Knoxville, TN
Vice President/Executive Editor
Whittle Communications

"One thing editorial art directors should do is not follow trends, but follow their audience."

CASEY CLAIR
Los Angeles, CA
V.P. of Print Advertising
West Coast at CBS

"Get an overview of what you're doing or plan to do . . . You need to know the whole process to contribute."

JOE DUFFY
Minneapolis, MN
The Duffy Design Group

"If there's one thing that kills the opportunity to do design, more than anything else, it's greed."

JUDY GARLAN
Knoxville, TN
Art Director
The Atlantic Monthly

"I'm most flattered when the
writer likes what we've done with
the art."

ROBIN GHELERTER
Los Angeles, CA
Creative Director
Hi-Tops Video

" . . . there's got to be a purpose
behind it [the marketing]; we are
trying to sell something."

JERI HEIDEN
Los Angeles, CA
Vice President / Creative Director
Warner Bros. Records

"What I look for is freshness. I
don't respond well to ugliness . . .
there [should be] a category called
'Good-Bad' where something is
intentionally bad—where it's so
bad it's wonderful."

ADVERTISING   *ENTERTAINMENT*   *ADVERTISING*

CHERYL HELLER
Boston, MA
President / Creative Director
Heller Breene

"I like things that aren't pretentious
. . . things that can inspire and
amuse and entertain."

MARTIN HESELOV
Los Angeles, CA
V.P. of Creative Advertising
Atlantic Entertainment

"You've got to put yourself into the
position of the public."

R. LYNN LIVINGSTON
Newport Beach, CA
President
Cochrane Chase Livingston

"I like to see . . . that we haven't lost
the concept of advertising, which
really is communication . . . that
we don't just get enamored of the
design."

SAM MACUGA
Washington, D.C.
President / Creative Director
Sohigian / Macuga

"Money is a short term motivator
. . . long term motivation comes
from the real sense of fulfillment
and enjoyment that you get in
this industry."

JAYME ODGERS
Los Angeles, CA

"One needs to be a real pioneer
spirit to create exceptional work
that stands apart from mere good."

KEN PARKHURST
Los Angeles, CA
President
Ken Parkhurst and Associates

"We have an image conscious
society that values image over
substance."

EDITORIAL   *EDITORIAL*   *DESIGN*

MARY SHANAHAN   FRED WOODWARD   TAMOTSU YAGI
New York, NY   *New York, NY*   *San Francisco, CA*
Art Director   *Art Director*   *Art Director*
GQ Magazine   *Rolling Stone Magazine*   *Esprit*

"I think for editorial, it's critical to   "Try and get as much information   "Real design is a creative endeavor
have a journalistic instinct."   about what you're doing as you   based on thousands of personality
                                            can."   details that become one's personal
                                                                                 style."

BERNARD REILLY
Curator
Library of Congress

This is the third year that the Library of Congress has made selections for its Permanent Collection from the ADLA Competition.

The Art Directors Club of Los Angeles provides one of the two sources in the country utilized by the Library for this purpose.

The Collection's Curator, Mr. Bernard Reilly, returned to Los Angeles to evaluate the entries based on typography and the book arts, including illustration, layout and other visual aspects of printing. He considered not only design excellence and originality but documentary significance, i.e. how a particular piece (or series) reflects societal values, trends and attitudes.

As last year, Mr. Reilly noted that building the national collections along these lines enables the Library to provide students, publishers, scholars, filmmakers and general researchers with a resource which is unmatched anywhere else in the country. .

Readers can identify the Library's selections by the ▲ symbols throughout the book.

Year after year, ADLA is supported by the generosity of many businesses. They contribute money, time, talent, creativity and moral support. Once again we thank all of them for their superb commitment to our organization and to our profession.

SPEAKERS

Mike Hicks
Hixo, Inc.

Primo Angeli
Primo Angeli, Inc.

Mario Donna
Keye/Donna/Pearlstein

Rex Peteet & Don Sibley
Sibley/Peteet Design, Inc.

Cheryl Heller
Heller Breene

Andrew Tomcik
Graphic Design Consultant
Design Educator

John Van Dyke
Van Dyke Company Designers

CONTRIBUTORS

Alpha Graphix
Andresen Typographics
Apple Computer, Inc.
B&G House of Printing
Capco Type
Donahue Printing Co., Inc.
Dupont Design Technologies, Inc.
Fox River Paper Co.
Ilan Geva
Gillian Gough
Mark Harmel Photography
Hopper Paper Co.
Mike Hough
Jetgraphix
Bill Kent
Kirk Paper
Linda Lennon
Lennon and Associates
Janet Levinson
David Levy Lithography
Libera and Associates
Cris Loudahl/Downtown Exposure
Scott Mednick & Associates
Gayle Miller
Mitsui Comtek Corp.
David Nakashita
Noland Paper Company
George Rice & Sons
Karen Ross/J.B. West & Associates
Simpson Paper Co.
Gary Valenti
Van Noy Group
Dennis Yurosek/Music Productions

AWARDS

ART DIRECTOR
Jim Berte
DESIGNER
Jim Berte
PRODUCER
Robert Miles Runyan
& Associates
DIRECTOR
Robert Miles Runyan
WRITER
Client
PHOTOGRAPHERS
Peter Kane
Cynthia Moore
CLIENT
Mead Paper
AGENCY/STUDIO
Robert Miles Runyan
& Associates
PRODUCTION COMPANY
Robert Miles Runyan

ART DIRECTOR
John Van Dyke
DESIGNER
John Van Dyke
WRITER
Bill Hays
PHOTOGRAPHERS
Terry Heffernan
Cliff Fiess
CLIENT
Weyerhaeuser
Paper Company
AGENCY/STUDIO
Van Dyke Company

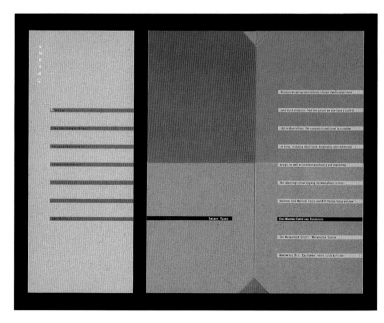

ART DIRECTOR
Ken White
DESIGNER
Lisa Levin
WRITER
Aileen Farnan
CLIENT
Cole Martinez Curtis
AGENCY/STUDIO
White & Associates

ART DIRECTOR
Mitchell Mauk
DESIGNER
Mitchell Mauk
WRITERS
Mitchell Mauk
Damien Martin
Raymond Burnham Jr.
CLIENT
Entertainment
Technologies
AGENCY/STUDIO
Mauk Design

ART DIRECTOR
Gwyn Smith
DESIGNERS
Kit Hinrichs
Niel Shakery
WRITER
John Dreyfuss
ACCD Development
PHOTOGRAPHERS
Jim Blackley
Steven A. Heller
CLIENT
Art Center College
of Design
AGENCY/STUDIO
Pentagram
▲

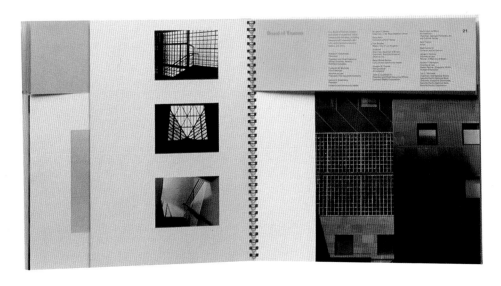

ART DIRECTORS
Tracey Shiffman
Roland Young
DESIGNER
Tracey Shiffman
PRODUCER
Kerry Buckley,
Director of Development,
MOCA
WRITER
Tom Pope
PHOTOGRAPHERS
R. Young
G. Mudford
D. Parker
D. Keeley
Squidds & Nunns
CLIENT
The Museum of
Contemporary Art
AGENCY/STUDIO
Tracey Shiffman
Roland Young Design
Group

ART DIRECTOR
James Sebastian
DESIGNERS
James Sebastian
Rose Biondi
INTERIOR DESIGNER
William Walter
PHOTOGRAPHER
Bruce Wolf
CLIENT
Martex/West Point
Pepperell
AGENCY/STUDIO
Designframe, Inc.
▲

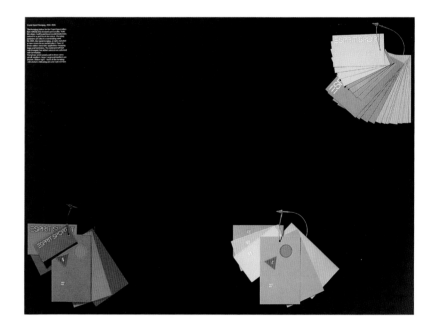

ART DIRECTOR
Tamotsu Yagi
DESIGNER
Tamotsu Yagi
PHOTOGRAPHERS
Robert Carra
Oliviero Toscani
CLIENT
Esprit Graphic Design
Studio
AGENCY/STUDIO
Esprit Graphic Design
Studio
PRODUCTION COMPANY
Nissha Printing
Company, Ltd.
▲

Best of Show

ART DIRECTOR
Kit Hinrichs
DESIGNER
Kit Hinrichs
WRITER
Delphine Hirasuna
PHOTOGRAPHER
Barry Robinson
ILLUSTRATOR
Various Historical
CLIENT
Pentagram Design
AGENCY/STUDIO
Pentagram Design

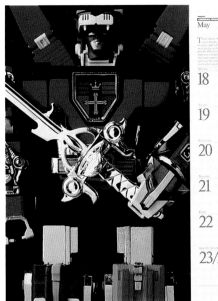

ART DIRECTOR
Kit Hinrichs

DESIGNERS
Kit Hinrichs
Gwyn Smith

WRITER
Peterson & Dodge

PHOTOGRAPHER
Terry Heffernan

CLIENT
American President
Companies

AGENCY/STUDIO
Pentagram Design

ART DIRECTOR
John Coy

DESIGNERS
John Coy
Kevin Consales

WRITER
Charles Labiner

PHOTOGRAPHER
COY, Los Angeles
& Richard Noble

ILLUSTRATOR
Scott Baldwin

CLIENT
Georgia Pacific Paper
Company

AGENCY/STUDIO
COY, Los Angeles

ART DIRECTOR
John C. Reger
DESIGNER
Dan Olson
CLIENT
Business Week
AGENCY/STUDIO
Design Center

ART DIRECTORS
Terence Mitchell
Yee-Ping Cho
DESIGNER
Yee-Ping Cho
WRITER
Various
PHOTOGRAPHERS
Jay Venezia
Chris Morland
CLIENT
Community
Redevelopment Agency
AGENCY/STUDIO
In-house

ART DIRECTOR
Kit Hinrichs
DESIGNER
Kit Hinrichs
WRITERS
Delphine Hirasuna
Steve Heller
PHOTOGRAPHERS
Michele Clement
Terry Heffernan
Barry Robinson
CLIENT
American Institute of
Graphic Arts
AGENCY/STUDIO
Pentagram Design

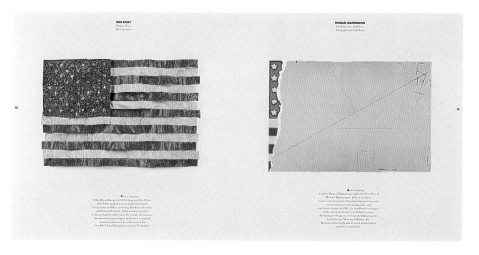

ART DIRECTOR
Cheryl Heller
DESIGNER
Cheryl Heller
WRITER
Peter Caroline
PHOTOGRAPHERS
Herb Ritts
Myron
CLIENT
S.D. Warren
AGENCY/STUDIO
Heller Breene

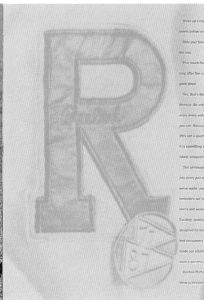

ART DIRECTOR
Cheryl Heller
DESIGNER
Cheryl Heller
WRITER
Jerry Cronin
PHOTOGRAPHER
Herb Ritts
CLIENT
Reebok
AGENCY/STUDIO
Heller Breene

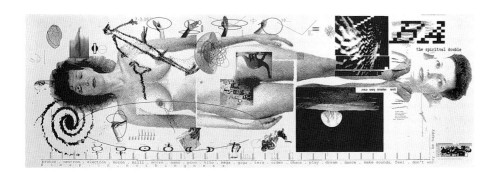

ART DIRECTOR
April Greiman
DESIGNER
April Greiman
PRODUCER
April Greiman
WRITER
April Greiman
PHOTOGRAPHER
Computer Graphic:
April Greiman
ILLUSTRATOR
Videographer:
April Greiman
CLIENT
Walker Art Center
AGENCY/STUDIO
April Greiman, Inc.

ART DIRECTOR
Primo Angeli
DESIGNERS
Primo Angeli
John Lodge
ILLUSTRATOR
Mark Jones
CLIENT
Lucca Delicatessen, Inc.
AGENCY/STUDIO
Primo Angeli, Inc.

ART DIRECTORS
Vance Studley
Stephen Levit
Lynn Easley
Suzanne Haddon
Trina Carter
Scott Allen
Ginny Egan
Jill Jacobson
Stacy Miereanu
Wendy Chism
Teal Rocco
Sean Ehringer
Jeff Hopfer
Sheri Myers Olmon
Nora Piibe
Charbel Bousraitt
DESIGNER
Vance Studley
WRITER
Edgar Allan Poe
CLIENT
Art Center College
of Design
AGENCY/STUDIO
ACCD Typography Class

ART DIRECTOR
Paul Pruneau
DESIGNERS
G. Chadwick
L. Sutton
R. Vaughn
PRODUCERS
Dorene Meadows
A. Kelley
J. Moran
WRITERS
Rich Binell
Mark Doyle
Eric Stouffer
Doug Gotthoffer
PHOTOGRAPHERS
K. Merfeld
P. Matsuda
T. Landecker
CLIENT
Apple Computer, Inc.
AGENCY/STUDIO
Apple Creative Services
PRODUCTION COMPANY
Apple Creative Services

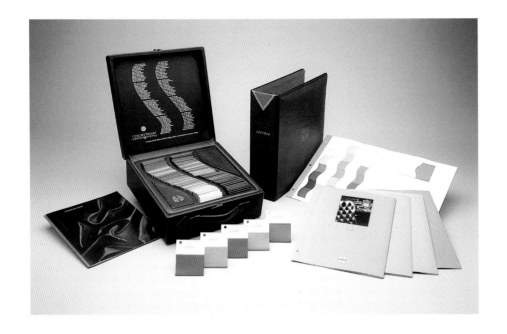

ART DIRECTOR
Dan Lennon
DESIGNERS
Joe Voltaggio
Dan Lennon
WRITER
Linda Lennon
CLIENT
Lackawanna
AGENCY/STUDIO
Lennon and Associates

ART DIRECTORS
Randall Hensley
Tom Bazzel
DESIGNERS
Tom Bazzel
Diana DeLucia
Randall Hensley
CREATIVE DIRECTOR
Randall Hensley
WRITERS
Robert S. Byer
Karen Wander
ILLUSTRATORS
Soren Arutunyan
Carol Ferrante
CLIENT
IBM Entry Systems
Division / P. Armstrong /
L.D. Green / M. Psaras
AGENCY/STUDIO
Muir Cornelius
Moore, Inc.

ART DIRECTOR
Randy Hipke
DESIGNERS
Randy Hipke
Brad Jansen
Keith Kaminski
CLIENT
Paramount Network
Television
AGENCY/STUDIO
5 Penguins Design, Inc.
PRINTER
A&L Graphico

ART DIRECTOR
Tamotsu Yagi

DESIGNER
Tamotsu Yagi

CLIENT
Esprit de Corp

AGENCY/STUDIO
Esprit Graphic
Design Studio

PRODUCTION COMPANY
Georgia Pacific

ART DIRECTOR
Tamotsu Yagi

DESIGNER
Tamotsu Yagi

CLIENT
Esprit de Corp

AGENCY/STUDIO
Esprit Graphic Design
Studio

PRODUCTION COMPANY
Nissha Printing Co., Ltd.

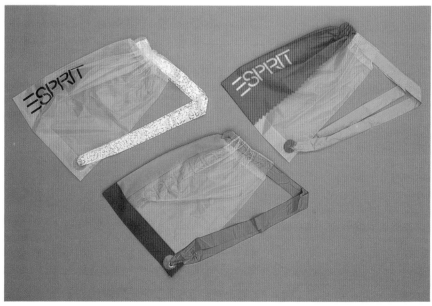

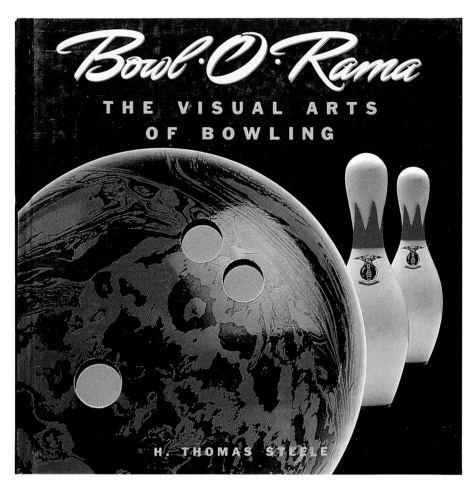

ART DIRECTOR
Tommy Steele

DESIGNER
Tommy Steele

WRITER
Tommy Steele

PHOTOGRAPHERS
Tommy Steele
Dennis Keeley

CLIENT
Abbeville Press, Inc.

AGENCY/STUDIO
SteeleWorks Design, Inc.

Best of Show

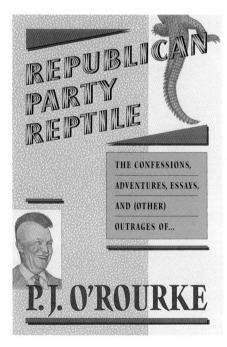

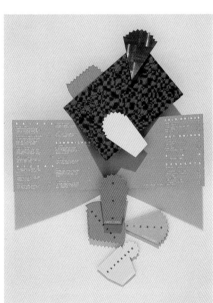

ART DIRECTOR
Robin Schiff

DESIGNERS
Keith Sheridan
Marie Barab
Craig Warner

ILLUSTRATOR
Kevin Sprouls

CLIENT
Atlantic Monthly Press

AGENCY/STUDIO
Keith Sheridan
Assoc., Inc.

ART DIRECTOR
Tamotsu Yagi

DESIGNER
Tamotsu Yagi

CLIENT
Esprit de Corp.

AGENCY/STUDIO
Esprit Graphic Design
Studio

PRODUCTION COMPANY
Menu:
Charles Douglas
Printing, diecutting
shape:
Golden State Embossing
Company, Inc.

ART DIRECTORS
Bob Kuperman
Melinda Kanipe
Rich Bess
DESIGNERS
Rich Bess
Bob Kuperman
Melinda Kanipe
CREATIVE DIRECTORS
Bob Kuperman
Pacy Markman
WRITER
Pacy Markman
CLIENT
Drug Free America
AGENCY/STUDIO
DDB Needham
Worldwide Los Angeles
PRODUCTION MANAGER
Barry Brooks

ART DIRECTOR
Rod Dyer
DESIGNER
Harriett Baba
WRITER
Tommy Steele
PHOTOGRAPHERS
Tommy Steele
Jim Heimann
CLIENT
Abbeville Press, Inc.
AGENCY/STUDIO
Dyer/Kahn, Inc.

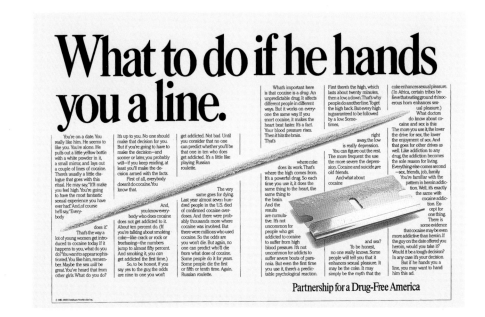

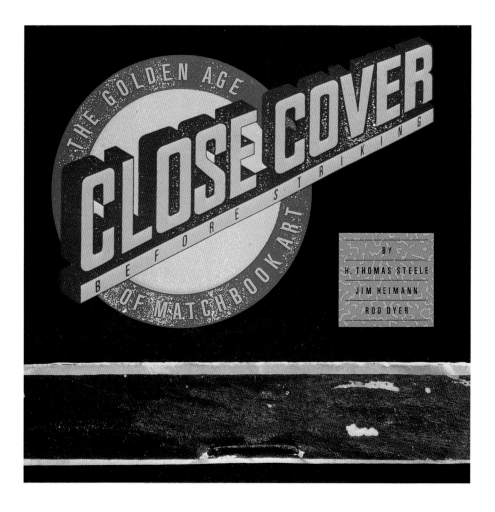

It can sing like Caruso, talk like Barrymore and calculate like Einstein.

Our newest Apple will be unveiled September 27th. You've never seen–or heard–anything quite like it.

It can play Beethoven, the stock market and eighteen holes of golf.

Our newest Apple will be unveiled September 27th. You've never seen–or heard–anything quite like it.

It can paint like Kandinski, play like Paderewski, and teach you who both of them are.

At noon today, your authorized Apple dealer will unveil the new Apple IIe Personal Computer. You'll want to be there. Because you've never seen–or heard–anything quite like it.

ART DIRECTOR
Yvonne Smith
DESIGNER
Yvonne Smith
PRODUCER
Joe Sosa
DIRECTOR
Steve Hayden
WRITER
Steve Hayden
Laurie Brandalise
CLIENT
Apple Computer, Inc.
AGENCY/STUDIO
BBDO
▲

ART DIRECTOR
Gunther Maier
DESIGNER
Gunther Maier
WRITER
Ted Baker
PHOTOGRAPHER
Jeff Zwart
CLIENT
Mercedes-Benz of
North America, Inc.
AGENCY/STUDIO
McCaffrey and McCall
▲

THE MERCEDES-BENZ 190 CLASS: NO MATTER HOW HARD YOU DRIVE, YOU NEVER LEAVE CIVILIZATION BEHIND.

You did not expect it to be this way, pounding over a remote back road peppered with unexpected dips and turns and unvisited by the county road crew for the better part of a decade.

You should feel tentative; instead, you feel elated. The 190 Class sedan executes its moves with calm exactitude, as if it were an athlete who had trained many years for precisely this event. And in fact, Mercedes-Benz engineers had just such a road in mind as they tuned their ingenious multi-link independent rear suspension concept, over five arduous years, on the special test vehicle depicted above. Their aim – to blend the handling surety of a Formula One racing car with the riding comfort of a Mercedes-Benz. You marvel that the drama visible through the windshield has so little apparent effect on the car. You flow through curves. Bumps lose their sting. Civilization is preserved.

All the while the cabin remains uncannily quiet, engine noise only a muted hum from behind a double firewall. The telltale sounds of a car being punished are not in evidence—no squeaks, rattles or groans, body and chassis held in rigid unity by 4,000-plus individual welds and sinews of high-strength, low-alloy steel. Endowed with such a constitution, the 190 Class sedan can run a gauntlet like this and barely seem challenged.

Even the atmosphere in the cabin is civilized, the climate kept cool and fresh by microprocessor control. Your seat is so comfortably supportive, so subtly contoured to your body that you no longer consciously think about it. As you brake and downshift and steer through turns, every move comes so easily and naturally that you almost sense a cooperative intelligence working with you—an impression the engineers have cultivated through relentless attention to ergonomic details.

The stop sign ahead signals that you are coming up on the smooth, predictable main highway. In another car, you might feel relieved. But now you feel a little downhearted. Until you remember that later today, you will come this way again.

Engineered like no other car in the world

THE MERCEDES-BENZ 300 CLASS: MICROCHIPS, SPATIAL KINEMATICS, ERGONOMICS AND THE HUMAN SPIRIT.

The suspension elements interacted in perfect geometric harmony. The engine's microprocessor intelligence network functioned flawlessly. Every equation balanced; the computer screens could go blank at last. The 300 Class was clearly destined to be the most technologically advanced series of automobiles ever built by Mercedes-Benz.

Then came the most critical phase of development. Engineers slipped into a fleet of prototype 300 Class sedans. Set off in search of every conceivable driving extreme. And themselves became the test instruments—even more sensitive and discerning than those they left behind in their laboratories.

It was during long autobahn treks, protracted Alpine climbs, in the searing heat of the American West and bitter Arctic cold that the six-cylinder engines proved their mettle—thriving under adversity, forging an unprecedented blend of speed and silence. Corkscrew mountain passes and corrugated gravel paths vindicated the engineers' inspired application of spatial kinematics—a multilink independent rear suspension that promoted quick, sure handling without sacrificing the fabled Mercedes-Benz ride. On slick downhill grades and snow-covered turns, the Anti-lock Braking System (ABS) turned potential drama into controlled, unruffled stops. And the technology proved not only remarkably advanced, but remarkably reliable as well.

All of which might have satisfied less ambitious engineers. But to these engineers, the triumphs of technology were only a platform from which to reach higher. To nudge the 300 Class closer to perfection.

So they continued to drive, to record their impressions, to rework their formulas. And in the process, the seats became subtly more supportive. Handling, even more reassuringly predictable. Steering, so responsive that it seemed "connected directly to your optic system," as one journalist would later put it. And by gradual, painstaking steps, a very advanced design evolved into a full-fledged Mercedes-Benz.

The effort consumed eight long years, but no engineer would begrudge an hour of that time. Because now the familiar saying, "Nothing feels like a Mercedes-Benz," means more than it ever has before.

Engineered like no other car in the world

MANY AUTOMOBILE MAKERS ITCH TO BUILD THE PERFECT CAR. THE MERCEDES-BENZ S-CLASS IS PROOF THAT SOME SIMPLY ITCH MORE THAN OTHERS.

It is a curious fact that not everyone who seeks the very best in a large sedan is fully aware of just how much sedan this entitles today's buyer to demand.

Some still opt for the overbearing "luxury" sedan in all its bulk and ostentation, unaware that big today can also mean fast, agile and responsive. Somewhat better off are those who have moved up to vivid big-sedan performance—but then go no further.

Then there are those who choose the sedans of the S-Class. The Mercedes-Benz overview is their overview: a large sedan—sufficiently well engineered—can balance triple-digit performance with hushed driving ease. Agile handling with an unruffled ride. The fragrance of leather upholstery and the richness of handworked woods with the tactile pleasures and keen precision of a true driver's car.

And the rewards that follow are theirs to enjoy every mile: swift and sure-footed automotive travel on vast highways and unpaved byways alike. Experienced amid sumptuously comfortable surroundings. And in a blissful state of near silence.

The rewards continue—because the S-Class is, after all, built by Mercedes-Benz. And thus is welded, brazed, filed, sanded, polished and nit-picked to completion along an assembly route lined with enough inspections (and inspectors) to make this the most demanding trip of its life, if not any car's life. The S-Class aims not only for the glamour of high technology, but also the reassurance of high technological reliability. And reflects almost fifty years of basic Mercedes-Benz safety research and engineering.

You can choose from three S-Class sedans—the 560 SEL and 420 SEL V-8s, and the stunning six-cylinder 300 SDL Turbo. Their character subtly differs from one to another; their blend of high performance and high driving civilization differs from all other large sedans in the world.

Engineered like no other car in the world

"PIE IN FACE"

MAN: Most paper plates will hold up to maybe one serving of pie.

SFX: (WHOOSH)

MAN: After that, they become soggy…
…and limp.

But Good Sense plastic plates stay rigid and don't leak.

SFX: (WHOOSH)

MAN: So you can go back for seconds.

SFX: (WHOOSH)

MAN: And thirds.

SFX: (WHOOSH)

ANNCR: Good Sense plastic plates. The best things you'll ever throw out.

SUPER: The best things you'll ever throw out.

ANNCR: By the way, we also make plastic cups.

ART DIRECTOR
Peter Cohen

DESIGNER
Peter Cohen

PRODUCER
Rachel Novack

DIRECTOR
Mark Story

WRITER
Larry Spector

CLIENT
Webster Industries—
Good Sense

PRODUCTION COMPANY
Story, Guliner, Piccolo
Prod.

AGENCY/STUDIO
Levine, Huntley, Schmidt
& Beaver

Best of Show

Most birds fly south for winter

Wimps!

In fact, we're having a special Winter Festival

at Sea World

All for $4.95 for adults and $3.95 for kids.

Such a deal.

WINTER FESTIVAL AT SEA WORLD
Nov. 28 – Dec. 24
Discount coupons at McDonald's.

That's why Murray's here.

He's my agent.

ART DIRECTOR
Jean Robaire
CREATIVE DIRECTOR
Bob Kuperman
PRODUCER
Shannon Silverman
DIRECTORS
Jean Robaire
John Stein
WRITER
John Stein
DIRECTOR OF PHOTOGRAPHY
Peter Brown
CLIENT
Sea World-Ohio
AGENCY/STUDIO
DDB Needham
Worldwide Los Angeles
PRODUCTION COMPANY
Hand Held Productions

"WINTERFEST"

SFX: Various shots of penguins on screen throughout making noises (as if speaking).

"DOG"

Open on beautiful park at dusk. Dog is lying in center.
Close-up of dog.
Slow move in as dog begins to dig a hole.
Dog digging deeper. Move in continues.
Dog no longer visible.
We see book in tunnel.
Move in tight on book as it closes.
NBC logo.
ANNCR: Discover the Wonder.
Monday nights on *NBC.*

ART DIRECTOR
Rick Boyko
PRODUCER
Richard O'Neill
DIRECTOR
Ken Davis
WRITER
Jaime Seltzer
CLIENT
Amblin Entertainment
PRODUCTION COMPANY
RSA Films
AGENCY/STUDIO
Chiat/Day Advertising
▲

ART DIRECTOR
Tony Lamonte

SENIOR CREATIVE DIRECTOR
Charlie Miesmer

CREATIVE DIRECTOR
John Greenberger

PRODUCERS
B. Mullins
K. O'Brien
A. Chinich

DIRECTOR
Steve Horn

WRITERS
Micheal Shevack
Charlie Miesmer

CLIENT
Apple Computer, Inc.

AGENCY/STUDIO
BBDO

PRODUCTION COMPANY
Steve Horn, Inc. N.Y.

"LEFT BRAIN/RIGHT BRAIN"

ANNCR: Imagine a brain whose left side is as brilliant as its right. A brain as artistic as it is logical. That can create. As well as calculate. Such a brain exists...in the remarkable new Apple IIGS.

Brilliant graphics, brilliant color, brilliant sound.

To help you use both sides of the most personal computer of all...your mind.

"FENCE COMBO"

MAN: Hey, y'know what? Somebody told me that there was Penguin's in my neighborhood, so I built this small but effective fence. I found out that this Penguin's stuff is frozen yogurt. Can you believe it? No threat at all. Hope it don't have no fishy taste.

ANNCR: Penguin's. Tastes like ice cream. About half the calories.

MAN: Remember me, with the fence? You know how they make Penguin's yogurt? A big walrus comes in and squeezes the little suckers' neck. (Laughs) See ya Tuesday.

Penguin's. Locations everywhere.

ART DIRECTOR
Jordin Mendelsohn

PRODUCER
Michelle Miller

DIRECTOR
Norman Seeff

WRITERS
Jordin Mendelsohn
Perrin Lam
Jim Boelse

CLIENT
Penguin's Frozen Yogurt

AGENCY/STUDIO
Mendelsohn/
Zein Advertising

PRODUCTION COMPANY
Richard Marlis
Productions

PRODUCERS
Karl Fischer
Vicki Halliday

DIRECTOR
Fred Petermann

WRITERS
Phil Dusenberry
Ted Sann

CLIENT
Apple Computers, Inc.

AGENCY/STUDIO
BBDO

PRODUCTION COMPANY
Petermann/Dektor

*SENIOR CREATIVE
DIRECTOR*
Ted Sann

CREATIVE DIRECTOR
Phil Dusenberry

"POWER IMAGES"

ANNCR: Think of all the power on this earth…
The power of nature and human endurance…
The power of spirit…and then realize that of
all this power…and speed…and determination
…none is more potent than the power that
resides within the minds of us all…The power
to learn…to communicate…to imagine…to
create…the power to be your best.

"FENCE I"

MAN: How are ya. Y'know what, I found out that there was these Penguin's in my neighborhood, so I built this small but effective fence. Y'know what, I found out that Penguin's was frozen yogurt. Can you believe it? Somebody lied to me.

Penguin's. Tastes like ice cream. About half the calories.

ART DIRECTOR
Jordin Mendelsohn

PRODUCER
Michelle Miller

DIRECTOR
Norman Seeff

WRITERS
Jordin Mendelsohn
Perrin Lam
Jim Boels

CLIENT
Penguin's Frozen Yogurt

AGENCY/STUDIO
Mendelsohn/
Zein Advertising

PRODUCTION COMPANY
Richard Marlis
Productions

ART DIRECTOR
Rick Strand (SF)

PRODUCER
Gene Lofaro

DIRECTOR
Joe Pytka

WRITER
Cynthia Franco (SF)

CREATIVE DIRECTOR
Alex Cichy (SF)

CLIENT
Apple Computer, Inc.

AGENCY/STUDIO
BBDO

PRODUCTION COMPANY
Pytka Prod. (LA)

"THE REPORT"

MAN 1: Yes, I know but…I understand, but I still want our attorneys to handle it. Fine.

MAN 2: Isn't that thing settled yet?

MAN 1: It looks like it's going to drag on forever. What do you think of Jensen's report?

MAN 2: It looks okay.

MAN 1: Okay?

MAN 2: Alright, it looks terrific; what do you want me to say? This is great work.

MAN 1: I thought so, too.

MAN 2: It's nice to see our computer system is finally earning its keep.

MAN 1: I wish that were true.

MAN 2: What do you mean?

MAN 1: Marketing isn't using our system anymore.

MAN 2: They're not? Then how did they do this?

MAN 1: They did it on their own system, the one they got a month ago.

MAN 2: They put this together in a month?

MAN 1: Well, not quite Frank, they did it in a week.

SUPER: (APPLE® LOGO)
Macintosh.® The power to be your best.

"THE RED-EYE"

(V.O.): Uh, this is the Captain again; we now expect to arrive at Kennedy Airport at around 6:40am.

MAN 1: I see you've got homework, too.

MAN 2: It never ends; you'd think when you get to this point things would get easier.

MAN 1: Yeah, I know—that looks like that was quite a project.

MAN 2: Yeah, it was. Have a look, no trade secrets here.

MAN 1: Thanks. Impressive. I wish we could do work like this, but we have to crank it out every week.

MAN 2: We do ours every week.

MAN 1: Well, we can't afford to farm ours out, we have to do them on a computer.

MAN 2: We did this on our computer.

MAN 1: You did that on a computer?

MAN 2: Of course, if we farmed them out I couldn't afford to ride up here.

SUPER: (APPLE® LOGO)
Macintosh® The power to be your best.

ART DIRECTOR
Rick Strand (SF)

CREATIVE DIRECTOR
Alex Cichy

PRODUCER
Gene Lofaro

DIRECTOR
Joe Pytka

WRITERS
Cynthia Franco
Steve Diamant

CLIENT
Apple Computer, Inc.

AGENCY/STUDIO
BBDO

PRODUCTION COMPANY
Pytka Prod. (LA)

ART DIRECTORS
Rick Boyko
Laura Della Sala
PRODUCER
Francesca Cohn
DIRECTOR
Jeff Gorman
WRITER
Richard Kelley
CLIENT
Foster Farms
PRODUCTION COMPANY
Johns + Gorman Films
AGENCY/STUDIO
Chiat/Day Advertising

"BARBECUED CHICKEN"

SUPER: (FOSTER FARMS® LOGO) You can't argue about the chicken.

MAN: For the best barbecued chicken, you don't need any fancy sauces. All you need is a little salt and pepper. Some fresh, plump chicken. Make sure the coal's just right. You need to know when to put the chicken on. And exactly when to take it off. *(CHUCKLES)* There's no doubt about it. I make the best barbecued chicken there is. But, you can ah, see that for yourself.

ANNCR. V.O.: You can argue about the recipe but you can't argue about the chicken. Foster Farms.

"MOTHER-IN-LAW"

DAUGHTER: My husband John loves my Chicken Parmesan. It's the best. First take fresh, plump chicken breasts, and cut them in half.

MOTHER-IN-LAW: Uh-huh, quarters.

DAUGHTER: Then, add garlic and oregano.

MOTHER-IN-LAW: Parsley and basil.

DAUGHTER: But what makes it, is fresh parmesan.

MOTHER-IN-LAW: Shredded mozzarella. That's how I always made it for my Johnny.

DAUGHTER: That's why your son Johnny's living with me now.

ANNCR: You can argue about the recipe. But you can't argue about the chicken. Foster Farms.

ART DIRECTORS
Rick Boyko
Laura Della Sala
PRODUCER
Francesca Cohn
DIRECTOR
Jeff Gorman
WRITER
Richard Kelley
CLIENT
Foster Farms
PRODUCTION COMPANY
Johns + Gorman Films
AGENCY/STUDIO
Chiat/Day Advertising

ART DIRECTORS
Rick Boyko
Laura Della Sala
PRODUCER
Francesca Cohn
DIRECTOR
Jeff Gorman
WRITER
Richard Kelley
CLIENT
Foster Farms
PRODUCTION COMPANY
Johns + Gorman Films
AGENCY/STUDIO
Chiat/Day Advertising

"TWO AUNTS"

AUNT #1 You want good chicken you don't need no foreign recipes. All you need is my Chicken Dumplings. Now first you get fresh plump chicken, you boil it, and let it steam. And then you make your dumplin's you put it in. Now that's Chicken Dumplin's. And everybody thinks it's the best. Mm. Mm. Mm.

AUNT #2: Mm, Mm Uh.

ANNCR.: You can argue about the recipe. But you can't argue about the chicken. Foster Farms.

**It was the
first summer
after college**

**I was living with her
in an old rundown
apartment near
Harvard Square**

**We'd sit up at night
and play the radio**

**And talk about
how we'd spend our
life together**

**I always think of her
when that song comes on**

But I never tell my wife

WMJX
106.7 FM
We play the great songs

"HARVARD SQUARE"

(MUSIC THROUGHOUT)
James Taylor Sings:
Fire and Rain.

ART DIRECTOR
Keith Lane
PRODUCER
Wendy Schwartz
WRITER
Michael Fortuna
Eric Haggman
CLIENT
WMJX FM Radio
PRODUCTION COMPANY
Vizwiz / Soundtrack
AGENCY / STUDIO
Emerson Lane Fortuna
▲

My husband and I
are in the middle of
an incredibly stupid
argument.

I mean we are
really losing it.

All of a sudden
God puts this song
on the radio.

Stopped us right
in our tracks.

I went out and
bought the album.

106.7

We play the great songs

ART DIRECTOR
Keith Lane
PRODUCER
Wendy Schwartz
WRITER
Michael Fortuna
Eric Haggman
CLIENT
WMJX FM Radio
PRODUCTION COMPANY
Vizwiz / Soundtrack
AGENCY/STUDIO
Emerson Lane Fortuna
▲

"ARGUMENT"

(MUSIC THROUGHOUT)
Dionne Warwick Sings:
That's What Friends Are For.

8 pounds, 6 ounces.

10 fingers, 10 toes.

We have a daughter.

I left the hospital
to meet my brother
for a beer.

The radio in the bar
has this song on.

Another miracle.

"TEN FINGERS, TEN TOES"

(MUSIC THROUGHOUT)
Stevie Wonder Sings:
Isn't She Lovely.

ART DIRECTOR
Keith Lane
PRODUCER
Wendy Schwartz
WRITER
Michael Fortuna
Eric Haggman
CLIENT
WMJX FM Radio
PRODUCTION COMPANY
Vizwiz / Soundtrack
AGENCY / STUDIO
Emerson Lane Fortuna
▲

PRODUCER
Craig Murray
DIRECTOR
Robert Jahn
AGENCY/STUDIO
Walt Disney Studio
▲

VO EDDIE: "He's got . . ."
Vince looking straight toward camera.
VO EDDIE: ". . . the eyes, . . ."
Vince makes a shot on pool table; camera pans to left along cue stick as cue ball hits other racked balls.
VO EDDIE: ". . . he's got the stroke, . . ."
Vince holding cue stick up and kissing it.
VO EDDIE: ". . . he's got the flake."
Vince kissing Carmen.
CARMEN: "This is the best."
Up angle Carmen and Vince as he takes his cue stick and mimics a Ninja warrior in battle then making the "kill."
Vince looking toward camera.
VO EDDIE: "You gotta . . ."
Vince's cue stick case; camera pans up to reveal Vince's face; he turns.
VO EDDIE: ". . . resource here, . . . a thoroughbred, . . ."
Reverse angle; Carmen and Eddie.
EDDIE: ". . . you make him feel good, I teach . . ."
Reverse angle; Eddie and Carmen.
EDDIE: ". . . him how to run."
Low angle as Vince breaks a rack of balls on the pool table.

Down angle; Eddie about to break rack of balls; camera zooms in on cluster.
Eddie hitting cue ball.
Vince and Eddie at pool table as cue ball hits racked balls.
VO MAN: "Let's see some Eddie legend action."
Carmen and Eddie.
EDDIE: "I want his best game."
Vince.
VINCE: "You want my game? You couldn't deal with my game Jack, you're out manned."
Carmen and Eddie.
EDDIE: "I'm gonna beat him you know."
Vince looking down.
VINCE: "What makes you so sure."
Eddie at pool table; he rises to face Vince.
Cue stick hitting cue ball in slow-motion.
Nine ball as camera zooms in on it.
Vince, Carmen and Eddie.
EDDIE: "Do you smell what I smell?"
VINCE: "Smoke?"
CARMEN: "Money."
Red title animates over black b.g.

"PLATOON"

PICTURE: B&W photo of Oliver Stone with members of his platoon in Vietnam slowly zooms back against black, then jungle canopy with rays of sunlight dissolves in. Montage of the men of Platoon in battle and behind the lines follows—set to "Tracks of My Tears."

AUDIO: In 1967, Oliver Stone was a combat infantry man in Vietnam. During his tour he received a bronze star for gallantry. Ten years later in Hollywood he was picking up an Oscar for the screenplay of MIDNIGHT EXPRESS.

Now he has another story to tell, a movie that grew out of his own experience.

Stone has come a long way from Vietnam, but he has not left it behind.

SONG: "Tracks of My Tears."

The first real casualty of war is innocence.
The first real movie about the war in Vietnam is *PLATOON.*

CREATIVE DIRECTORS
Charles O. Glenn
Michael Kaiser

ART DIRECTORS
Tony Silver
Larry Lurin
Sam Alexander

WRITERS
Tony Silver
Michael Kaiser
Charles O. Glenn

PRODUCERS
Barbara Glazer
Linda Habib

DIRECTOR
Tony Silver

EDITOR
Barbara Glazer

STUDIO/PRODUCTION COMPANY
Tony Silver Films, Inc.

CLIENT
Orion Pictures
Corporation

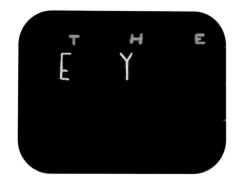  

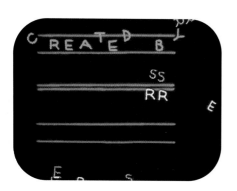  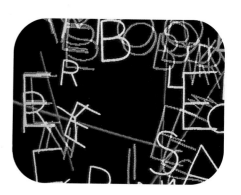

ART DIRECTOR
Gabor Csupo

DESIGNER
Jeffrey Townsend

PRODUCER
Margot Pipkin

DIRECTOR
Gabor Csupo

MUSIC
George Clinton

ANIMATION
Bill Hedge

ANIMATORS
David Blum
Gabor Csupo

CLIENT
Fox Broadcasting

AGENCY/STUDIO
Gracie Films

PRODUCTION COMPANY
Klasky Csupo, Inc.

 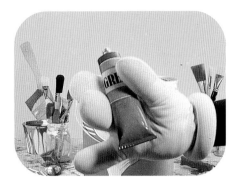 

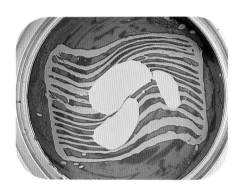 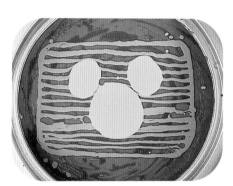

ART DIRECTORS
Michael Nichols
Carl Willat

DESIGNERS
Michael Nichols
Carl Willat
Heather Selick

PRODUCER
Chris Whitney

DIRECTORS
Carl Willat
Heather Selick

PHOTOGRAPHERS
Melissa Mullin
John Gazdik

CLIENT
The Disney Channel

AGENCY/STUDIO
Direct

PRODUCTION COMPANY
Colossal Pictures

Best of Show

ADVERTISING

ADVERTISING

NEWSPAPER

ART DIRECTORS
David Fox

PRODUCER
Ruby Polnau

WRITER
Jerry Fury

PHOTOGRAPHER
Tom Berthiaume

CLIENT
North Memorial
Medical Center

AGENCY/STUDIO
Clarity Coverdale Rueff

ART DIRECTOR
Jac Coverdale

PRODUCER
Ruby Polnau

WRITER
Jerry Fury

PHOTOGRAPHER
Jim Arndt

CLIENT
YMCA—Metro

AGENCY/STUDIO
Clarity Coverdale Rueff

ART DIRECTOR
Chip Kettering

PRODUCER
Dean Pasch

WRITER
Ed Lottero

PHOTOGRAPHER
Jay Fries

ILLUSTRATORS
Bob August
Joel Levirne

CLIENT
Mexicana

AGENCY/STUDIO
J. Walter Thompson

ART DIRECTOR
Chip Kettering

PRODUCER
Dean Pasch

WRITER
Ed Lottero

PHOTOGRAPHER
Panuska

ILLUSTRATORS
Bob August
Joel Levirne

CLIENT
Mexicana

AGENCY/STUDIO
J. Walter Thompson

In an unpredictable world,
there are still some things
you can count on.

NEWSPAPER

ART DIRECTOR
Andy Dijak
WRITER
Phil Lanier
PHOTOGRAPHER
Dennis Ashlock
CLIENT
Porsche Cars
North America
AGENCY/STUDIO
Chiat/Day Advertising

ART DIRECTORS
Andy Dijak
John Vitro
WRITERS
Phil Lanier
John Robertson
ILLUSTRATOR
Richard Leech
CLIENT
Porsche Cars
North America
AGENCY/STUDIO
Chiat/Day Advertising

ART DIRECTOR
David Bartels
DESIGNER
Chuck Hart
WRITER
Donn Carstens
PHOTOGRAPHER
Bill Vuksanovich
ILLUSTRATOR
Master Typographers
CLIENT
Bartels & Carstens
AGENCY/STUDIO
Bartels & Carstens

ART DIRECTORS
Robert Prins
Greg Harrison
DESIGNER
Ed Segura
WRITER
Bob Wilson
PHOTOGRAPHER
Lamb & Hall
Photography
CLIENT
So. Calif. Honda Dealers
Association
AGENCY/STUDIO
Robert Elen & Associates

ADVERTISING

NEWSPAPER

ART DIRECTOR
Beth McConnell

WRITER
Susan Lee

PHOTOGRAPHER
Cycle News

CLIENT
Yamaha Motor
Corp., USA

AGENCY/STUDIO
Chiat/Day Advertising

ART DIRECTOR
Kathy Grubb

DESIGNER
Kathy Grubb

WRITER
Chip Willis

CLIENT
Gray Baumgarten
Layport, Inc.

AGENCY/STUDIO
Sundown Studios

If you want to see who finished second, stare at this page for thirty minutes.

DRIVE DRUNK AND THE BEST PARKING SPOTS IN TOWN COULD BE YOURS.

ART DIRECTORS
Robert Prins
Greg Harrison

DESIGNER
Ed Segura

WRITER
Bob Wilson

PHOTOGRAPHER
Lamb & Hall
Photography

CLIENT
So. Calif. Honda Dealers
Association

AGENCY/STUDIO
Robert Elen & Associates

You can buy a cheaper car, but can you afford the cost?

Southern California Honda Dealers
As dependable as the cars we sell.

ART DIRECTOR
John Vitro

WRITER
John Robertson

PHOTOGRAPHER
Paul Gersten

CLIENT
Foster Farms

AGENCY/STUDIO
Chiat/Day Advertising

You won't believe your ears, either.

What makes our Christmas package so attractive is this lovely green paper.

The power to be your best.

How to get people who work together to work together.

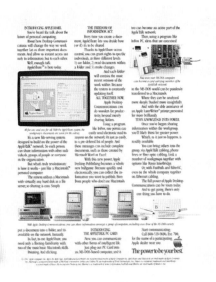

The power to be your best.

THE ACURA LEGEND WOULD COMPARE EQUALLY TO A MERCEDES 560 SEC IF ONLY IT WASN'T MISSING A $40,000 PART.

ACURA

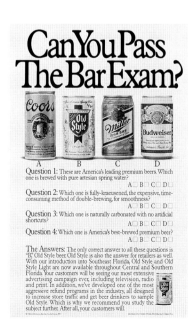

Can You Pass The Bar Exam?

ADVERTISING

NEWSPAPER

ART DIRECTORS
Pam Cunningham
Laura Della Sala

WRITERS
Steve Rabosky
David Lubars
Ed Cole

CLIENT
Fox Broadcasting

AGENCY/STUDIO
Chiat/Day Advertising

Tape this to your television screen to improve the picture until Sunday night, April 5th.

*NEWSPAPER
CAMPAIGN*

ART DIRECTOR
Jerry Gentile

DIRECTOR
Bob Kuperman

WRITER
Barbara DeSantis

CLIENT
Cigna Healthplan

AGENCY/STUDIO
DDB Needham
Worldwide Los Angeles

PRODUCTION COMPANY
Paul Newman:
Production Manager

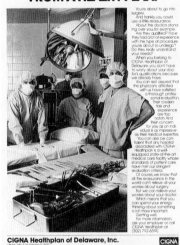

AT A TIME LIKE THIS THERE'S ONLY ONE BENEFIT YOU WANT FROM A HEALTH PLAN.

CIGNA Healthplan of Delaware, Inc.

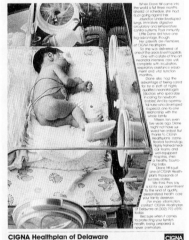

DIANE HILL SPENT SIX MONTHS IN HER MOTHER'S WOMB. AND TWO MONTHS IN OURS.

CIGNA Healthplan of Delaware

AT CIGNA HEALTHPLAN, TREATING HEART DISEASE ISN'T ALWAYS A MAJOR OPERATION.

CIGNA Healthplan of Delaware, Inc.

NEWSPAPER
CAMPAIGN

ART DIRECTORS
Robert Prins
Greg Harrison

DESIGNER
Ed Segura

WRITER
Bob Wilson

PHOTOGRAPHER
Lamb & Hall
Photography

CLIENT
So. Calif. Honda
Dealers Association

AGENCY/STUDIO
Robert Elen & Associates

Let's hope that in the long run, you hold up as well.

Buying a new car is a little like falling in love. Whether you'll feel the same a year or so later
depends on the car you buy.
If it's a Honda, your passion will very likely continue to burn bright. Because as you probably
already know, a Honda is as famous for maintaining its value as it is for reliability.
So, take care of both yourself and your Honda, and the two of you can live happily ever after.

Ⅲ Southern California Honda Dealers
As dependable as the cars we sell.

You can buy a cheaper car, but can you afford the cost?

The low price of certain new cars can turn out to be the start of something big. As repair bills mount, along with your blood pressure, you wonder what kind of deal you really got.
To calculate the true long-term cost of a car, add maintenance and repairs to what you paid for it. Then subtract the resale price. That's when the old truth will hit home about getting what you pay for.
Happily, you get plenty when you buy a Honda.

For starters, there's Honda's legendary reliability. Plus, Hondas have a demonstrated history of performance that lower priced upstarts do not.
When it comes time to sell, if you can bear to part with your Honda, the facts and figures are on your side. Hondas retain their value better than most cars on the road.
If you'd like to know what Honda owners themselves think about their Hondas, consider this.

In 1986, Honda owners rated their Hondas #1 in the prestigious Customer Satisfaction Index. Honda was also rated #1 in customer loyalty, as it has been year after year after year.
Those are two of the reasons why in 1986 Honda was also #1 in import nameplate passenger car sales.
So if you're in the market for a new car, yes, you can find one cheaper than a Honda.
And that's exactly what you'll get.

Ⅲ Southern California Honda Dealers
As dependable as the cars we sell.

In an unpredictable world, there are still some things you can count on.

Mom. Your blue blazer. Aunt Bessie's apple strudel. Your best friend. Your Honda Civic.

Ⅲ Southern California Honda Dealers
As dependable as the cars we sell.

NEWSPAPER
CAMPAIGN

ART DIRECTOR
Jac Coverdale

PRODUCER
Ruby Polnau

WRITER
Jerry Fury

PHOTOGRAPHER
Jim Arndt

CLIENT
YMCA—Metro

AGENCY/STUDIO
Clarity Coverdale Rueff

Add on a new family room.

With a family membership to the YMCA, you don't have to do any remodeling. Yet you create all kinds of room for family entertainment. Like swimming, youth sports, racquetball, aerobics, Nautilus, and family programs.

YMCA

See less of your family.

When you get a family membership to the YMCA, you'll end up seeing more of your family even though there'll actually be less of them to see.

YMCA

How to be a role model instead of a roll model.

Let's face it, healthy habits start at a young age. So set a good example for your kids by getting a family membership to the YMCA.

YMCA

It can play Beethoven, the stock market and eighteen holes of golf.

Our newest Apple will be unveiled September 27th.
You've never seen—or heard—anything quite like it.

It can paint like Kandinski, play like Paderewski, and teach you who both of them are.

At noon today, your authorized Apple dealer will unveil the new Apple IIes Personal Computer.
You'll want to be there. Because you've never seen—or heard—anything quite like it.

It can sing like Caruso, talk like Barrymore and calculate like Einstein.

Our newest Apple will be unveiled September 27th.
You've never seen—or heard—anything quite like it.

Apple and the Apple logo are registered trademarks of Apple Computer, Inc.

NEWSPAPER
CAMPAIGN

ART DIRECTOR
Yvonne Smith
DESIGNER
Yvonne Smith
PRODUCER
Joe Sosa
DIRECTOR
Steve Hayden
WRITER
Steve Hayden
Laurie Brandalise
CLIENT
Apple Computer, Inc.
AGENCY/STUDIO
BBDO
▲

ADVERTISING

NEWSPAPER
CAMPAIGN

ART DIRECTOR
Richard Crispo

WRITER
Martin MacDonald

PHOTOGRAPHER
Bo Hylen

ILLUSTRATOR
Randy Glass

CLIENT
American Hondamotor
Company, Inc.

AGENCY/STUDIO
Ketchum Advertising

LAST WINTER WAS EUROPE'S WORST IN A CENTURY. SPRING BROUGHT AN EVEN BIGGER PROBLEM.

It rolled in with force enough to rival that of nature. Like the best of a renaissance creation, making its mark on science and art. As Europe shuddered even while the weather turned warm.

And so the Acura Legend coupe made its entrance with the spring. Heralded immediately in the United States with the Motor Trend Magazine Import Car of the Year award.

All to the great consternation of those fine automakers who have become accustomed to dominating the luxury sports coupe market. And who may have spent a little too much of the winter in hibernation.

From a distance, the coupe's beauty is readily apparent. Meticulous styling. Grace in the line. And on closer look, the pleasure increases. The studied attention to ergonomics puts every driving decision at your fingertips, while the L-option package envelopes you in plush leather. A turn of the key and you are poised to command the kind of power and performance not often associated with luxury this complete.

The Acura Legend coupe's 4-valve technology, programmed fuel injection and variable intake manifold enables the 2.7 liter V-6 to produce 161 horsepower at 5900 rpm. Its 0 to 60 time is 8 short seconds, with a track tested top speed of 134 miles per hour.

Enough to recommend it very highly. But since we were then in the process of redefining the world class luxury sports coupe, we had to go further. Far beyond what was merely expected.

A case in point, the new L-option Anti-Lock Braking (ALB) system. In even the most inclement weather, on even the most recalcitrant roads, it prevents wheel lockup during severe braking. And at the same time, helps to retain stability and steering control. But superior braking under every condition is only part of the coupe's technological finesse. Innovations in handling have been just as substantial.

An independent double wishbone system, front and rear, results in a tenacious suspension. The kinks are taken out of the most twisted mountain roads as you are treated to the same stability you'll feel on a straightaway.

All of which goes toward creating a fairly substantial problem for Europe. Because when a luxury sports coupe is this formidable, nothing is able to undermine its performance. Not even the worst of winter.

Or the best of Europe.

Test drive the Acura Legend coupe exclusively at your Acura dealer. Call 1-800-TO ACURA for the location of the dealer nearest you.

ACURA
PRECISION CRAFTED AUTOMOBILES
A division of American Honda Motor Co., Inc.

HOW TO AVOID THE EUROPEAN COMMON MARKET.

In this modern day and age, there seems to be more than one European automobile manufacturer that trades on its reputation rather than its pure engineering know-how.

Granted, these autobahn autocrats produce their share of luxury cars. And yes, they do have a propensity to charge dearly for the marque. Not to mention the service.

Happily, there now exists a viable alternative. Introducing the Acura Legend sports coupe. Motor Trend Magazine's Import Car of the Year.

Its styling is truly classic. Its appointments, beyond reproach. Its price, starting around $22,000.

The Legend coupe's 2.7 liter fuel injected 24-valve V-6 produces 161 horsepower.

And with a track test speed of 134 miles per hour, words like "quick" and "fast" begin to sound like mere understatement.

The Legend sports coupe provides an environment for the driver that could only be designed by enthusiasts. The white on black analog gauges remain easily and constantly within your field of vision. The controls at your fingertips. And in our luxurious L option package, finest leather abounds. There's also a power driver's seat, a driver information center with the ability to monitor eight separate functions, and a very protective anti-theft system.

As you'd expect, the Legend sports coupe also offers handling features that make those inviting, lonely country roads take on new character, new meaning. Fully independent front and rear double wishbone suspension. Rack and pinion steering. And to prevent wheel lock-up during severe braking, Honda's own Anti-Lock Braking (ALB) system is available.

This system also helps you to retain stability and steering control in the event of a panic stop.

The Acura Legend sports coupe. As they put it at Motor Trend Magazine, "This is the best blend of innovation, performance and fun-to-drive we have seen in almost a decade."

With the arrival of the award-winning Acura Legend sports coupe, the European tradition is broken. Through technological innovation and stylized sophistication, it keeps you well ahead of the status quo. Both literally. And figuratively.

Test drive the new Acura Legend sports coupe exclusively at your Acura dealer.

Call us at 1-800-TO-ACURA for the location of the dealer nearest you.

ACURA
PRECISION CRAFTED AUTOMOBILES
A division of American Honda Motor Co., Inc.

There is no second place.

At Acura, a new division of American Honda, we respect technology that exemplifies precision. We salute the drive and determination that make for a superior product. We understand what motivates those who set out, often against overwhelming odds, to win.

In other words, our hat's off to those who are contending for the America's Cup. Those who know, that in the pursuit of excellence, there is no easy way.

You see, we have set some extremely tough, very demanding standards for ourselves. Standards based on a philosophy that precision craftsmanship neither comes easy nor cheap; excellence is something you strive for.

Whether it's building automobiles, racing yachts, or a business relationship.

A prime example, the Acura Legend V-6 shown here was engineered around the basic ideas that a luxury sedan can be both fast and quiet. In this case, a 0 to 50 time of 6.1 seconds. And an interior noise level at 55 mph almost equal to that of the main reading room of the New York City Public Library.

Then there's the Acura Integra. Its 16-valve DOHC engine and programmed fuel injection are both descended from the engine technology used in our Formula 1 racing program.

Had we let anything but precision craftsmanship set our standards, had we decided to take the easy way out, there would be no Legend or Integra.

On that note, we salute you, the men and women who are pursuing America's Cup. The men and women, who, in chasing precision, are pursuing excellence. We salute you and your quest for America's Cup.

Test drive the Acura Legend and Integra exclusively at your Acura dealer.

Call 1-800-TO-ACURA for the location of the dealer nearest you.

ACURA
PRECISION CRAFTED AUTOMOBILES
A division of American Honda Motor Co., Inc.

MAGAZINE

ART DIRECTOR
John O'Brien
DESIGNER
John O'Brien
WRITER
Lissa Walker
ILLUSTRATOR
Mike Hashimoto
CLIENT
Capitol Records, Inc.
AGENCY/STUDIO
Capitol Records, Inc.

I'm not asking for a father.
Just a friend.

BIG BROTHERS OF GREATER LOS ANGELES.

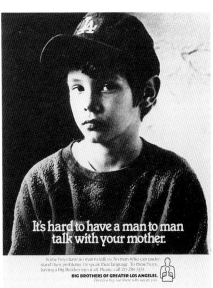

It's hard to have a man to man
talk with your mother.

BIG BROTHERS OF GREATER LOS ANGELES.

ART DIRECTOR
Kathy Sjogren
CREATIVE DIRECTOR
Peter Coutroulis
WRITER
Cary Sacks
PHOTOGRAPHER
Stock—IBID
CLIENT
Big Brothers of
Greater Los Angeles
AGENCY/STUDIO
DJMC, Inc.

ART DIRECTOR
Kathy Sjogren
CREATIVE DIRECTOR
Peter Coutroulis
WRITER
Cary Sacks
PHOTOGRAPHER
Stock—IBID
CLIENT
Big Brothers of
Greater Los Angeles
AGENCY/STUDIO
DJMC, Inc.

MAGAZINE

ART DIRECTOR
David Heise

DESIGNER
David Heise

PRODUCER
Nancy Williams

WRITER
Pieter Reeves

PHOTOGRAPHER
David Rawcliffe

CLIENT
ARCO

ENGRAVER
Mission Engraving, Inc.

AGENCY/STUDIO
Kresser, Craig/D.I.K.

ART DIRECTOR
Rony Herz

DESIGNER
Rony Herz

WRITER
Richard Gamer

CLIENT
IBM Corp.

AGENCY/STUDIO
Lord, Geller, Federico,
Einstein, Inc.

CREATIVE DIRECTOR
Arthur Hecht

DESIGNER
Jeff Cohen

ART DIRECTOR
Jeff Cohen

WRITER
Paula Mermelstein

ILLUSTRATOR
Dave Frankel

CLIENT
NBC Corporate Relations

AGENCY/STUDIO
NBC (In-House)

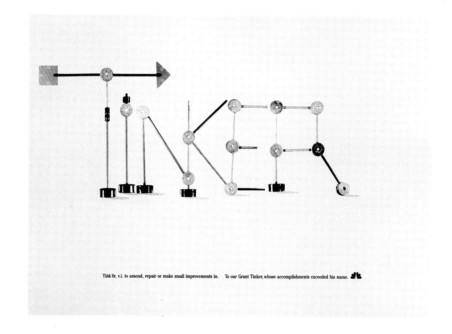

ART DIRECTOR
Jill Kohut

PRODUCER
Nancy Williams

WRITER
Wendi Knox

PHOTOGRAPHER
Ron Avery

CLIENT
ARCO/
LA Central Library

PRODUCTION COMPANY
1312 Productions

AGENCY/STUDIO
Kresser, Craig/D.I.K.

ART DIRECTOR
Cheryl Heller

DESIGNER
Cheryl Heller

WRITER
Jerry Cronin

PHOTOGRAPHER
Herb Ritts

CLIENT
Reebok

AGENCY/STUDIO
Heller Breene

MAGAZINE

ART DIRECTOR
Tracy Wong
DESIGNER
Tracy Wong
WRITER
Mike LaMonica
PHOTOGRAPHER
Chuck LaMonica
CLIENT
Le Menu Frozen Foods
AGENCY/STUDIO
Ogilvy & Mather

ART DIRECTOR
Marten Tonnis
WRITER
Steve Rabosky
PHOTOGRAPHER
Bo Hylen
CLIENT
Mitsubishi Electric
Sales America
AGENCY/STUDIO
Chiat/Day Advertising

ART DIRECTORS
Bob Kuperman
Melinda Kanipe
Rich Bess
DESIGNERS
Bob Kuperman
Melinda Kanipe
Rich Bess
CREATIVE DIRECTORS
Bob Kuperman
Pacy Markman
WRITER
Pacy Markman
CLIENT
Drug Free America
AGENCY/STUDIO
DDB Needham
Worldwide Los Angeles
PRODUCTION MANAGER
Barry Brooks

HOGAN. NOT JUST CLUBS FOR BETTER PLAYERS, BUT CLUBS TO MAKE ANY PLAYER BETTER.

In 1953, Ben Hogan began his equipment company because he believed that he could design and manufacture better clubs than were then available.

In the 34 years since, Hogan clubs have earned a singular reputation for quality and performance that makes them among the most sought-after clubs in the world.

Unfortunately, they've also become known as clubs exclusively for "better players."

An understandable mistake, given Ben Hogan's own legendary playing status, and the Ben Hogan Company's long association with the PGA Tour through our tour blades.

But, in fact, for the past several years, we've offered an excellent choice of clubs for golfers of all handicaps willing to make a serious investment in their games.

At Hogan, we offer this selection because we believe quality and sound design are fundamental to better and more consistent golfing. Or, as Mr. Hogan puts it, with the right equipment, a player of any skill level can improve.

In 1987, the "right equipment" includes Apex, our traditional irons and persimmon woods preferred by low handicap and scratch golfers. Also Radial, our popular cambered-sole, easy-to-hit club. And Magnum, our most forgiving club ever, for golfers who want to put more good hits in every round.

You see, Hogan clubs aren't exclusively for the better player. But they're an excellent idea if you'd like to work on becoming one.

Ask your pro about the right Hogan club for your game.

Hogan

NOW YOU CAN MAKE 1898 FACES IN ONE HOUR.

Our new washless 721 photo system prints 79 rolls in one hour.

Actually, it can do 79 rolls and 2 prints an hour. But why quibble. It is very, very fast. In more ways than one.

Thanks to new rapid access chemistry, its dry-to-dry time is just 20 minutes and 20 seconds.

You might think that our new minilab is so fast you'd have to run around like crazy just to keep up. Well, you're terribly mistaken.

Because the new 721 does just about everything all by itself.

It automatically turns itself on, replenishes the chemistry, senses the film size, threads the paper, sorts the prints and prices the orders.

It even automatically dead-heats if you happen to know what that is.

Toot-a-lu problem negatives.

The 721 comes with a built-in color negative scanner. So you don't have to think twice about compensating for dominant colors. Back-lit scenes. Incandescent or fluorescent lights. Or flash shots against a dark background. In other words, you always get terrific prints. No matter who's running your system.

Our new lab handles everything from disc to 120. It also switches between 3½-, 4- and 5-inch paper in less than five minutes. And you still get our reliable self-support drive mechanism.

You'd figure a minilab that can do all of the above would be as big as your average Winnebago.

Actually, it has a footprint of just 38 square feet. That's about the same size as some photo systems with half its capacity.

What about all those EP-2 fans out there? Well, we've got something terrific for them, too.

Introducing the 713.

Our new 713 photo system has all the features of the 721. Except it's a little bigger. Uses standard EP-2 chemistry. And prints 71 rolls an hour. That's over 1700 faces.

Just like all of our equipment, the 721 and 713 come with the best support in the industry. And that's not just our opinion. In a recent Photo Marketing Association *Photaphinion* poll, we ranked highest in customer service satisfaction. We also had the fewest hours of down time.

Want to know more about our new minilabs? Well, don't just sit there with a silly look on your face.

Give us a call at (714) 521-9040. Or send us this coupon.

Please tell me more about the 713 and 721 photo systems.

Name

Company

Address

City

State

Zip

Phone

Noritsu America
Corporation
6900 Noritsu Ave.,
Buena Park, CA
90622-5039

THE 700 SERIES BY NORITSU.

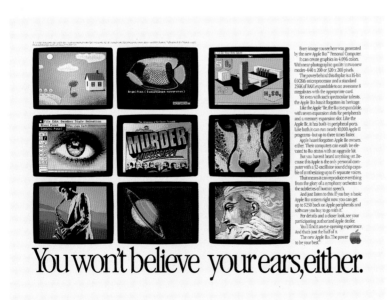

Every image you see here was generated by the new Apple IIGS™ Personal Computer.

It can create graphics in 4,096 colors. With new photographic quality in two new modes—640 x 200 or 320 x 200 pixels.

The power behind this display is a 16-bit 65C816 microprocessor and a standard 256K of RAM, expandable to an awesome 8 megabytes with the appropriate card.

Yet even with such spectacular talents, the Apple IIGS hasn't forgotten its heritage.

Like the Apple IIe, the IIGS is expandable with seven expansion slots for peripherals and a memory expansion slot. Like the Apple IIc, it has built-in peripheral ports. Like both, it can run nearly 10,000 Apple II programs—but up to three times faster.

Apple hasn't forgotten Apple IIe owners, either. Their computers can easily be elevated to IIGS status with an upgrade kit.

But you haven't heard anything yet. Because this Apple is the only personal computer with a 32-oscillator sound chip capable of synthesizing up to 15 separate voices.

That means it can reproduce everything from the glory of a symphony orchestra to the subtleties of human speech.

And just listen to this: If you buy a basic Apple IIGS system right now you can get up to $250 back on Apple peripherals and software you buy to go with it.

For details and a closer look, see your participating authorized Apple dealer.

You'll find it an eye-opening experience. And that's just the half of it.

The new Apple IIGS. The power to be your best.™

You won't believe your ears, either.

MAGAZINE

ART DIRECTOR
James Dalthorp

WRITER
Galen Greenwood

PHOTOGRAPHER
Mike Chessier
Jules Alexander

CLIENT
Ben Hogan Co.

AGENCY/STUDIO
Tracy-Locke

ART DIRECTOR
Preuit Holland

DESIGNER
Preuit Holland

WRITER
Marc Deschenes

PHOTOGRAPHER
Lamb & Hall Photography

CLIENT
Noritsu America
Corporation

AGENCY/STUDIO
(213) 827-9695 and
Associates

PRODUCTION COMPANY
The Production
Company

ART DIRECTOR
Yvonne Smith

DESIGNER
Gina Norton

PRODUCER
Joe Sosa

DIRECTOR
Steve Hayden

WRITERS
Laurie Brandalise
Marc Deschenes

PHOTOGRAPHER
Dan Wolfe

CLIENT
Apple Computer, Inc.

AGENCY/STUDIO
BBDO

ADVERTISING

MAGAZINE
ART DIRECTORS
Bob Kuperman
Melinda Kanipe
Rich Bess
DESIGNERS
Rich Bess
Bob Kuperman
Melinda Kanipe
CREATIVE DIRECTORS
Bob Kuperman
Pacy Markman
WRITER
Pacy Markman
CLIENT
Drug Free America
AGENCY/STUDIO
DDB Needham
Worldwide Los Angeles
PRODUCTION MANAGER
Barry Brooks

ART DIRECTOR
Michael Pitzer
PRODUCER
Sally Lagman
DIRECTOR
Alex Cichy
WRITER
Michael Fineberg
PHOTOGRAPHER
Aaron Jones
CLIENT
Apple Computer, Inc.
AGENCY/STUDIO
BBDO

ART DIRECTOR
John Vitro
WRITER
John Robertson
PHOTOGRAPHER
Bill Werts Studio
CLIENT
Yamaha Motor
Corp., USA
AGENCY/STUDIO
Chiat/Day Advertising

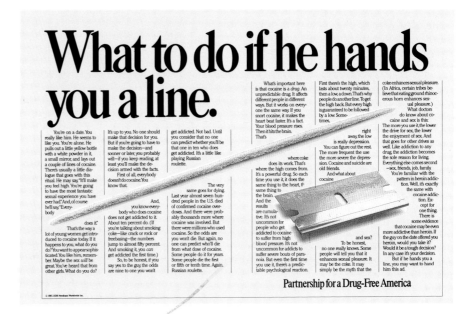

Zero to sixty, 5.5 seconds.
Top speed, 157 miles per hour.

For nearly four decades it has been Professor Porsche's philosophy that a car should do more than simply move people from one point to another.

Much more.

And anyone who's ever had the good fortune to drive a car like the one on the left knows exactly what he had in mind.

Since its introduction in 1974 the race-bred, rear-engine 911 Turbo has stood alone as the fastest, most powerful production Porsche ever built.

The ultimate expression of Professor Porsche's philosophy.

But now turn your attention to the car on the right. The new 928S 4.

With its front-mounted, liquid-cooled V-8 engine and rear-mounted transmission, it's as different from the 911 Turbo as it could possibly be. A fact which did not

911 Turbo: 6-cylinder, horizontally opposed, two overhead camshafts, air-cooled rear engine with turbocharger and intercooler, 3299cc, 282 hp. Weight: 2978 lbs. 0-60 mph: 5.5 sec. Top speed: 157 mph.

Zero to sixty, 5.7 seconds.
Top speed, 165 miles per hour.

escape the attention of surprised Porsche enthusiasts when the first 928 was introduced in 1977.

But, like the 911 Turbo, the 928S 4 started as a breakthrough in sports car design. A design that promised even more than a new level of performance.

It promised a totally new driving experience. Different from the challenge of the 911 Turbo, yet every bit as rewarding.

Since then, it has evolved, year by year, to higher and higher levels of performance. Incorporating, at every step, the most advanced technology our engineers could devise.

And so today, it is the 928S 4 which stands alone as the fastest, most powerful production Porsche ever built.

The ultimate expression of Professor Porsche's philosophy.

928S 4: 8-cylinder, 90 degree V, four overhead camshafts, four valves per cylinder, liquid-cooled front engine, 4957cc, 316 hp, transaxle design. Weight: 3505 lbs. 0-60 mph: 5.7 sec. Top speed: 165 mph. (performance figures with manual transmission).

You've seen television this good before. But never this big before.

History's first 35-inch conventional-tube television. You can see it all only at an authorized Mitsubishi dealer.

▲ MITSUBISHI

Mitsubishi Electric Sales America, Inc., 5757 Plaza Drive, Cypress, CA 90630-0007.

MAGAZINE

ART DIRECTORS
Andy Dijak
Jeff Roll
WRITERS
Phil Lanier
David Butler
PHOTOGRAPHER
Lamb & Hall Photography
CLIENT
Porsche Cars
North America
AGENCY/STUDIO
Chiat/Day Advertising

ART DIRECTOR
Rick Boyko
WRITER
Bill Hamilton
PHOTOGRAPHER
Dennis Manarchy
CLIENT
Mitsubishi Electric
Sales America
AGENCY/STUDIO
Chiat/Day Advertising

ADVERTISING

MAGAZINE CAMPAIGN

ART DIRECTOR
Rick Boyko

WRITERS
Bill Hamilton
Bob Fosse
Billy Wilder
Jim Henson

PHOTOGRAPHER
Norman Seeff

CLIENT
Mitsubishi Electric
Sales America

AGENCY/STUDIO
Chiat/Day Advertising

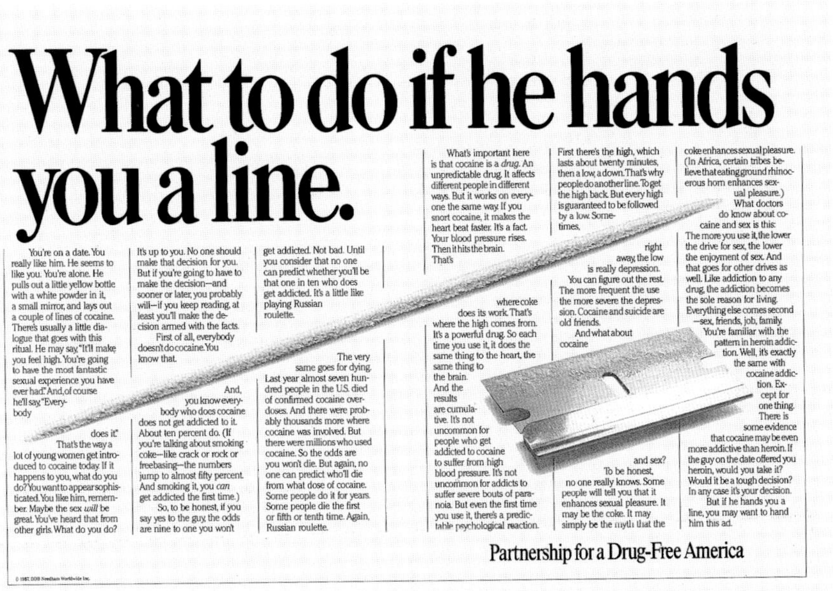

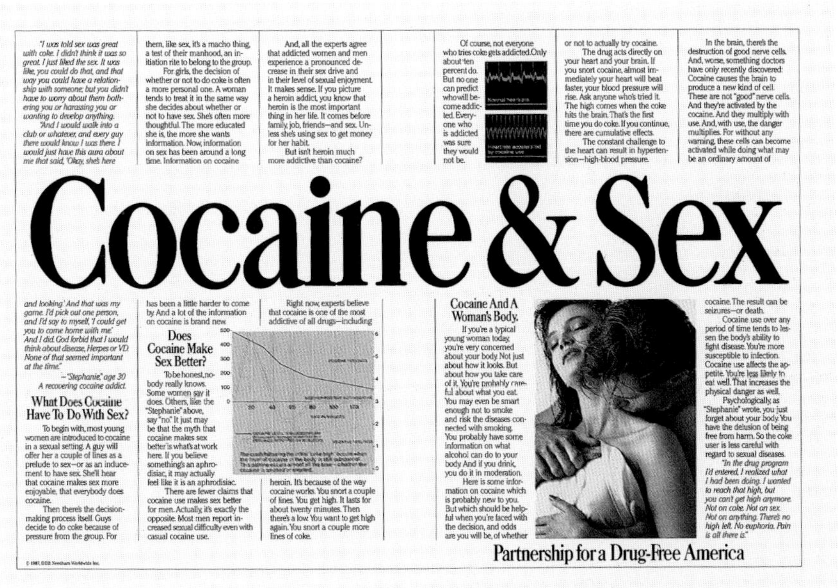

What to do if he hands you a line.

You're on a date. You really like him. He seems to like you. You're alone. He pulls out a little yellow bottle with a white powder in it, a small mirror, and lays out a couple of lines of cocaine. There's usually a little dialogue that goes with this ritual. He may say, "It'll make you feel high. You're going to have the most fantastic sexual experience you have ever had." And, of course he'll say, "Everybody

does it." That's the way a lot of young women get introduced to cocaine today. If it happens to you, what do you do? You want to appear sophisticated. You like him, remember. Maybe the sex will be great. You've heard that from other girls. What do you do?

It's up to you. No one should make that decision for you. But if you're going to have to make the decision—and sooner or later, you probably will—if you keep reading, at least you'll make the decision armed with the facts.

First of all, everybody doesn't do cocaine. You know that.

And, you know everybody who does cocaine does not get addicted to it. About ten percent do. (If you're talking about smoking coke—like crack or rock or freebasing—the numbers jump to almost fifty percent. And smoking it, you can get addicted the first time.)

So, to be honest, if you say yes to the guy the odds are nine to one you won't

get addicted. Not bad. Until you consider that no one can predict whether you'll be that one in ten who does get addicted. It's a little like playing Russian roulette.

The very same goes for dying. Last year almost seven hundred people in the U.S. died of confirmed cocaine overdoses. And there were probably thousands more where cocaine was involved. But there were millions who used cocaine. So the odds are you won't die. But again, no one can predict who'll die from what dose of cocaine. Some people do it for years. Some people die the first or fifth or tenth time. Again, Russian roulette.

What's important here is that cocaine is a *drug*. An unpredictable drug. It affects different people in different ways. But it works on everyone the same way. If you snort cocaine, it makes the heart beat faster. It's a fact. Your blood pressure rises. Then it hits the brain. That's

where coke does its work. That's where the high comes from. It's a powerful drug. So each time you use it, it does the same thing to the heart, the same thing to the brain. And the results are cumulative. It's not uncommon for people who get addicted to cocaine to suffer from high blood pressure. It's not uncommon for addicts to suffer severe bouts of paranoia. But even the first time you use it, there's a predictable psychological reaction.

First there's the high, which lasts about twenty minutes, then a low, a down. That's why people do another line. To get the high back. But every high is guaranteed to be followed by a low. Sometimes,

right away, the low is really depression. You can figure out the rest. The more frequent the use the more severe the depression. Cocaine and suicide are old friends.

And what about cocaine

and sex? To be honest, no one really knows. Some people will tell you that it enhances sexual pleasure. It may be the coke. It may simply be the myth that the

coke enhances sexual pleasure. (In Africa, certain tribes believe that eating ground rhinoceros horn enhances sexual pleasure.)

What doctors do know about cocaine and sex is this: The more you use it, the lower the drive for sex, the lower the enjoyment of sex. And that goes for other drives as well. Like addiction to any drug, the addiction becomes the sole reason for living. Everything else comes second —sex, friends, job, family. You're familiar with the pattern in heroin addiction. Well, it's exactly the same with cocaine addiction. Except for one thing. There is some evidence that cocaine may be even more addictive than heroin. If the guy on the date offered you heroin, would you take it? Would it be a tough decision? In any case it's your decision.

But if he hands you a line, you may want to hand him this ad.

Partnership for a Drug-Free America

Beauty and the Beast

"I used to go into the bathroom and talk to the person in the mirror. And it was really weird because the person in the mirror was stone sober. I would have conversations with this person in the mirror who was trying to tell me what I was doing to myself. At first, it was, 'Mary, this is ridiculous, what are you doing?' type things. 'You're dying, stop doing coke, get help.' Talk with somebody. Then we had fifteen minute conversations. The physical me would be leaning up against the wall, but I'd see her moving in the mirror, waving her hands, yelling. And I'd walk away, and sit at my desk and do a toot. Try to get over what happened there."
— *Mary, age 35*
A recovering cocaine addict

If you knew Mary at sixteen, you wouldn't have noticed anything unusual

about her. She was pretty. And smart. Her family wasn't particularly rich or poor. Her childhood wasn't unusual. She was probably a lot like you or your

friends. It could have happened at a party. Or on a date. Someone said, "Want to do a line?" There's not much more to the beginning than that. Because up until a couple of years ago, there were lots of people, smart people, who were convinced you couldn't get addicted to cocaine. That

cocaine was a glamourous drug. It didn't put you into a stupor like heroin. Or make you move in slow motion like pot. It made you feel great. Look great. It was a real high. It was beautiful. It was too good to be true. It's not true.

What do we know that we didn't know before? Well, nobody's saying cocaine isn't an addictive drug anymore. Far from it. It's psychologically addictive. More so than almost any other drug.

They do tests with laboratory animals and various drugs. The ones on cocaine will push the lever for the drugs more and more often. Until they die. That doesn't even happen with heroin or PCP.

And though for years people have died from cocaine use, it took a couple of highly-publicized, tragic deaths to get the message home to everyone. You

can die the first time or the tenth time or the fiftieth time you do coke. Because of the way the brain processes the drug, you can do the same dose week after week, and one day *that* dose will kill you.

No one can predict who will die or who won't. There's no such thing as "safe snorting." The truth is every time you do a line of coke, you risk dying.

In fact, the only thing about cocaine that's predictable is its unpredictability. Ten percent of the people who try the drug get addicted... like Mary. But no expert can predict who will or won't get addicted. And, of course, everyone who did was sure they wouldn't.

There's nothing glamourous about the way cocaine works. It goes one of two ways. You do some coke. Get high. Then about twenty minutes later, you

feel low. Irritable. Some people can walk away from the drug then. But there are the others who are driven to recapture the high. For them, each time,

it takes more coke to get there. And the more coke they do, the deeper the lows. Irritation becomes depression. Or worse.

Lots of people who get addicted to coke experience periods of real paranoia. The feeling that they're being chased. Some become frightened at the

sight of a policeman. Of course, that's partly because cocaine possession is illegal. And, in most states, the penalties are very stiff.

And cocaine addiction can get even uglier. The person who truly needs cocaine now needs nothing else. Not food. So the appetite goes. Not friends. Not sex. You know how someone on heroin behaves. Getting the drug is everything. Where you get the drug, what lies you have to tell, what you'll do to get the money—everything is secondary to getting the drug. The picture's no prettier with coke. It's almost exactly the same as heroin. The dependency, the deception, the irrational fear, the loss of self. You look in the mirror and someone else is looking out at you. Coke is a real scary drug.

That's the truth.

Partnership for a Drug-Free America

"I was told sex was great with coke. I didn't think it was so great. I just liked the sex. It was like, you could do that, and that way you could have a relationship with someone, but you didn't have to worry about them bothering you or harassing you or wanting to develop anything. 'And I would walk into a club or whatever, and every guy there would know I was there. I would just have this aura about me that said, 'Okay, she's here

and looking.' And that was my game. I'd pick out one person, and I'd say to myself, I could get you to come home with me.' And I did. God forbid that I would think about disease, Herpes or VD. None of that seemed important at the time."
— *Stephanie, age 30*
A recovering cocaine addict.

What Does Cocaine Have To Do With Sex?

To begin with, most young women are introduced to cocaine in a sexual setting. A guy will offer her a couple of lines as a prelude to sex—or as an inducement to have sex. She'll hear that cocaine makes sex more enjoyable, that everybody does cocaine.

Then there's the decision-making process itself. Guys decide to do coke because of pressure from the group. For

them, like sex, it's a macho thing, a test of their manhood, an initiation rite to belong to the group.

For girls, the decision of whether or not to do coke is often a more personal one. A woman tends to treat it in the same way she decides about whether or not to have sex. She's often more thoughtful. The more educated she is, the more she wants information. Now, information on sex has been around a long time. Information on cocaine

has been a little harder to come by. And a lot of the information on cocaine is brand new.

Does Cocaine Make Sex Better?

To be honest, nobody really knows. Some women say it does. Others, like the "Stephanie" above, say "no." It just may be that the myth that cocaine makes sex better is what's at work here. If you believe something's an aphrodisiac, it may actually feel like it is an aphrodisiac.

There are fewer claims that cocaine use makes sex better for men. Actually, it's exactly the opposite. Most men report increased sexual difficulty even with casual cocaine use.

And, all the experts agree that addicted women and men experience a pronounced decrease in their sex drive and in their level of sexual enjoyment. It makes sense. If you picture a heroin addict, you know that heroin is the most important thing in her life. It comes before family, job, friends—and sex. Unless she's using sex to get money for her habit.

But isn't heroin much more addictive than cocaine?

Right now experts believe that cocaine is one of the most addictive of all drugs—including

heroin. It's because of the way cocaine works. You snort a couple of lines. You get high. It lasts for about twenty minutes. Then there's a low. You want to get high again. You snort a couple more lines of coke.

Of course, not everyone who tries coke gets addicted. Only about ten percent do. But no one can predict who will become addicted. Everyone who is addicted was sure they would not be.

or not to actually try cocaine. The drug acts directly on your heart and your brain. If you snort cocaine, almost immediately your heart will beat faster, your blood pressure will rise. Ask anyone who's tried it. The high comes when the coke hits the brain. That's the first time you do coke. If you continue, there are cumulative effects. The constant challenge to the heart can result in hypertension—high-blood pressure.

In the brain, there's the destruction of brain nerve cells. And, worse, something doctors have only recently discovered: Cocaine causes the brain to produce a new kind of cell. These are not "good" nerve cells. And they're activated by the cocaine. And they multiply with use. And, with use, the danger multiplies. For without any warning, these cells can become activated while doing what may be an ordinary amount of

Cocaine & Sex

Cocaine And A Woman's Body.

If you're a typical young woman today you're very concerned about your body. Not just about how it looks. But about how you take care of it. You're probably careful about what you eat. You may even be smart enough not to smoke and risk the diseases connected with smoking. You probably have some information on what alcohol can do to your body. And if you drink, you do it in moderation.

Here is some information on cocaine which is probably new to you. But which should be helpful when you're faced with the decision, and odds are you will be when

cocaine. The result can be seizures—or death.

Cocaine use over any period of time tends to lessen the body's ability to fight disease. You're more susceptible to infection. Cocaine use affects the appetite. You're less likely to eat well. That increases the physical danger as well.

Psychologically, as "Stephanie" wrote, you just forget about your body. You have the delusion of being free from harm. So the coke user is less careful with regard to sexual diseases.

"In the drug program I'd entered, I realized what I had been doing. I wanted to reach that high, but you can't get high anymore. Not on coke. Not on sex. Not on anything. There's no high left. No euphoria. Pain is all there is."

Partnership for a Drug-Free America

MAGAZINE
CAMPAIGN

ART DIRECTORS
Bob Kuperman
Melinda Kanipe
Rich Bess
DESIGNERS
Bob Kuperman
Melinda Kanipe
Rich Bess
CREATIVE DIRECTORS
Bob Kuperman
Pacy Markman
WRITER
Pacy Markman
CLIENT
Drug Free America
AGENCY/STUDIO
DDB Needham
Worldwide Los Angeles
PRODUCTION MANAGER
Barry Brooks

ADVERTISING

*MAGAZINE
CAMPAIGN*

ART DIRECTOR
Gunther Maier

DESIGNER
Gunther Maier

WRITER
Ted Baker

PHOTOGRAPHER
Jeff Zwart

CLIENT
Mercedes-Benz of
North America, Inc.

AGENCY/STUDIO
McCaffrey and McCall

THE MERCEDES-BENZ 190 CLASS:
THE SUBTLE DIFFERENCE BETWEEN MASTERING
THE ROAD AND MERELY COPING WITH IT.

The road passes beneath you as always, but the sensations are markedly different. So is your state of mind. This is your first experience with a 190 Class sedan, but already you are driving with calm confidence. The car has earned your trust.

It feels resolutely stable, going precisely where you steer it, refusing to waver off course or wallow over potholes. Even the severest bumps seem only a minor disturbance as the suspension gently quells the violence underneath. Negotiating a run of switchback turns seems more routine business than high drama as the car shifts direction nimbly in response to your steering commands. Sports sedans might occasionally handle this adroitly, but they seldom feel this composed.

Suddenly the pavement deteriorates into washboard gravel, but the car tracks steadfastly ahead, curiously unfazed by the change in terrain. It occurs to you that you have yet to hear a squeak or rattle. The engine remains almost subliminally quiet, wind noise a faint whisper when you hear it at all. You normally feel an urge to stretch your legs after sitting for so long, but now you feel the urge to keep driving.

Even if you chose the automatic transmission, you still find it easy to shift manual-style when the mood strikes, locating each gear by feel without glancing downward. Your driving has become pleasurably instinctive, as driving at its best should be.

This ostensibly mystical exaltation of the driving experience springs from such technological advances as "the most sophisticated steel suspension ever put into volume production" (Britain's *Car* Magazine). And the simple fact that a 190 Class sedan is built like every Mercedes-Benz—not one ergonomic or safety principle sacrificed for the sake of cosmetic luxury or digital showmanship. Every detail of construction and assembly meeting universally envied standards.

The result is a sedan that does not "challenge" you in the macho sports-sedan tradition, but rather serves as a congenial and supremely capable ally—at once exciting and obedient, responsive and considerate. The road provides challenge enough.

Engineered like no other car in the world

THE MERCEDES-BENZ 300 CLASS:
SO TECHNOLOGICALLY ADVANCED, YOU BARELY
NOTICE THE TECHNOLOGY.

Microcircuits silently work their millisecond miracles. Hydraulics, pneumatics, kinematics, aerodynamics and myriad other disciplines interact with a synergy born of computer design, human inspiration, and eight arduous years of development and testing. Yet you drive oblivious to all this technology, savoring only its results. Precisely as Mercedes-Benz engineers intended.

Technology that intruded into your driving life could never have found its way into the 300 Class. Because it would then run counter to the sole justification for technology—enhancing the car's ability to transport its occupants with maximum efficiency, pleasure and safety.

Thus, you might never notice the five individual steel links that guide the movements of each rear wheel, comprising the most sophisticated steel suspension extant, as illustrated above. But you do notice their effect: handling prowess sufficient to "challenge many high-priced sports and GT cars," according to one automotive journal. A ride on rough surfaces that is "nothing short of magical," in the words of another.

Onboard electronics serve higher purposes than orchestrating dashboard pyrotechnics: continuously recalibrating the gasoline fuel-injection system for changing conditions and driver demands. Governing the ABS Anti-lock Braking System to help thwart wheel lockup during sudden hard stops. Monitoring the Mercedes-Benz Supplemental Restraint System (SRS), ready to deploy its driver's-side air bag and front seat belt emergency tensioning retractors within an eyeblink of a major frontal impact.

Nothing that you see or hear or feel seems overtly "technological." And yet that aerodynamically immaculate body all but banishes wind noise from the cabin. Your seat still feels comfortable after hours of driving. You find that every control falls logically to hand. And that your outward vision is reassuringly clear even in a rainstorm.

Advanced technology is at work all around you, but you do not think of it as technology. You think of it as the rewards of driving a 300 Class Mercedes-Benz.

Engineered like no other car in the world

THE MERCEDES-BENZ S-CLASS
AND THE MYSTIQUE OF THE "BIG MERCEDES."

From era to era over the decades, few automobile series have been accorded the admiration verging on awe that surrounds the premier sedans of Mercedes-Benz.

Shown in descending order at left are examples dating from 1955 to 1963 to 1972 to the 1987 S-Class sedan in the foreground. The "big Mercedes," they are popularly called. Not so much in tribute to their size—substantial but never excessive—as to their prowess. Powerful in a silky way, baronially comfortable rather than garishly luxurious, a big Mercedes manages to blend the dignity of a limousine with what one journal terms "the innate ability to leap yawning stretches of landscape in single, effortless bounds." The big sedan as marathoner, in brief. With the stamina to endlessly devour the miles on any highway in the world, at a pace that might exhaust the drivers of lesser cars. If not the cars themselves.

A big Mercedes of any era is remarkable. The current series, the S-Class, is the most remarkable yet. For its choice of three models, crowned by the 5.6-liter gasoline V-8 560SEL. For one of the slipperiest aerodynamic shapes ever bestowed on a large sedan. For its library quiet within 100 sumptuous cubic feet of living space.

For its brilliant use of electronics—to activate its Anti-lock Braking System (ABS), for example. And to deploy its Supplemental Restraint System (SRS)—with driver's-side air bag and front seat belt emergency tensioning retractors—within a fraction of a second of a major frontal impact.

And at root, it represents Mercedes-Benz: no mere assemblage of trendy technological hardware but a specimen of automotive integrity. In every seam and sinew, in every glossy inch of its hand-rubbed finish.

To drive an S-Class sedan is to partake of one of the timeless motoring traditions. More important, it is to experience a synthesis of high performance and high refinement matched by no other automobile.

Engineered like no other car in the world

MAGAZINE
CAMPAIGN

ART DIRECTOR
James Dalthorp
WRITER
Galen Greenwood
PHOTOGRAPHERS
Jules Alexander
Mike Chessier
CLIENT
Ben Hogan Co.
AGENCY/STUDIO
Tracy-Locke

FROM A GOLFER WHO MADE HITTING LOOK EASY, THE CLUB THAT'S EASY TO HIT.

Few golfers have ever understood the art of striking a ball as well as Ben Hogan.

A student of the game, Hogan spent years learning about shot-making, from the mechanics of the swing, to the design of the club itself.

This is the experience that shapes the Hogan Radial. A club specifically made to be easy to hit, for golfers who don't find hitting that easy.

When we introduced Radial five years ago, it represented a breakthrough in club design. The four-way sole gave golfers better contact from any lie. And it offered the traditional look and feel of a forged club.

This past year, we've made significant improvements. The long irons have wider soles and are weighted lower, to help you get the ball up, when typically it's the most difficult. So now, we can boast long irons that are truly easy to hit.

At the same time, our short irons are even better scoring clubs. They feature progressively smaller soles and higher weight distribution, and play with improved accuracy and control. All the clubs are also progressively offset, to better position your hands and set up more solid shots.

And as with all Hogan clubs, Radial meets the industry's tightest specifications for weighting, balance point, flex point, loft and lie.

Ask your pro about our latest edition of the Hogan Radial. We can't promise that you'll hit as easily as Mr. Hogan. But by playing Radial, at least you'll be off to a good start.

Hogan
PLAY THE BEST YOU CAN PLAY

WHEN IT CAME TO MAKING METALWOODS, BEN HOGAN WAS HIS OWN BEST INSPIRATION.

Introducing Series 56. The new line of metalwoods from the Ben Hogan Company, based on one of Mr. Hogan's most successful club designs ever, our classic 1956 woods.

Why did we adapt a traditional wood design to metalwoods?

Simple. We believe it makes a better club. Shaped by Ben Hogan's years of playing experience, the 1956 Hogan wood became a classic because of its excellent playability. It was the natural model for these metalwoods.

Borrowing from the traditional design, Series 56 metalwoods set up visually square and allow you to align the ball better.

Yet, they feature perimeter weighting for tremendous distance, even with off-center hits. They're also the only metalwoods available with our exclusive Apex shafts.

And, as with all Hogan clubs (including the original '56 woods), our metalwoods meet the tightest specifications in the industry for weighting, balance point, flex point, loft, and lie.

Uncompromising standards set by Ben Hogan himself.

Ask your pro about the new Hogan Series 56 line of metalwoods.

The only metalwoods we know of that've been 31 years in the making. And, we might add, are better clubs for it.

Hogan
PLAY THE BEST YOU CAN PLAY

WHY A GOLFER KNOWN FOR CONSISTENCY BUILDS A CLUB FOR GOLFERS WHO AREN'T.

During his years on Tour, Ben Hogan was known as a golfer who spent countless hours on the practice tee honing his competitive edge. The author of the definitive book on swing mechanics. The man with the classic swing.

As clubmakers, we at the Ben Hogan Company recognize that not all golfers are ready for the Tour. And that many of you play for the sheer pleasure of the game. But that doesn't mean you can't play better and even

enjoy the game more, by playing a club gifted with Hogan quality and performance. In this case, Magnum, our most forgiving club ever.

Magnum's head design distributes weight toward the toe of the clubhead, creating a generous sweetspot, and producing more solid impacts, even with off-center hits. The design also helps reduce slicing.

The full offset promotes a "hands ahead" position to help you hit down and through the ball. Each Magnum also features Hogan's exclusive Apex shafts.

And, as with every Hogan club, Magnum is subject to the tightest weighting, balance point, flex point, loft, and lie specifications in golf.

Uncompromising standards set down by Ben Hogan himself.

Now that you know that the Ben Hogan Co. makes a club for golfers like yourself, talk to your pro about playing Magnum irons and woods. The clubs for players who'd like to be more consistent, from the man who wrote the book on the subject.

Hogan
PLAY THE BEST YOU CAN PLAY

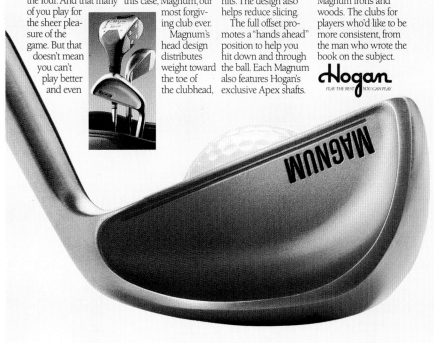

ADVERTISING

MAGAZINE CAMPAIGN

ART DIRECTOR
Marce Mayhew

DESIGNER
Marce Mayhew

SET DIRECTOR
Michael Hartog

PHOTOGRAPHER
Doug Taub

CLIENT
Jaguar

AGENCY/STUDIO
Geer DuBois

EVOLUTION OF THE SPECIES

The New Breed Jaguar XJ6

Strong. Silent. Sensual. The 1988 Jaguar XJ6 is completely new, yet it reflects all the very finest traits of its forebears.

True to Jaguar tradition, its new, fuel injected six cylinder engine has double overhead cams. However, the added sophistication of 24 valves further enhances power and high-speed response. Unique "pendulum" isolation refines Jaguar's renowned fully independent suspension. A Bosch anti-lock (ABS) system supplements its four wheel power disc brakes. And an ingenious J-gate selector lets the driver take full advantage of the ZF four speed/overdrive automatic transmission by offering a choice of fully automatic shifting, or the manual selection of gears two through four.

In the totally redesigned XJ6, the Old World splendor of supple leather and polished burl walnut is complemented by truly enlightened engineering. There are seven microprocessors to regulate mechanical and driver information systems, which include a trip computer and a Vehicle Condition Monitor that continually checks 27 vehicle functions. The front seats are orthopedically designed and adjust electrically in eight directions. Its computer-controlled heating and air conditioning can even regulate cabin humidity.

A most advanced species, the new XJ6 is also the most thoroughly proven sedan ever introduced by Jaguar. It is covered by an extensive three year/36,000 mile warranty and Jaguar's new Service-On-Site™ Roadside Assistance Plan. For details of this uniquely comprehensive program and Jaguar's limited warranty, applicable in North America, visit our showroom. We invite you to experience the evolution of a legendary species—the new breed Jaguar XJ6.

ENJOY TOMORROW. BUCKLE UP TODAY.

JAGUAR
A BLENDING OF ART AND MACHINE.

MAGAZINE
CAMPAIGN

ART DIRECTOR
Robert E. MacIntosh
DESIGNER
Robert E. MacIntosh
WRITER
Carol Lasky
PHOTOGRAPHER
Kurt Stier
CLIENT
Monadnock Paper
Mills, Inc.
AGENCY/STUDIO
Rob MacIntosh
Communications, Inc.

R A D I A N C E

The eloquence of white on white. The brilliance is Astrolite.®

MONADNOCK PAPER MILLS
Bennington, New Hampshire 03442

I M P A C T

P O I S E

MAGAZINE CAMPAIGN

ART DIRECTOR
Rick Boyko

WRITER
Richard Kelly

PHOTOGRAPHER
Dennis Manarchy

ILLUSTRATOR
Michael Bull

CLIENT
Foster Farms

AGENCY/STUDIO
Chiat/Day Advertising

MAGAZINE
CAMPAIGN

ART DIRECTOR
Neil Raphan

DESIGNER
Neil Raphan

WRITER
Larry Chase

PHOTOGRAPHER
Peter Johansky

CLIENT
Borden

AGENCY/STUDIO
DDB Needham
Worldwide

THE MERCEDES-BENZ 190 CLASS:
NO MATTER HOW HARD YOU DRIVE, YOU NEVER
LEAVE CIVILIZATION BEHIND.

You did not expect it to be this way, pounding over a remote back road peppered with unexpected dips and turns and unvisited by the county road crew for the better part of a decade.

You should feel tentative; instead, you feel elated. The 190 Class sedan executes its moves with calm exactitude, as if it were an athlete who had trained many years for precisely this event. And in fact, Mercedes-Benz engineers had just such a road in mind as they tuned their ingenious multi-link independent rear suspension concept, over five arduous years, on the special test vehicle depicted above. Their aim—to blend the handling surety of a Formula One racing car with the riding comfort of a Mercedes-Benz. You marvel that the drama visible through the windshield has so little apparent effect on the car. You flow through curves. Bumps lose their sting. Civilization is preserved.

All the while the cabin remains uncannily quiet, engine noise only a muted hum from behind a double firewall. The telltale sounds of a car being punished are not in evidence—no squeaks, rattles or groans, body

 and chassis held in rigid unity by 4,000-plus individual welds and sinews of high-strength, low-alloy steel. Endowed with such a constitution, the 190 Class sedan can run a gauntlet like this and barely seem challenged.

Even the atmosphere in the cabin is civilized, the climate kept cool and fresh by microprocessor control. Your seat is so comfortably supportive, so subtly contoured to your body that you no longer consciously think about it. As you brake and downshift and steer through turns, every move comes so easily and naturally that you almost sense a cooperative intelligence working with you—an impression the engineers have cultivated through relentless attention to ergonomic details.

The stop sign ahead signals that you are coming up on the smooth, predictable main highway. In another car, you might feel relieved. But now you feel a little downhearted. Until you remember that later today, you will come this way again.

Engineered like no other car in the world

THE MERCEDES-BENZ 300 CLASS:
MICROCHIPS, SPATIAL KINEMATICS, ERGONOMICS
AND THE HUMAN SPIRIT.

The suspension elements interacted in perfect geometric harmony. The engine's microprocessor intelligence network functioned flawlessly. Every equation balanced; the computer screens could go blank at last. The 300 Class was clearly destined to be the most technologically advanced series of automobiles ever built by Mercedes-Benz.

Then came the most critical phase of development. Engineers slipped into a fleet of prototype 300 Class sedans. Set off in search of every conceivable driving extreme. And themselves became the test instruments—even more sensitive and discerning than those they left behind in their laboratories.

It was during long autobahn treks, protracted Alpine climbs, in the searing heat of the American West and bitter Arctic cold that the six-cylinder engines proved their mettle—thriving under adversity, forging an unprecedented blend of speed and silence. Corkscrew mountain passes and corrugated gravel paths vindicated the engineers' inspired application of spatial kinematics—a multilink independent rear suspension that promoted quick, sure handling without sacrificing the fabled Mercedes-Benz ride. On slick downhill grades and snow-covered turns, the Anti-lock Braking System

(ABS) turned potential drama into controlled, unruffled stops. And the technology proved not only remarkably advanced, but remarkably reliable as well.

All of which might have satisfied less ambitious engineers. But to these engineers, the triumphs of technology were only a platform from which to reach higher. To nudge the 300 Class closer to perfection. So they continued to drive, to record their impressions, to rework their formulas. And in the process, the seats became subtly more supportive. Handling, even more reassuringly predictable. Steering, so responsive that it seemed "connected directly to your optic system," as one journalist would later put it. And by gradual, painstaking steps, a very advanced design evolved into a full-fledged Mercedes-Benz.

The effort consumed eight long years, but no engineer would begrudge an hour of that time. Because now the familiar saying, "Nothing feels like a Mercedes-Benz," means more than it ever has before.

Engineered like no other car in the world

MANY AUTOMOBILE MAKERS ITCH
TO BUILD THE PERFECT CAR.
THE MERCEDES-BENZ S-CLASS IS PROOF THAT
SOME SIMPLY ITCH MORE THAN OTHERS.

It is a curious fact that not everyone who seeks the very best in a large sedan is fully aware of just how much sedan this entitles today's buyer to demand.

Some still opt for the overbearing "luxury" sedan in all its bulk and ostentation, unaware that big today can also mean fast, agile and responsive. Somewhat better off are those who have moved up to vivid big-sedan performance—but then go no further.

Then there are those who choose the sedans of the S-Class. The Mercedes-Benz overview is their overview: a large sedan—sufficiently well engineered—can *balance* triple-digit performance with hushed driving ease. Agile handling with an unruffled ride. The fragrance of leather upholstery and the richness of handworked woods with the tactile pleasures and keen precision of a true drivers car.

And the rewards that follow are theirs to enjoy every mile: swift and sure-footed automotive travel on vast highways and unpaved byways alike. Experienced amid sumptuously comfortable surroundings.

 And in a blissful state of near silence.

The rewards continue—because the S-Class is, after all, built by Mercedes-Benz. And thus is welded, brazed, filed, sanded, polished and nit-picked to completion along an assembly route lined with enough inspections (and inspectors) to make this the most demanding trip of its life, if not any car's life. The S-Class aims not only for the glamour of high technology but also the reassurance of high technological reliability. And reflects almost fifty years of basic Mercedes-Benz safety research and engineering.

You can choose from three S-Class sedans—the 560 SEL and 420 SEL V-8s, and the stunning six-cylinder 300 SDL Turbo. Their character subtly differs from one to another; their blend of high performance and high driving civilization differs from all other large sedans in the world.

Engineered like no other car in the world

*MAGAZINE
CAMPAIGN*

ART DIRECTOR
Gunther Maier
DESIGNER
Gunther Maier
WRITER
Ted Baker
PHOTOGRAPHER
Jeff Zwart
CLIENT
Mercedes-Benz of
North America, Inc.
AGENCY/STUDiO
McCaffrey and McCall
▲

ADVERTISING

MAGAZINE
CAMPAIGN

ART DIRECTORS
Jeff Gold
Chuck Beeson

DESIGNER
Donald Krieger

WRITER
Jeff Gold

PHOTOGRAPHER
Various

CLIENT
A&M Records, Inc.

AGENCY/STUDIO
A&M Records, Inc.

Best Performance in a pair of Reeboks February 12, 1982

Best Performance in a pair of Reeboks October 6, 1983

Best Performance in a pair of Reeboks December 10, 1985

*MAGAZINE
CAMPAIGN*

ART DIRECTOR
Cheryl Heller
DESIGNER
Cheryl Heller
DIRECTOR
Jerry Cronin
WRITER
Herb Ritts
CLIENT
Reebok
AGENCY/STUDIO
Heller Breene

ADVERTISING

*MAGAZINE
CAMPAIGN*

ART DIRECTOR
Todd McVey

DESIGNER
Todd McVey

WRITERS
Lee Garfinkel
Rochelle Klein

PHOTOGRAPHER
Beth Galton

CLIENT
Citizen Watches

AGENCY/STUDIO
Levine, Huntley, Schmidt
& Beaver, Inc.

What's on your arm should be as beautiful as who's on it.

Finally, great works of art that will be appreciated in their own time.

You can tell a lot about a person by the look on their face.

MAGAZINE
CAMPAIGN

ART DIRECTOR
Anne Rhodes

CREATIVE DIRECTOR
Terri Small

WRITER
Dan Balazs

CLIENT
JanSport

AGENCY/STUDIO
Elgin Syferd

CARRYING JANSPORT CAN DO THE SAME FOR YOUR SALES CURVE.

BEFORE OUR PRODUCTS GO ANYWHERE WITH YOU, THEY GO THROUGH HELL WITH US.

WE'VE TAKEN PEOPLE PLACES NO SELF-RESPECTING PACK HORSE WOULD GO.

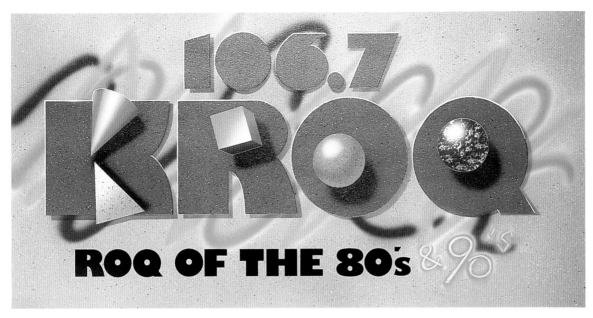

OUTDOOR

ART DIRECTOR
Jim Fittipaldi

DESIGNER
Jim Fittipaldi

ILLUSTRATOR
Jim Fittipaldi

CLIENT
Infinity Broadcasting
KROQ Radio

AGENCY/STUDIO
Jim Fittipaldi Design

ART DIRECTOR
Peter Coutroulis

WRITER
David Bishop

ILLUSTRATOR
Bob Hickson

CLIENT
MarineWorld

AGENCY/STUDIO
DJMC, Inc.

ART DIRECTOR
John Lee Wong

DESIGNER
John Lee Wong

WRITER
Ken Fitzgerald

PHOTOGRAPHER
Gerry Wilson

CLIENT
Kentucky Fried Chicken
Southern Calif. Co-Op

AGENCY/STUDIO
DYR

ADVERTISING

OUTDOOR
ART DIRECTORS
Richard Crispo
Dennis Lim
David Ryoshima
WRITERS
Gail Smith
Cami Cohen
Martin MacDonald
PHOTOGRAPHER
Michael Justice
CLIENT
Los Angeles
Herald Examiner
AGENCY/STUDIO
Ketchum Advertising

ART DIRECTOR
Richard Caraballo
CREATIVE DIRECTOR
Aurelio Saiz
WRITER
Aurelio Saiz
PHOTOGRAPHER
Abe Seltzer
CLIENT
American Express
AGENCY/STUDIO
Ogilvy & Mather Direct

OOPS.

Health care shouldn't be a bad break. ✚ Blue Cross of Washington and Alaska

OUTDOOR

ART DIRECTOR
Anne Rhodes
CREATIVE DIRECTOR
Terri Small
WRITER
Dan Balazs
CLIENT
Blue Cross of
Washington and Alaska
AGENCY/STUDIO
Elgin Syferd

RUNAWAYS
DO
FIND A HOME.

THE INTERNATIONAL MISSING
CHILDREN'S FOUNDATION

ART DIRECTOR
Glenn O. Dayton III
DESIGNER
Trish Stratton
DIRECTOR
Glenn O. Dayton III
WRITER
Arthur Bradshaw
PHOTOGRAPHER
David Kramer
CLIENT
International Missing
Children's Foundation
AGENCY/STUDIO
Dayton Associates

RUNAWAYS DO
BECOME
MOVIE STARS.

THE INTERNATIONAL MISSING
CHILDREN'S FOUNDATION

OUTDOOR
ART DIRECTOR
Terri Small
CREATIVE DIRECTOR
Terri Small
WRITER
Margy Tylczak
CLIENT
Blue Cross of
Washington and Alaska
AGENCY/STUDIO
Elgin Syferd

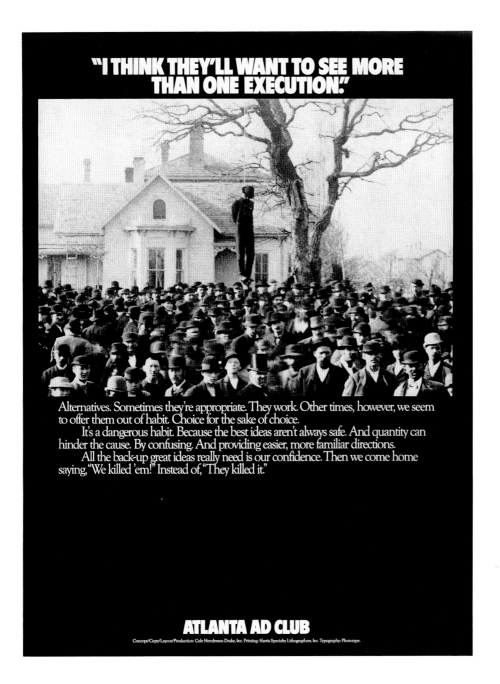

"I THINK THEY'LL WANT TO SEE MORE THAN ONE EXECUTION."

Alternatives. Sometimes they're appropriate. They work. Other times, however, we seem to offer them out of habit. Choice for the sake of choice.

It's a dangerous habit. Because the best ideas aren't always safe. And quantity can hinder the cause. By confusing. And providing easier, more familiar directions.

All the back-up great ideas really need is our confidence. Then we come home saying, "We killed 'em!" Instead of, "They killed it."

ATLANTA AD CLUB

Concept/Copy/Layout/Production: Cole Henderson Drake, Inc. Printing: Harris Specialty Lithographers, Inc. Typography: Phototype.

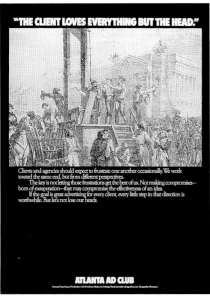

"THE CLIENT LOVES EVERYTHING BUT THE HEAD."

Clients and agencies should expect to frustrate one another occasionally. We work toward the same end, but from different perspectives.

The key is not letting those frustrations get the best of us. Not making compromises—born of exasperation—that may compromise the effectiveness of an idea.

If the goal is great advertising for every client, every little step in that direction is worthwhile. But let's not lose our heads.

ATLANTA AD CLUB

Concept/Copy/Layout/Production: Cole Henderson Drake, Inc. Printing: Harris Specialty Lithographers, Inc. Typography: Phototype.

"LET'S SEE HOW IT DOES IN FOCUS GROUP."

Beware the research explosion. An onslaught of numbers we sometimes allow to make decisions for us.

Numbers can't replace a writer's wit. An art director's eye. The savvy of a media planner. Or an account executive's insight.

Research: It's a tool. Not gospel. After all, who is more qualified to make an advertising decision? Five housewives, a plumber and a night watchman. Or you?

ATLANTA AD CLUB

Concept/Copy/Layout/Production: Cole Henderson Drake, Inc. Printing: Harris Specialty Lithographers, Inc. Typography: Phototype.

DIRECT MAIL

ART DIRECTOR
Jim Condit
WRITER
Ken Lewis
PHOTOGRAPHER
Minnesota Historical Society
CLIENT
Atlanta Ad Club
AGENCY/STUDIO
Cole Henderson Drake, Inc.

ART DIRECTOR
Jim Condit
WRITER
Ken Lewis
CLIENT
Atlanta Ad Club
AGENCY/STUDIO
Cole Henderson Drake, Inc.

ART DIRECTOR
Jim Condit
WRITER
Ken Lewis
PHOTOGRAPHER
The Mercury News Press
CLIENT
Atlanta Ad Club
AGENCY/STUDIO
Cole Henderson Drake, Inc.

DIRECT MAIL

ART DIRECTOR
Jim Van Noy

DESIGNER
Sam Beeson

WRITERS
Wendy Marks
Howie Cohen

ILLUSTRATORS
Gretchen Schields
Rob Colvin
Gary Lund

CLIENT
Western States
Advertising Agencies
Association

AGENCY/STUDIO
The Van Noy Group

ART DIRECTOR
Jann Church

DESIGNER
Jann Church

CLIENT
ESRI

AGENCY/STUDIO
Jann Church

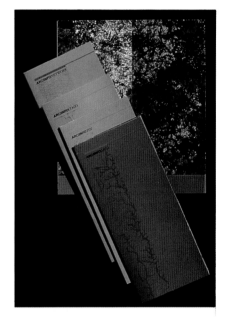

ART DIRECTOR
Cheryl Heller

DESIGNER
Cheryl Heller

WRITER
Peter Caroline

PHOTOGRAPHER
Clint Clemens

ILLUSTRATOR
Michael Orzech

CLIENT
S.D. Warren

AGENCY/STUDIO
Heller Breene

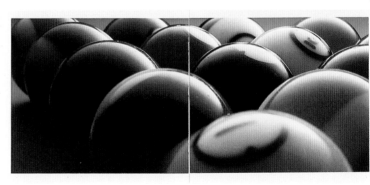

DIRECT MAIL
ART DIRECTOR
Cheryl Heller
DESIGNER
Cheryl Heller
WRITER
Peter Caroline
PHOTOGRAPHERS
Herb Ritts
Myron
CLIENT
S.D. Warren
AGENCY/STUDIO
Heller Breene

ART DIRECTORS
Paul Pruneau
Liz Sutton
DESIGNER
Liz Sutton
PRODUCER
Dorene Meadows
DIRECTOR
Liz Sutton
WRITER
Rich Binell
PHOTOGRAPHER
Paul Matsuda
ILLUSTRATOR
Dorene Meadows
CLIENT
Apple Computer, Inc.
AGENCY/STUDIO
Apple Creative Services
PRODUCTION COMPANY
Apple Creative Services

POINT OF PURCHASE,
DISPLAY

ART DIRECTOR
Yvonne Smith

DESIGNER
Yvonne Smith

WRITER
Marc Deschenes

PHOTOGRAPHER
Lamb & Hall Photography

CLIENT
Noritsu American
Corporation

AGENCY/STUDIO
(213) 827-9695 and
Associates

PRODUCTION COMPANY
The Production
Company

CAN WE ENLARGE SOMETHING FOR YOU?
We'd be more than happy to make 5x7, 8x10 or 11x14 enlargements of your favorite prints.

ART DIRECTOR
Jim Van Noy

DESIGNERS
Lauren Swits-Harger
Mutsumi Gregg

CLIENT
McGuire-Nicholas
Manufacturing Co.

AGENCY/STUDIO
The Van Noy Group

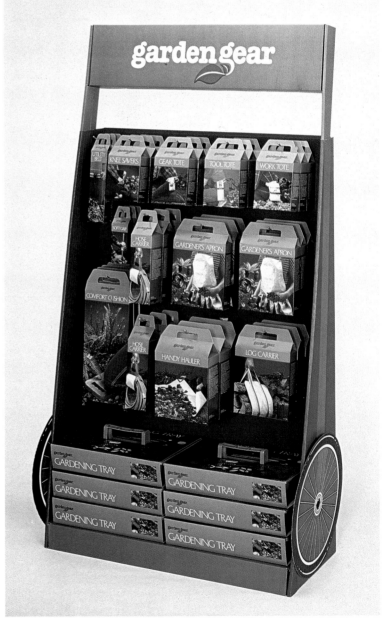

SALES KIT, PRESS KIT

ART DIRECTOR
Dan Lennon
DESIGNERS
Joe Voltaggio
Dan Lennon
WRITER
Linda Lennon
CLIENT
Lackawanna
AGENCY/STUDIO
Lennon and Associates

ART DIRECTORS
Randall Hensley
Tom Bazzel
DESIGNERS
Tom Bazzel
Diana DeLucia
Randall Hensley
CREATIVE DIRECTOR
Randall Hensley
WRITERS
Robert S. Byer
Karen Wander
ILLUSTRATORS
Soren Arutunyan
Carol Ferrante
CLIENT
IBM Entry Systems
Division / P. Armstrong /
L.D. Green / M. Psaras
AGENCY/STUDIO
Muir Cornelius
Moore, Inc.

ART DIRECTOR
Paul Pruneau
DESIGNERS
G. Chadwick
L. Sutton
R. Vaughn
PRODUCERS
Dorene Meadows
A. Kelley
J. Moran
WRITERS
Rich Binell
Mark Doyle
Eric Stouffer
Doug Gotthoffer
PHOTOGRAPHERS
K. Merfeld
P. Matsuda
T. Landecker
CLIENT
Apple Computer, Inc.
AGENCY/STUDIO
Apple Creative Services
PRODUCTION COMPANY
Apple Creative Services

BROCHURE, FOLDER

ART DIRECTOR
Jack Anderson

DESIGNERS
Jack Anderson
Heidi Hatlestad

WRITER
Dan Balazs

PHOTOGRAPHERS
Mark Burnside
Todd Pearson

ILLUSTRATORS
Tim Kilian
John Fortune

CLIENT
Mac B Sports

AGENCY/STUDIO
Hornall Anderson
Design Works

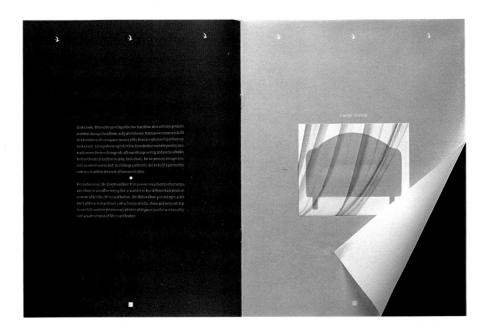

ART DIRECTOR
Maureen Erbe

DESIGNER
Maureen Erbe

PHOTOGRAPHER
Henry Blackham

CLIENT
Scandiline
Furniture Corp.

AGENCY/STUDIO
Maureen Erbe Design

ART DIRECTOR
Craig Fuller

DESIGNER
Craig Fuller

WRITER
Terri Roders

PHOTOGRAPHER
Nishihira Photography

CLIENT
U.S. Grant Hotel

AGENCY/STUDIO
Crouch+Fuller, Inc.

BROCHURE, FOLDER

ART DIRECTOR
Don Sibley

DESIGNER
Don Sibley

WRITER
Lee Herrick

PHOTOGRAPHER
Joe Aker

ILLUSTRATOR
Mark Domiteaux

CLIENT
Trammell Crow
Company

AGENCY/STUDIO
Sibley/Peteet
Design, Inc.

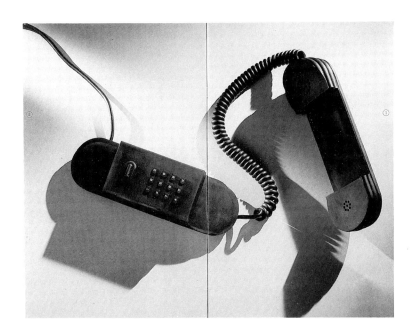

ART DIRECTOR
Robert Valentine

DESIGNER
Robert Valentine

WRITER
Kathy Mack

PHOTOGRAPHER
Charles Purvis

CLIENT
Walker Art Center
Book Shop

AGENCY/STUDIO
Robert Valentine, Inc.

ART DIRECTOR
John C. Reger

DESIGNER
Dan Olson

CLIENT
Business Week

AGENCY/STUDIO
Design Center

BROCHURE, FOLDER

ART DIRECTOR
Cheryl Heller

DESIGNER
Cheryl Heller

WRITER
Jerry Cronin

PHOTOGRAPHER
Herb Ritts

CLIENT
Reebok

AGENCY/STUDIO
Heller Breene

ART DIRECTOR
David Bartels

DESIGNER
Buck Smith

WRITER
Donn Carstens

PHOTOGRAPHERS
Don Vanderbeeck
Jean Early
David Sheldon
Jim Jacobs

ILLUSTRATORS
T.P. Speer
Buddy Hickerson

CLIENT
S.W. Bell Telephone

AGENCY/STUDIO
Bartels & Carstens

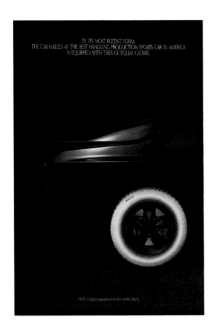

IN ITS MOST POTENT FORM,
THE CAR HAILED AS THE BEST HANDLING PRODUCTION SPORTS CAR IN AMERICA
IS EQUIPPED WITH TIRES OF EQUAL CALIBRE.

TO MAKE IT FLY THEY GAVE THE NEW M5 6 CYLINDERS 24 VALVES AND A TOP SPEED OF 150 MPH.
TO KEEP IT ON THE GROUND, THEY GAVE IT PIRELLIS.

POSTER

ART DIRECTOR
Michael Arola

CREATIVE DIRECTORS
Michael Arola
Kip Klappenback

WRITER
Kip Klappenback

PHOTOGRAPHER
Dennis Gray

RETOUCHER
Joe Kennedy

CLIENT
Pirelli Tire Corporation

AGENCY/STUDIO
Cochran Chase
Livingston

ART DIRECTORS
Mike Arola
Mike Kelly

CREATIVE DIRECTOR
Kip Klappenback

WRITER
Kip Klappenback

PHOTOGRAPHER
Dennis Gray

RETOUCHER
Rob Lawrence

CLIENT
Pirelli Tire Corporation

AGENCY/STUDIO
Cochran Chase
Livingston

FRANK XAVIER HAIR IS ALWAYS ON HIS MIND

FRANK XAVIER HAIR IS ALWAYS ON HIS MIND

ART DIRECTOR
Cheryl Heller

DESIGNERS
Cheryl Heller
Nick Kaldenbaugh

WRITER
Jerry Cronin

PHOTOGRAPHER
Myron

ILLUSTRATOR
Cheryl Heller

CLIENT
Xavier Hair Salon

AGENCY/STUDIO
Heller Breene

CAN WE ENLARGE SOMETHING FOR YOU?
We'd be more than happy to make 5x7, 8x10 or 11x14 enlargements of your favorite prints.

ART DIRECTOR
Yvonne Smith

DESIGNER
Yvonne Smith

WRITER
Marc Deschenes

PHOTOGRAPHER
Lamb & Hall Photography

CLIENT
Noritsu America
Corporation

AGENCY/STUDIO
(213) 827-9695 and
Associates

PRODUCTION COMPANY
The Production
Company

one hundred three

TELEVISION—PRODUCT

ART DIRECTOR
Larry Reinschmiedt

PRODUCER
Erin Ragan Johnson

DIRECTOR
Phil Marco

WRITER
Diane Fannon

CLIENT
The McIlhenny Co.

AGENCY/STUDIO
Tracy-Locke

PRODUCTION COMPANY
Phil Marco Prod., Inc.

"THE BIG DROP"

TEEN: Mom, I hate meatloaf. Can't you do
something to make it taste a little better?
…thank you.

ANNCR: TABASCO brand pepper sauce. It's for
more than you thought it was for.

"FROM ZERO TO ZERO"

MUSIC: (SUBTLE, RHYTHMIC THROUGHOUT.)

SFX: SOUNDS OF 928S 4 VERY FAR AWAY.

SFX: (928S 4 SOUNDS GET LOUDER.)

SFX: (AND LOUDER)

SFX: (AND LOUDER.)

ANNCR VO: In under 10 seconds, the new Porsche 928S 4 can go from zero to sixty...

SFX: (APPROPRIATE.)

ANNCR VO: ...and back to zero.

ART DIRECTORS
Jeff Roll
Andy Dijak
PRODUCER
Susan Ashmore
DIRECTOR
Mark Coppos
WRITERS
David Butler
Phil Lanier
CLIENT
Porsche Cars
North America
PRODUCTION COMPANY
Coppos Films
AGENCY/STUDIO
Chiat/Day Advertising

ART DIRECTOR
Deidre Huberty

PRODUCER
Janis Gabbert

DIRECTOR
Steve Horn

WRITERS
Alan Dummer

CLIENT
National Dairy Board

PRODUCTION COMPANY
Steve Horn, Inc. NY

AGENCY/STUDIO
McCann-Erickson, Inc.

"LATE BLOOMER"

GIRL: Michael Martin, I don't even exist in your eyes.

'Cause all you see is a person's outside. Well, I'm a beautiful person inside.

VOICE SLIGHTLY OLDER: And I'm drinking milk. Do you know what that means? I'm growing fast in these years.

TEEN'S VOICE: And milk's giving me a lot of what I need for strong bones, beautiful skin, and a great smile.

MATURE VOICE: And by the time my outside catches up with my inside, I'll have long since outgrown you.

GIRL'S VOICE: And you'll be history.

ANNCR: Milk. It does a body good.

"BARBECUED CHICKEN"

SUPER: (FOSTER FARMS® LOGO) You can't argue about the chicken.

MAN: For the best barbecued chicken, you don't need any fancy sauces. All you need is a little salt and pepper. Some fresh, plump chicken. Make sure the coal's just right. You need to know when to put the chicken on. And exactly when to take it off. (*CHUCKLES*) There's no doubt about it. I make the best barbecued chicken there is. But, you can ah, see that for yourself.

ANNCR. V.O.: You can argue about the recipe but you can't argue about the chicken. Foster Farms.

ART DIRECTOR
Rick Boyko
PRODUCER
Francesca Cohn
DIRECTOR
Jeff Gorman
WRITER
Richard Kelley
CLIENT
Foster Farms
PRODUCTION COMPANY
Johns + Gorman Films
AGENCY/STUDIO
Chiat/Day Advertising

TELEVISION—PRODUCT

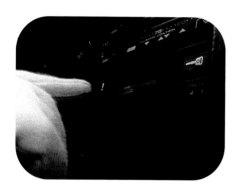  

ART DIRECTORS
Jeff Roll
Andy Dijak
PRODUCER
Susan Ashmore
DIRECTOR
Mark Coppos
WRITERS
David Butler
Phil Lanier
CLIENT
Porsche Cars
North America
PRODUCTION COMPANY
Coppos Films
AGENCY/STUDIO
Chiat/Day Advertising

"PERFORMANCE"

SFX: (PORSCHE 928S 4 ACCELERATING. ALL SUBSEQUENT SOUNDS ARE APPROPRIATE TO THE ACTION.)
MUSIC: (UP-TEMPO MUSIC STARTS SUDDENLY.)
SFX: (CONTINUE.)
MUSIC: (CONTINUES.)
MUSIC: (CONTINUES.)
SFX: (CONTINUE.)
MUSIC: (CONTINUES.)
SFX: (CONTINUE.)
ANNCR: The preceding performance
MUSIC (STOPS ABRUPTLY.)
ANNCR: has been brought to
you…by Porsche.
SFX: (THE 928S 4 IDLING.)

"COW"

ANNCR: The revolutionary Yamaha Clavinova keyboard is unlike anything you've ever heard. So we've compared it to a cow, both being black and white and standing on four legs. But where the cow makes but one sound…

SFX: (MOO)

ANNCR: …Thank you…the new Yamaha Clavinova makes up to sixteen. Piano, guitar, harpsichord, drums…a roomful of instruments that never go out of tune, best of all…

SFX: (MOO)

ANNCR: …It's housebroken

SFX: (GIGGLE)

ANNCR: The Yamaha Clavinova keyboard.

ART DIRECTOR
Ken Sakoda
CREATIVE DIRECTORS
Ken Sakoda
Scott Montgomery
WRITER
Scott Montgomery
CLIENT
Yamaha International
AGENCY/STUDIO
Reyes Art Works
PRODUCTION COMPANY
Spungbuggy

TELEVISION—PRODUCT

ART DIRECTORS
Larry Yearsley
Lon Davis
PRODUCER
Michael Portis
DIRECTOR
Mark Rasmussen
WRITER
Joel Prescott
CLIENT
Los Angeles Mitsubishi
Dealer Advertising
Association
AGENCY/STUDIO
Grey Advertising, Inc.
Orange County
PRODUCTION COMPANY
Riverrun Films

"SURPRISING GALANT"

ANNCR: One of these Japanese luxury sedans comes with a 2.4 liter electronically fuel injected engine...

SFX: (ENGINE STARTS)

ANNCR: One comes with a 6-speaker AM/FM stereo cassette system at no extra charge...

SFX: (MUSIC UP BRIEFLY)

ANNCR: One supplies a theft-deterrent system as standard equipment...

SFX: (HORN BLOWS)

ANNCR: And one retained a phenomenal 99% of its original retail value over the past year.

Which one?

The less expensive one. Mitsubishi Galant. Immediate delivery now available at your Mitsubishi Motors Dealer!

"PIE IN FACE"

MAN: Most paper plates will hold up to maybe one serving of pie.

SFX: (WHOOSH)

MAN: After that, they become soggy…
…and limp.

But Good Sense plastic plates stay rigid and don't leak.

SFX: (WHOOSH)

MAN: So you can go back for seconds.

SFX: (WHOOSH)

MAN: And thirds.

SFX: (WHOOSH)

ANNCR: Good Sense plastic plates. The best things you'll ever throw out.

SUPER: The best things you'll ever throw out.

ANNCR: By the way, we also make plastic cups.

ART DIRECTOR
Peter Cohen

DESIGNER
Peter Cohen

PRODUCER
Rachel Novack

DIRECTOR
Mark Story

WRITER
Larry Spector

CLIENT
Webster Industries—
Good Sense

PRODUCTION COMPANY
Story, Guliner, Piccolo
Prod.

AGENCY/STUDIO
Levine, Huntley, Schmidt
& Beaver
▲

Best of Show

TELEVISION—PRODUCT

ART DIRECTOR
Peter Cohen

DESIGNER
Peter Cohen

PRODUCER
Rachel Novack

DIRECTOR
Mark Story

WRITER
Larry Spector

CLIENT
Webster Industries-
Good Sense

PRODUCTION COMPANY
Story, Guliner,
Piccolo Prod.

AGENCY/STUDIO
Levine, Huntley, Schmidt
& Beaver, Inc.

"ELEPHANT"

MAN: When the people at Good Sense asked
me to stand under one of their garbage bags,
filled with 58 pounds of elephant fertilizer…

I said forget it!

When they said they'd pay me a fortune, I said
…maybe.

Then they told me their bags were made of a
super tough plastic to resist punctures and tears.
Obviously…that took a big load off my mind.

ANNCR: Good Sense. The best things you'll
ever throw out.

SUPER: The best things you'll ever throw out.

"THE SHORTEST DISTANCE"

MUSIC: (APPROPRIATE THROUGHOUT.)

SFX: (NATURAL THROUGHOUT.)

ANNCR: Anyone who subscribes to the theory…

…that the shortest distance

between two points…

…is a straight line…

…has obviously never driven…

…a Porsche.

ART DIRECTOR
Jeff Roll
PRODUCER
Susan Ashmore
DIRECTOR
John Marles
WRITER
David Butler
CLIENT
Porsche Cars
North America
PRODUCTION COMPANY
RSA Films Limited
AGENCY/STUDIO
Chiat/Day Advertising

TELEVISION—PRODUCT

CREATIVE DIRECTOR
Ian Blain

SET DESIGNER
Rob Einfrank

EXECUTIVE PRODUCER
Dick Kerns

DIRECTOR
Stu Hagmann

WRITER
Geoffrey Seebeck

EDITOR
Scott Wollin
Wollin Productions

CLIENT
Foster's Lager

AGENCY/STUDIO
George Patterson
Advertising
Melbourne-AC&R
DHB & BESS

PRODUCTION COMPANY
Hisk Productions

AGENCY PRODUCER
Norman Zuppicich

"COUNTDOWN"

PAUL HOGAN: G'day.

In about 30 seconds, I'm going to be enjoying this.

The famous Foster's. Try it the next time you're having a beer.

'Course, you can't actually drink in commercials.

That's fair enough. This is one taste that's worth waiting for.

How long to go, mate?

MATE: Five seconds, Paul.

HOGAN: Four, three, two...Fade to black.

VO: Foster's. It's Australian for beer, mate.

"WINTERFEST"

SFX: Various shots of penguins on screen throughout making noises (as if speaking).

ART DIRECTOR
Jean Robaire

CREATIVE DIRECTOR
Bob Kuperman

PRODUCER
Shannon Silverman

DIRECTORS
Jean Robaire
John Stein

WRITER
John Stein

DIRECTOR OF
PHOTOGRAPHY
Peter Brown

CLIENT
Sea World-Ohio

AGENCY/STUDIO
DDB Needham
Worldwide Los Angeles

PRODUCTION COMPANY
Hand Held Productions

TELEVISION—PRODUCT

ART DIRECTOR
Jean Robaire

CREATIVE DIRECTOR
Bob Kuperman

PRODUCER
Beth Hagen

DIRECTOR
Jordan Cronenwith

WRITER
John Stein

CLIENT
Sea World San Diego

AGENCY/STUDIO
DDB Needham
Worldwide Los Angeles

PRODUCTION COMPANY
Riverrun Films

"OVERVIEW/UNDERVIEW"

SFX: (A PIECE OF MUSIC THAT STARTS OUT QUIETLY AND PEACEFULLY.)

ANNCR: Sea World. An overview.

SFX: (MUSIC CHANGES FAIRLY DRAMATI-CALLY. IT IS NOW QUICK AND VERY DYNAMIC.)

SFX: (MUSIC IS PEACEFUL—JUST AS IT WAS AT THE BEGINNING OF THE COMMERCIAL.)

ANNCR: Sea World. An underview.

SFX: (AS IN THE "OVERVIEW" SECTION, THE MUSIC CHANGES AND BECOMES FAST AND DRAMATIC.)

ANNCR: Sea World. No other day makes you feel this way.

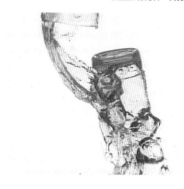

"TUMBLING TUMBLERS"

ANNCR: Tupperware's® Deluxe Tumblers® are
so elegant

they're perfect for cocktail parties,

dinner parties,

pool parties,
barbeque parties,

little kids' parties,

or any party who's (just) a little clumsy.
Because, Tupperware® tumblers are

the fine tumblers
that are guaranteed to last a lifetime.

Tupperware.® We're in the White Pages.

ART DIRECTORS
Tom Shortlidge
Parker Leinh
WRITER
Mike Faems
CLIENT
Tupperware Home Parties
AGENCY/STUDIO
Pat McNaney
PRODUCTION COMPANY
Peter Elliott Productions

TELEVISION—PRODUCT

ART DIRECTOR
Roberto Bojorgez
EXECUTIVE PRODUCER
Marcie Malooly
PRODUCER
Doug Magallon
DIRECTOR
Nick Mendoza
WRITER
Andy Sullivan
CLIENT
Miller Brewing Co.
AGENCY/STUDIO
Mendoza, Dillon &
Associados
PRODUCTION COMPANY
Nick Mendoza
Productions

"LITE—WEST COAST"

BERRY: A todos nos une el Espanol y nuestra Miller Lite, la unica que llena menos con este gran sabor.

(English): We're all brought together by our Miller Lite, the only one that's less filling with this great taste.

SUPER: Oiga, mi socio, del sabor de Lite hay que hablar en Cubano, que es el Espanol mas sabroso…Okay?

(English): Listen, my friend, when speaking of the taste of Miller Lite, one has to speak in Cuban, which is the tastiest Spanish.

WILLIE: Sabrosa la musica…y el Espanol Puertorriqueno es el mas musical!

(English): Tasty is the music…and Puerto Rican Spanish is the most musical!

PIPORRO: Pâ Espanol cantado y taconeado, el Mexicano! Abusado!

(English): For Spanish with song and dance make it Mexican!

LOC (VO): En cualquier Espanol solo hay una cerveza Lite, Miller Lite.

(English): In any Spanish there is only one Lite beer, Miller Lite.

PIPORRO: Para musica la Polka, la Redoba, el Corrido.

(English): For music, the "Polka," the "Redoba," the "Corrido."

WILLIE: La Salsa!

(English): The "Salsa!"

BERRY: La Ranchera!

(English): The "Ranchera"!

SUPER: La Guaracha! Aqui todos estamos de acuerdo.

(English): The "Guaracha"! I'm so glad we all agree.

"LEFT BRAIN/RIGHT BRAIN"

ANNCR: Imagine a brain whose left side is as brilliant as its right. A brain as artistic as it is logical. That can create. As well as calculate. Such a brain exists…in the remarkable new Apple IIGs.

Brilliant graphics, brilliant color, brilliant sound.

To help you use both sides of the most personal computer of all…your mind.

ART DIRECTOR
Tony Lamonte
SENIOR CREATIVE DIRECTOR
Charlie Miesmer
CREATIVE DIRECTOR
John Greenberger
PRODUCERS
B. Mullins
K. O'Brien
A. Chinich
DIRECTOR
Steve Horn
WRITERS
Micheal Shevack
Charlie Miesmer
CLIENT
Apple Computer, Inc.
AGENCY/STUDIO
BBDO
PRODUCTION COMPANY
Steve Horn, Inc. N.Y.

TELEVISION—PRODUCT

ART DIRECTORS
Rick Boyko
Laura Della Sala
PRODUCER
Francesca Cohn
DIRECTOR
Jeff Gorman
WRITER
Richard Kelley
CLIENT
Foster Farms
PRODUCTION COMPANY
Johns + Gorman Films
AGENCY/STUDIO
Chiat/Day Advertising

"MOTHER-IN-LAW"

DAUGHTER: My husband John loves my Chicken Parmesan. It's the best. Fist take fresh, plump chicken breasts, and cut them in half.

MOTHER-IN-LAW: Uh-uh, quarters.

DAUGHTER: Then, add garlic and oregano.

MOTHER-IN-LAW: Parsley and basil.

DAUGHTER: But what makes it, is fresh parmesan.

MOTHER-IN-LAW: Shredded mozzarella. That's how I always made it for my Johnny.

DAUGHTER: That's why your son Johnny's living with me now.

ANNCR: You can argue about the recipe. But you can't argue about the chicken. Foster Farms.

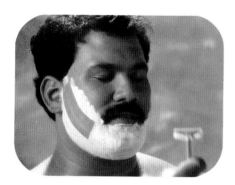 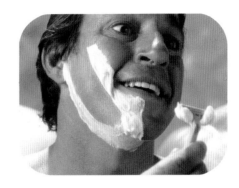 

"LUCHADORES"

ANNCR: A while back we met a group of professional wrestlers who had just reached the end of their Good Days!

We offered them Probak II, the new and economic razor with a double steel blade.

With Probak II the shave is so smooth, and so close day after day…that the pleasure rose to their heads.

Change to the new Probak II with a double steel blade, because with Probak II a happy face doesn't cost anything.

ART DIRECTOR
Carlos Mendez

EXECUTIVE PRODUCER
Marcie Malooly

PRODUCER
Alvaro Calderon

DIRECTOR
Nick Mendoza

WRITER
Robert Garni

DIRECTOR/
CAMERAMAN
Nick Mendoza

CLIENT
Gillette

AGENCY/STUDIO
McCann Erickson P.R.

PRODUCTION COMPANY
Nick Mendoza
Productions

TELEVISION—PRODUCT

ART DIRECTOR
Rick Strand (SF)

PRODUCER
Gene Lofaro

DIRECTOR
Joe Pytka

WRITER
Cynthia Franco (SF)

CREATIVE DIRECTOR
Alex Cichy (SF)

CLIENT
Apple Computer, Inc.

AGENCY/STUDIO
BBDO

PRODUCTION COMPANY
Pytka Prod. (LA)

"THE REPORT"

MAN 1: Yes, I know but...I understand, but
I still want our attorneys to handle it. Fine.

MAN 2: Isn't that thing settled yet?

MAN 1: It looks like it's going to drag on forever.
What do you think of Jensen's report?

MAN 2: It looks okay.

MAN 1: Okay?

MAN 2: Alright, it looks terrific; what do you
want me to say? This is great work.

MAN 1: I thought so, too.

MAN 2: It's nice to see our computer system
is finally earning its keep.

MAN 1: I wish that were true.

MAN 2: What do you mean?

MAN 1: Marketing isn't using our system
anymore.

MAN 2: They're not? Then how did they do
this?

MAN 1: They did it on their own system, the
one they got a month ago.

MAN 2: They put this together in a month?

MAN 1: Well, not quite Frank, they did it in
a week.

SUPER: (APPLE® LOGO)
Macintosh.® The power to be your best.

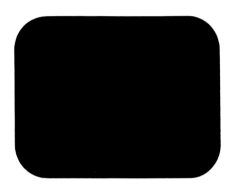  

"COUNTDOWN"

PAUL HOGAN: G'day.

In about 30 seconds, I'm going to be enjoying this.

The famous Foster's. Try it the next time you're having a beer.

'Course, you can't actually drink in commercials.

That's fair enough. This is one taste that's worth waiting for.

How long to go, mate?

MATE: Five seconds, Paul.

HOGAN: Four, three, two…Fade to black.

VO: Foster's. It's Australian for beer, mate.

CREATIVE DIRECTOR
Ian Blain

SET DESIGNER
Rob Einfrank

AGENCY PRODUCER
Norman Zuppicich

DIRECTOR
Stu Hagmann

WRITER
Geoffrey Seebeck

EDITOR
Scott Wollin,
Wollin Productions

EXECUTIVE PRODUCER
Dick Kerns

CLIENT
Foster's Lager

AGENCY/STUDIO
George Patterson
Advertising/
Melbourne—AC&R/
DHB & BESS

PRODUCTION COMPANY
Hisk Productions

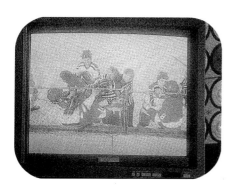  

CREATIVE DIRECTOR
Ian Blain

SET DESIGNER
Rob Einfrank

AGENCY PRODUCER
Norman Zuppicich

DIRECTOR
Stu Hagmann

WRITER
Geoffrey Seebeck

EDITOR
Scott Wollin,
Wollin Productions

EXECUTIVE PRODUCER
Dick Kerns

CLIENT
Foster's Lager

AGENCY/STUDIO
George Patterson
Advertising /
Melbourne—AC&R /
DHB & BESS

PRODUCTION COMPANY
Hisk Productions

"ICE HOCKEY"

PAUL HOGAN: G'day.

Ripper match! They'd love it back home.

Of course, you'd have to freeze the waterholes
and stop the crocodiles from joining in.

'Course, we've heard of Bobbie Wottsisname.
World famous.

Like Foster's. The Australian beer.

Goes down like a river of sunlight.

Oogh! I'm not sure the crocodiles would be
tough enough.

Foster's. It's Australian for beer, mate.

"ART GALLERY"

MAN: Intellectual, not cerebral. Concrete, not materialist.

PAUL HOGAN: G'day.

Nothing like an art show to stimulate the brain cells.

And there's nothing like a Foster's to stimulate the taste buds.

Australia's favourite…

the Mona Lisa of beers…

MAN: Look at that colour…that refreshing sparkle…that life.

HOGAN: Yep. Took the words right out of my mouth.

MAN: Sublime.

HOGAN: Foster's. It's Australian for beer, mate.

CREATIVE DIRECTOR
Ian Blain
SET DESIGNER
Rob Einfrank
AGENCY PRODUCER
Norman Zuppicich
DIRECTOR
Stu Hagmann
WRITER
Geoffrey Seebeck
EDITOR
Scott Wollin,
Wollin Productions
EXECUTIVE PRODUCER
Dick Kerns
CLIENT
Foster's Lager
AGENCY/STUDIO
George Patterson
Advertising/
Melbourne—AC&R/
DHB & BESS
PRODUCTION COMPANY
Hisk Productions

ART DIRECTORS
Gary Johnston
Barbara Schubeck

PRODUCER
Bob Schenkel

DIRECTOR
David Ashwell

WRITERS
Sharon Vanderslice
Kevin O'Neill
Elmer Skahan

CLIENT
IBM PS/2

PRODUCTION COMPANY
David Ashwell Films

AGENCY/STUDIO
Lord, Geller, Federico,
Einstein, Inc.

"SOLITAIRE"

SFX: (TELEPHONE RINGS.)

GARY: Hello. You want research? Uh, no problem. We work around the clock here. Hold on a second.

SFX: (KEYBOARD.)

SFX: (KEYBOARD.)

GARY: Research here. All trends are up. You're most welcome. Oops.

SFX: (TELEPHONE RINGS.)

GARY: Hello. Need a shipping date?

SFX: (TELEPHONE RINGS.)

GARY: Hold on a second.

GARY: Yo, price change? Yeah, ugh…let me switch you.

ANNCR. (V.O.): The IBM Personal System 2, Family.

SFX:

GARY: Shipping.

Yeah, It'll be out in 10 days.

ANNCR. (V.O.): The next generation…

of power, speed…

and graphics.

GARY: The price on that. The price is $89.99 effective Friday. No problem.

ANNCR. (V.O.): To help a company, a department, or a person get their work done.

GARY: Nice work everybody.

ANNCR. (V.O.): The Personal System 2 family from IBM.

"HAWAII"

SWIT: You do not have to visit our Hawaii office.

ROGERS: They need my expertise, my marketing magic.

SWIT: We can send your expertise without sending you. Our new IBM…

Personal System 2…

connects with all our other computers…

to send reports…plans

ROGERS: Yes, but I want to dangle my toes in the surf.

SWIT: Dangle your fingers right here. Everything's connected.

SWIT: Aloha.

ROGERS: Aloha.

FARR: Where do you want these?

ROGERS: Hey, ask him, he's the one going to Hawaii.

ANNCR. (V.O.): The Personal System 2 family, from IBM.

ART DIRECTORS
Gary Johnston
Barbara Schubeck
PRODUCER
Bob Schenkel
DIRECTOR
David Ashwell
WRITERS
Sharon Vanderslice
Kevin O'Neill
Elmer Skahan
CLIENT
IBM PS/2
PRODUCTION COMPANY
David Ashwell Films
AGENCY/STUDIO
Lord, Geller, Federico,
Einstein, Inc.

 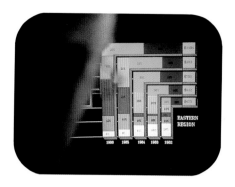 

ART DIRECTORS
Gary Johnston
Barbara Schubeck

PRODUCER
Bob Schenkel

DIRECTOR
David Ashwell

WRITERS
Sharon Vanderslice
Kevin O'Neill
Elmer Skahan

CLIENT
IBM PS/2

PRODUCTION COMPANY
David Ashwell Films

AGENCY/STUDIO
Lord, Geller, Federico,
Einstein, Inc.

"GRAPHICS"

ROGERS: Personally, I've always admired...

his use of yellow.

CHRISTOPHER: His merging of abstract shapes ...

and a multi-hued palette...

is one of the joys of our time. Yes, his subtle
shading, sensitivity...

to the grey spectrum...

CHRISTOPHER (V.O.): The stroke work of a
Rembrandt.

SWIT: Oh, it's so thrilling to see...

the new IBM Personal System...

2 family, in the hands of an old master.

MORGAN: Balderdash!

ANNCR. (V.O.): The IBM Personal System 2,
family, advancing the art of business.

"BARBECUED CHICKEN"

SUPER: (*FOSTER FARMS® LOGO*) You can't
argue about the chicken.

MAN: For the best barbecued chicken, you don't
need any fancy sauces. All you need is a little
salt and pepper. Some fresh, plump chicken.
Make sure the coal's just right. You need to
know when to put the chicken on. And exactly
when to take it off. (*CHUCKLES*) There's no
doubt about it. I make the best barbecued
chicken there is. But, you can ah, see that for
yourself.

ANNCR. V.O.: You can argue about the recipe
but you can't argue about the chicken. Foster
Farms.

ART DIRECTORS
Rick Boyko
Laura Della Sala
PRODUCER
Francesca Cohn
DIRECTOR
Jeff Gorman
WRITER
Richard Kelley
CLIENT
Foster Farms
PRODUCTION COMPANY
Johns + Gorman Films
AGENCY/STUDIO
Chiat/Day Advertising

TELEVISION—PRODUCT
CAMPAIGN

ART DIRECTORS
Rick Boyko
Laura Della Sala

PRODUCER
Francesca Cohn

DIRECTOR
Jeff Gorman

WRITER
Richard Kelley

CLIENT
Foster Farms

PRODUCTION COMPANY
Johns + Gorman Films

AGENCY/STUDIO
Chiat/Day Advertising

"MOTHER-IN-LAW"

DAUGHTER: My husband John loves my Chicken Parmesan. It's the best. First take fresh, plump chicken breasts, and cut them in half.

MOTHER-IN-LAW: Uh-huh, quarters.

DAUGHTER: Then, add garlic and oregano.

MOTHER-IN-LAW: Parsley and basil.

DAUGHTER: But what makes it, is fresh parmesan.

MOTHER-IN-LAW: Shredded mozzarella. That's how I always made it for my Johnny.

DAUGHTER: That's why your son Johnny's living with me now.

ANNCR: You can argue about the recipe. But you can't argue about the chicken. Foster Farms.

"TWO AUNTS"

AUNT #1 You want good chicken you don't need no foreign recipes. All you need is my Chicken Dumplings. Now first you get fresh plump chicken, you boil it, and let it steam. And then you make your dumplin's you put it in. Now that's Chicken Dumplin's. And everybody thinks it's the best. Mm. Mm. Mm.

AUNT #2: Mm, Mm Uh.

ANNCR.: You can argue about the recipe. But you can't argue about the chicken. Foster Farms.

ART DIRECTORS
Rick Boyko
Laura Della Sala
PRODUCER
Francesca Cohn
DIRECTOR
Jeff Gorman
WRITER
Richard Kelley
CLIENT
Foster Farms
PRODUCTION COMPANY
Johns + Gorman Films
AGENCY/STUDIO
Chiat/Day Advertising

TELEVISION—BRAND

ART DIRECTOR
Jordin Mendelsohn

PRODUCER
Michelle Miller

DIRECTOR
Norman Seeff

WRITERS
Jordin Mendelsohn
Perrin Lam
Jim Boels

CLIENT
Penguin's Frozen Yogurt

AGENCY/STUDIO
Mendelsohn/
Zein Advertising

PRODUCTION COMPANY
Richard Marlis
Productions

"FENCE I"

MAN: How are ya. Y'know what, I found out that there was these Penguin's in my neighborhood, so I built this small but effective fence. Y'know what, I found out that Penguin's was frozen yogurt. Can you believe it? Somebody lied to me.

Penguin's. Tastes like ice cream. About half the calories.

 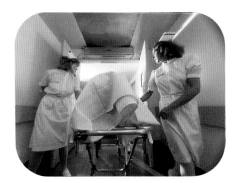 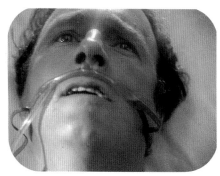

"AMI BRAND"

SFX SIRENE: (MUSIC THROUGHOUT)

NURSE: What have we got.

DOCTOR BACKGROUND: Auto accident with chest injuries.

WIFE: My husband?

DOCTOR BACKGROUND: Call Dr. Steward and get him into room 3.

DOCTOR: Since I was a kid I wanted to be a doctor.

DOCTOR BACKGROUND: I'm on my way.

DOCTOR: Yes it takes skill but it also takes...

DOCTOR BACKGROUND: Call surgery.

DOCTOR: compassion...

DOCTOR BACKGROUND: You're going to be alright.

DOCTOR: and dedication.

WIFE: Is he going to need surgery?

ANNCR: AMI hospitals are built around some of Denver's (City) best doctors. Doctors dedicated to good health.

DOCTOR BACKGROUND: Everything went fine...

ANNCR: Because AMI knows...

PATIENT: Thank's, Doc.

ANNCR: ...that good health requires good doctors.

ANNCR OVER: AMI hospitals, our doctors make the difference.

ART DIRECTOR
Ralph Price
DESIGNER
Ralph Price
PRODUCER
Susan Thurston
DIRECTOR
Michael Grasso
WRITER
Michael Wagman
CLIENT
AMI
AGENCY/STUDIO
Foote, Cone & Belding

ART DIRECTOR
Monique Risch

DESIGNER
Bob Kurtz

PRODUCER
Patti Dungen

DIRECTOR
Bob Kurtz

WRITER
Sharon Goldberg

CREATIVE DIRECTOR
Bob Browand

ILLUSTRATOR
Bob Kurtz

CLIENT
Lewis Browand

AGENCY/STUDIO
Kurtz & Friends

"I RECOMMEND COMPUTERLAND"

BRUNSWICK: As President, I recommend we buy a computer at Computerland.

LOOMIS: As Chairman, I must remind you of our frugal fiscal policy.

BRUNSWICK: As Comptroller, I assure you we'll be very fiscal. Save money too, heh, heh.

LOOMIS: As Personnel Director, I'd also like to know who'll teach us to use it, and if it breaks down, who'll fix it.

BRUNSWICK: As Research Director, I've found the answer to both…is Computerland.

LOOMIS: Then let's call Computerland. Where's the Secretary?

BRUNSWICK: It's your turn.

LOOMIS: Oh, yeah.

"PORTA COPY"

(MUSIC UNDER)

ANNCR: This is a portable copier. You can tell it's portable because it has wheels.

This is also a portable copier.

You can tell it's portable, because it fits on top of the portable copier with wheels.

And this is the new Silver Reed Porta Copy.

It runs on batteries

and makes clean, clear copies three inches wide

by as long as you need.

Porta Copy. You can tell it's portable, because we don't have to tell you it's portable.

(MUSIC OUT)

ART DIRECTOR
Tom Cordner
DESIGNER
Tom Cordner
PRODUCER
Leslie Zurla
DIRECTOR
Bill Werts
WRITER
Brent Bouchez
CLIENT
Silver Reed
AGENCY/STUDIO
Ogilvy & Mather, L.A.
PRODUCTION COMPANY
Bill Werts Productions

TELEVISION—BRAND

ART DIRECTOR
Jordin Mendelsohn

PRODUCER
Michelle Miller

DIRECTOR
Norman Seeff

WRITERS
Jordin Mendelsohn
Perrin Lam
Jim Boelse

CLIENT
Penguin's Frozen Yogurt

AGENCY/STUDIO
Mendelsohn/
Zein Advertising

PRODUCTION COMPANY
Richard Marlis
Productions

"FENCE COMBO"

MAN: Hey, y'know what? Somebody told me that there was Penguin's in my neighborhood, so I built this small but effective fence. I found out that this Penguin's stuff is frozen yogurt. Can you believe it? No threat at all. Hope it don't have no fishy taste.

ANNCR: Penguin's. Tastes like ice cream. About half the calories.

MAN: Remember me, with the fence? You know how they make Penguin's yogurt? A big walrus comes in and squeezes the little suckers' neck. (Laughs) See ya Tuesday.

Penguin's. Locations everywhere.

"POWER IMAGES"

ANNCR: Think of all the power on this earth…
The power of nature and human endurance…
The power of spirit…and then realize that of
all this power…and speed…and determination
…none is more potent than the power that
resides within the minds of us all…The power
to learn…to communicate…to imagine…to
create…the power to be your best.

PRODUCERS
Karl Fischer
Vicki Halliday

DIRECTOR
Fred Petermann

WRITERS
Phil Dusenberry
Ted Sann

CLIENT
Apple Computers, Inc.

AGENCY/STUDIO
BBDO

PRODUCTION COMPANY
Petermann/Dektor

*SENIOR CREATIVE
DIRECTOR*
Ted Sann

CREATIVE DIRECTOR
Phil Dusenberry

TELEVISION—BRAND

ART DIRECTORS
Rick Boyko
Miles Turpin

PRODUCERS
Richard O'Neill
David Prince

WRITERS
Elizabeth Hayes
Bill Hamilton
Harold Arlund

CLIENT
Home Savings of America

PRODUCTION COMPANY
Petermann/Dektor

AGENCY/STUDIO
Chiat/Day Advertising

"HAROLD ARLUND"

MUSIC: (UNDER THROUGHOUT.)

HAROLD: My philosophy of life…huh! Well, money's not going to grow out of a tree in the backyard, you gotta earn it. I made myself pretty secure, definitely have done that.

ANNCR: Harold Arlund, Home Savings Customer.

HAROLD: But like I told you, if I spend a buck I don't have to worry about making it back tomorrow. I'm not cheap, I'll spend a dollar, two dollars. But I want my money's worth. I hate to spend 5 dollars and get a dollar and a half's work.

HAROLD: I want to take another trip down to that Caribbean, it's nice sitting on that ol' ship and let her float down the line, can't beat it.

ANNCR: Harold Arlund doesn't take chances with his money, neither does Home Savings.

HAROLD: The kids won't have to fight over anything, I told 'em that when I go and take a trip, I said, I'm gonna spend your inheritance. They say go ahead and spend it.

"MOTHER'S DAY CARD"

ANNCR: of a young woman singing this song...
"M is for the many things you gave me.
O means one who's always there to hold.
T is for the tears that were shed to save me.
H is for her heart of purest gold.
E is for her eyes with love's light shining.
R means right and right she'll always be.
Put them all together, they spell MOTHER;
a word that means the world to me.

ART DIRECTOR
Joe Petruccio
CREATIVE GROUP HEAD
Jaqueline Push
PRODUCER
Tom Faxon
DIRECTOR
Maggie Condon
*CREATIVE DIRECTOR
AND WRITER*
Peggy Masterson
CLIENT
Pampers
AGENCY/STUDIO
DMB&B
PRODUCTION COMPANY
N. Lee Lacy

TELEVISION—BRAND

  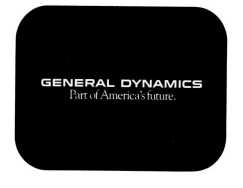

ART DIRECTOR
Jim Cox

PRODUCER
Jim Cox

DIRECTORS
Gary Johns
Jeff Gorman

WRITER
Tony Durket

CLIENT
General Dynamics

AGENCY/STUDIO
Knoth & Meads

PRODUCTION COMPANY
Johns + Gorman Films

"FARM HOUSE"

SFX: (CRICKETS, NATURAL SOUNDS)
ANNCR: The defense of our country is something most people don't think about every day.

We make sure they don't have to.

"THE RED-EYE"

(V.O.): Uh, this is the Captain again; we now expect to arrive at Kennedy Airport at around 6:40am.

MAN 1: I see you've got homework, too.

MAN 2: It never ends; you'd think when you get to this point things would get easier.

MAN 1: Yeah, I know—that looks like that was quite a project.

MAN 2: Yeah, it was. Have a look, no trade secrets here.

MAN 1: Thanks. Impressive. I wish we could do work like this, but we have to crank it out every week.

MAN 2: We do ours every week.

MAN 1: Well, we can't afford to farm ours out, we have to do them on a computer.

MAN 2: We did this on our computer.

MAN 1: You did that on a computer?

MAN 2: Of course, if we farmed them out I couldn't afford to ride up here.

SUPER: (APPLE® LOGO)
Macintosh.® The power to be your best.

ART DIRECTOR
Rick Strand (SF)

CREATIVE DIRECTOR
Alex Cichy

PRODUCER
Gene Lofaro

DIRECTOR
Joe Pytka

WRITERS
Cynthia Franco
Steve Diamant

CLIENT
Apple Computer, Inc.

AGENCY/STUDIO
BBDO

PRODUCTION COMPANY
Pytka Prod. (LA)

TELEVISION—BRAND

ART DIRECTOR
Chuck Stepner

PRODUCER
Chuck Stepner

DIRECTOR
Mark Story

WRITERS
K. Cox
Chuck Stepner

CLIENT
NBC Entertainment

AGENCY/STUDIO
NBC Advertising
& Promotion

PRODUCTION COMPANY
Story, Piccolo, Guliner
Prod.

"APPLIANCES"

ANNCR: The vacuum cleaner turned on you at 9 A.M.

ANNCR: The food processer threw a temper tantrum at 10 A.M.

ANNCR: And the washing machine tried to clean the whole house at 11 A.M.

ANNCR: Some days…you really need Days of Our Lives.

ANNCR: A daytime drama you can count on. Weekdays on NBC.

The Rivalry

"THE RIVALRY"

MAN 1: Come on, admit it, it was a great shot.

MAN 2: For a beginner.

MAN 1: Beginner? Two out of three pal, two out of three.

MAN 2: I think you're still trying to get even because I had the higher grade point average.

MAN 1: And as I recall, the lowest starting salary.

MAN 2: Yea, but at the hottest shop in town.

MAN 1: Yeah, as an assistant to an assistant.

MAN 2: Oh, okay, okay—so who first as a Vice President?

MAN 1: And last with a corner office.

MAN 2: But if I can land the North Bay project—

MAN 1: Yeah?

MAN 2: I'm talking senior partnership.

MAN 1: Really, how's it look?

MAN 2: You tell me.

MAN 1: What a production, you guys must have had outside help on this one.

MAN 2: No way, we put the whole thing together ourselves.

MAN 1: Come on.

MAN 2: No really, we did everything on our computer.

MAN 1: Revenue projections, impact studies?

MAN 2: Everything.

MAN 1: So uh, what kind of computer?

MAN 2: Oh, I'm running late.

MAN 1: No, what kind of computer?!

SUPER: (APPLE® LOGO)
Macintosh.® The power to be your best.

ART DIRECTOR
Mike Campbell
PRODUCER
Gene Lofaro
DIRECTOR
Gary Graf
CLIENT
Apple Computer, Inc.
AGENCY/STUDIO
BBDO
PRODUCTION COMPANY
Pytka Prod. (LA)

ART DIRECTOR
Tony Lamonte

*SENIOR CREATIVE
DIRECTOR*
Charlie Miesmer

CREATIVE DIRECTOR
John Greenberger

PRODUCERS
B. Bullins
K. O'Brian
A. Chinich

DIRECTOR
Steve Horn

WRITERS
Michael Shevack
C. Meismer

CLIENT
Apple Computer, Inc.

AGENCY/STUDIO
BBDO

PRODUCTION COMPANY
Steve Horn Prod.

"LEFT BRAIN/RIGHT BRAIN"

ANNCR: Imagine a brain whose left side is as brilliant as its right. A brain as artistic as it is logical. That can create. As well as calculate. Such a brain exists... in the remarkable new Apple IIGS.

Brilliant graphics, brilliant color, brilliant sound.

To help you use both sides of the most personal computer of all... your mind.

It was the
first summer
after college

I was living with her
in an old rundown
apartment near
Harvard Square

We'd sit up at night
and play the radio

And talk about
how we'd spend our
life together

I always think of her
when that song comes on

But I never tell my wife

"HARVARD SQUARE"

(MUSIC THROUGHOUT)
James Taylor Sings:
Fire and Rain.

ART DIRECTOR
Keith Lane
PRODUCER
Wendy Schwartz
WRITER
Michael Fortuna
Eric Haggman
CLIENT
WMJX FM Radio
PRODUCTION COMPANY
Vizwiz / Soundtrack
AGENCY/STUDIO
Emerson Lane Fortuna
▲

My husband and I
are in the middle of
an incredibly stupid
argument.

I mean we are
really losing it.

All of a sudden
God puts this song
on the radio.

Stopped us right
in our tracks.

I went out and
bought the album.

We play the great songs

ART DIRECTOR
Keith Lane
PRODUCER
Wendy Schwartz
WRITER
Michael Fortuna
Eric Haggman
CLIENT
WMJX FM Radio
PRODUCTION COMPANY
Vizwiz / Soundtrack
AGENCY / STUDIO
Emerson Lane Fortuna
▲

"ARGUMENT"

(MUSIC THROUGHOUT)
Dionne Warwick Sings:
That's What Friends Are For.

8 pounds, 6 ounces.

10 fingers, 10 toes.

We have a daughter.

I left the hospital
to meet my brother
for a beer.

The radio in the bar
has this song on.

Another miracle.

"TEN FINGERS, TEN TOES"

(MUSIC THROUGHOUT)
Stevie Wonder Sings:
Isn't She Lovely.

ART DIRECTOR
Keith Lane
PRODUCER
Wendy Schwartz
WRITER
Michael Fortuna
Eric Haggman
CLIENT
WMJX FM Radio
PRODUCTION COMPANY
Vizwiz / Soundtrack
AGENCY / STUDIO
Emerson Lane Fortuna
▲

ART DIRECTORS
Monique Risch
Tyler Vogel

DESIGNER
Bob Kurtz

PRODUCERS
Patti Dungen
Cindy Fluitt

DIRECTOR
Bob Kurtz

WRITER
Sharon Goldberg

CREATIVE DIRECTOR
Bob Browand

ILLUSTRATOR
Bob Kurtz

CLIENT
Computerland

AGENCY/STUDIO
Lewis Browand &
Associates

PRODUCTION COMPANY
Kurtz & Friends

"COMPUTERLAND CAN"

BRUNSWICK: Well, here we are, our very first staff meeting.

LOOMIS: And we're both here.

BRUNSWICK: How's the computer committee coming?

LOOMIS: I've found one, cheap. Maybe even a little less than if we bought it at Computerland.

BRUNSWICK: Ah. But can they teach us to use it like say Computerland?

LOOMIS: Well no, but.

BRUNSWICK: Fix it if it breaks? Like Computerland?

LOOMIS: Ah, no…

BRUNSWICK: How about talk to us?

LOOMIS: Noooooo, but…

BRUNSWICK: Think maybe we should just go to Computerland? (pause)

LOOMIS: All in favor of Computerland, say aye.

BOTH: Aye!

BRUNSWICK: Opposed?

LOOMIS: Got our way on that one didn't we, Max.

"I RECOMMEND COMPUTERLAND"

BRUNSWICK: As President, I recommend we buy a computer at Computerland.

LOOMIS: As Chairman, I must remind you of our frugal fiscal policy.

BRUNSWICK: As Comptroller, I assure you we'll be very fiscal. Save money too, heh, heh.

LOOMIS: As Personnel Director, I'd also like to know who'll teach us to use it, and if it breaks down, who'll fix it.

BRUNSWICK: As Research Director, I've found the answer to both…is Computerland.

LOOMIS: Then let's call Computerland. Where's the Secretary?

BRUNSWICK: It's your turn.

LOOMIS: Oh, yeah.

ART DIRECTORS
Monique Risch
Tyler Vogel
DESIGNER
Bob Kurtz
PRODUCERS
Patti Dungen
Cindy Fluitt
DIRECTOR
Bob Kurtz
WRITER
Sharon Goldberg
CREATIVE DIRECTOR
Bob Browand
ILLUSTRATOR
Bob Kurtz
CLIENT
Computerland
AGENCY/STUDIO
Lewis Browand &
Associates
PRODUCTION COMPANY
Kurtz & Friends

ART DIRECTORS
Monique Risch
Tyler Vogel

DESIGNER
Bob Kurtz

PRODUCERS
Patti Dungen
Cindy Fluitt

DIRECTOR
Bob Kurtz

WRITER
Sharon Goldberg

CREATIVE DIRECTOR
Bob Browand

ILLUSTRATOR
Bob Kurtz

CLIENT
Computerland

AGENCY/STUDIO
Lewis Browand & Associates

PRODUCTION COMPANY
Kurtz & Friends

"MOVING UP"

BRUNSWICK: Well, Fred, our little company's moving up.

LOOMIS: Ohhh, yeah, Max. Bright young staff. New clients.

BRUNSWICK: Fortune 500, here we come!

LOOMIS: Well, on our way to the top, let's stop back at Computerland. We need a new computer.

BRUNSWICK: (*THOUGHTFULLY*) Hmm. Computerland *was* easy on the ole budget.

LOOMIS: (*BRIGHTENING*) Friendly, too.

BRUNSWICK: (*GETTING EXCITED*) Great at service and training.

LOOMIS: Yeah. Even taught *you* to use it. Heh, heh.

BACKGROUND VOICES: Mr. Loomis, Mr. Brunswick…

BRUNSWICK: Fred, remember when it was just you, me and the computer?

LOOMIS: Yeah, great computer?

BRUNSWICK: Ummm.

"GOING TO WORK"

MAN 1: They here yet?

MAN 2: Plenty of time, it's only 7:45.

MAN 1: What's so interesting?

MAN 2: Those two down there.

MAN 1: Oh, that's Wilson and Bennet, a couple of hotshots from finance.

MAN 2: What are they carrying?

MAN 1: Oh, those are computers.

MAN 2: Computers? They're taking our computers home at night?

MAN 1: Not exactly; they're bringing their computers in.

MAN 2: You're kidding. What for?

MAN 1: Well for one thing, that's how they put together these killer forecasts.

MAN 2: You mean we can't do this on our system?

MAN 1: Nope, not like this.

MAN 2: Okay, two questions: What kind of computers are they using?

MAN 1: And?

MAN 2: And why don't we have them?

ART DIRECTOR
Rick Strand (SF)

CREATIVE DIRECTOR
Alex Cichy

PRODUCER
Gene Lofaro

DIRECTOR
Cynthia Franco (SF)

CLIENT
Apple Computer, Inc.

AGENCY/STUDIO
BBDO

PRODUCTION COMPANY
Pytka Prod. (LA)

ART DIRECTOR
Rick Strand (SF)

CREATIVE DIRECTOR
Alex Cichy

PRODUCER
Gene Lofaro

DIRECTOR
Cynthia Franco (SF)

CLIENT
Apple Computer, Inc.

AGENCY/STUDIO
BBDO

PRODUCTION COMPANY
Pytka Prod. (LA)

"THE REPORT"

MAN 1: Yes, I know but…I understand, but I still want our attorneys to handle it. Fine.

MAN 2: Isn't that thing settled yet?

MAN 1: It looks like it's going to drag on forever. What do you think of Jensen's report?

MAN 2: It looks okay.

MAN 1: Okay?

MAN 2: Alright, it looks terrific; what do you want me to say? This is great work.

MAN 1: I thought so, too.

MAN 2: It's nice to see our computer system is finally earning its keep.

MAN 1: I wish that were true.

MAN 2: What do you mean?

MAN 1: Marketing isn't using our system anymore.

MAN 2: They're not? Then how did they do this?

MAN 1: They did it on their own system, the one they got a month ago.

MAN 2: They put this together in a month?

MAN 1: Well, not quite Frank, they did it in a week.

SUPER: (APPLE® LOGO)
Macintosh.® The power to be your best.

"THE RED-EYE"

(V.O.): Uh, this is the Captain again; we now expect to arrive at Kennedy Airport at around 6:40am.

MAN 1: I see you've got homework, too.

MAN 2: It never ends; you'd think when you get to this point things would get easier.

MAN 1: Yeah, I know—that looks like that was quite a project.

MAN 2: Yeah, it was. Have a look, no trade secrets here.

MAN 1: Thanks. Impressive. I wish we could do work like this, but we have to crank it out every week.

MAN 2: We do ours every week.

MAN 1: Well, we can't afford to farm ours out, we have to do them on a computer.

MAN 2: We did this on our computer.

MAN 1: You did that on a computer?

MAN 2: Of course, if we farmed them out I couldn't afford to ride up here.

SUPER: (APPLE® LOGO)
Macintosh.® The power to be your best.

ART DIRECTOR
Rick Strand (SF)
CREATIVE DIRECTOR
Alex Cichy
PRODUCER
Gene Lofaro
DIRECTOR
Cynthia Franco (SF)
CLIENT
Apple Computer, Inc.
AGENCY/STUDIO
BBDO
PRODUCTION COMPANY
Pytka Prod. (LA)

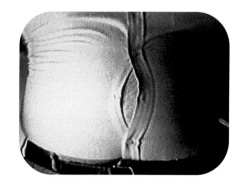

ART DIRECTOR
Jac Coverdale

WRITER
Jerry Fury

PRODUCTION COMPANY
Northwest
Teleproductions

AGENCY/STUDIO
Clarity Coverdale Rueff

"SPARETIRE"

Simple instructions for changing your
spare tire.
Join the YMCA.

"PAPER DOLLS"

SFX: (MUSIC OVER AND THROUGHOUT)

ANNCR: More and more families are moving closer and closer to our forests. That's why if you're careless with fire when you go to the forest you could burn a lot more than trees. Only you can prevent forest fires.

ART DIRECTOR
Ralph Price
DESIGNER
Ralph Price
PRODUCER
Mark Filippo
DIRECTOR
Phil Marco
WRITER
Peter Angelos
CLIENT
U.S. Forest Service
AGENCY/STUDIO
Foote, Cone & Belding
PRODUCTION COMPANY
Phil Marro Productions

ART DIRECTORS
Tery Norton
Ed Zelinsky

PRODUCER
Bruce Daman

DIRECTOR
David Greenfield

WRITER
David Perkins

CLIENT
Maine Teenage Males
Preventing Pregnancy

AGENCY/STUDIO
Megaphone

PRODUCTION COMPANY
WPXT-TV

"TEENS"

BOY 1: I don't care if she's pregnant. It's not my problem.

BOY 2: Hey, birth control is up to the girl.

BOY 3: But I'm too young to make a girl pregnant.

BOY 4: She had sex with a lot of guys. They can't prove it's mine.

BOY 5: It's her baby. She's gotta pay for it.

BOY 1: It's not my problem.

MAN (V.O.): Becoming a teenage father is your problem. Get the facts about preventing pregnancy. Because sex is nothing to kid around with.

"JR. CD"

ANNCR: For as long as there have been chores to do, parents have taught their children how to earn money.

BOY: Dad . . .

DAD: Yeah.

BOY: I just mowed the doggy.

DAD: (preoccupied) Good boy, here's a quarter.

ANNCR: But while parents' dollars multiplied handsomely, invested in CDs, the children's small fortunes languished unprosperously in the bellies of small plastic pigs.

SFX: (Coin dropped in piggybank.)

ANNCR: Until now. Introducing the Lincoln Savings Jr. CD.

BOY: Dad . . .

DAD: Yeah.

BOY: I just waxed the couch.

DAD: Fine, here's a quarter.

ANNCR: If you know someone 16 or under, that little someone can now invest as little as $100, from 7 days to 10 years or anywhere in between.

BOY: Dad . . .

DAD: Yeah.

BOY: I just painted the kitty.

DAD: That's nice, here's a quarter.

ANNCR: Their Lincoln Jr. CD enjoys the same rates as our adult CDs. And it's compounded daily. It's an excellent way to teach your future tycoon how to both earn money . . .

BOY: Dad . . .

DAD: Yeah.

BOY: I just washed your shoes.

ANNCR: And save it, as well. Stop by any of Lincoln's 24 branches for details. The new Jr. CD from Lincoln. The only savings institution big enough to think this small.

DAD: (loudly) Honey, have you seen my shoes?

BOY: Member FSLIC.

"1001 NIGHTS"

ANNCR: For the most part behaviorists have been able to identify four different screams. The "hysterical" scream . . .

SFX: (SCREAM.)

ANNCR: . . . with its piercing shrieking quality. The "gutteral" scream . . .

SFX: (SCREAM.)

ANNCR: . . . as if deep from within. And the "silent" scream . . .

SFX: (QUIET.)

ANNCR: . . . perhaps the most frightened of all.

No one can say which scream you'll make when you ride "A Thousand and One Nights." We'll just have to wait and see.

"A Thousand and One Nights" at Boardwalk and Baseball. It's ready if you are.

CREATIVE DIRECTORS
Ken Sakoda
Scott Montgomery
WRITER
Scott Montgomery
CLIENT
Lincoln Savings
AGENCY/STUDIO
Reyes Art Works
PRODUCTION COMPANY
LA Studios

RADIO

PRODUCER
Beth Hagen
CREATIVE DIRECTOR
Bob Kuperman
WRITER
John Stein
CLIENT
Boardwalk & Baseball
AGENCY/STUDIO
DDB Needham
Worldwide Los Angeles

RADIO

PRODUCER
Gabby Gruen

DIRECTOR
Gabby Gruen

WRITER
Gabby Gruen

CLIENT
The Factory
Fashion Works

PRODUCTION COMPANY
Gabby Gruen
Creative Services

AGENCY/STUDIO
Gabby Gruen
Creative Services

DIRECTOR
Christine Coyle

WRITER
Dick Orkin's Radio Ranch

CLIENT
Kroger Stores

AGENCY/STUDIO
Campbell Mithun
Chicago

PRODUCTION COMPANY
Dick Orkin's Radio Ranch

"SUMMMER OF SLOTH"

MUSIC: (LEISURELY JAZZ SLOWED TO A WOBBLE)

ANNCR: Sloth. First discovered on a sofa. In May. During a nap.

CATATONIA: Whatcha' doin,' Bobby?

BOBBY: Nothin.'

CATATONIA: Cool.

ANNCR: Today, Sloth is celebrated on beaches and in back yards, in union halls and the halls of Congress. Wherever it's easier said than done, you'll find sloth.

BOBBY: Hey. I got my heart rate down to 4 beats a minute.

CATATONIA: You animal.

ANNCR: Of course, once you get your sloth moves down, you have to dress the part. And for that you need the help of The Factory Fashion Works.

(STORE SFX)

BOBBY: Is this Print Shirt $10? Miss? You're lying down.

SALESGIRL: To serve you better.

ANNCR: It's The Factory's "Summer of Sloth" Sale. With almost no effort and just a few bucks, you sloths and slothettes can look like the best of the breed. For example, just $10 buys you Colored Bermuda Shorts. Casual Chambray Pleated Pants, just $15 bucks.

SFX: (BIRDS TWEET)

BOBBY: I got this Oxford Work Shirt for just $10.

ANNCR: Sloth season runs through May 25th at The Factory Fashion Works, Downtown and Sherman Oaks.

CATATONIA: (SCORNFUL) Work...shirt?

BOBBY: It's just an expression.

"TWO LITTLE WORDS"

SFX: DOOR OPENS

MAN: How ya doin birthday girl?

WOMAN: Aah George, you remembered my birthday.

MAN: Heh heh. Ya know I was gonna get ya some flowers or something but I forgot.

WOMAN: Ah well— that's okay hon.

MAN: You're not mad?

WOMAN: Ah no. Just the words happy birthday is enough.

MAN: Ah good. Happy birthday.

WOMAN: (Half laugh) well...you're a busy man...you don't have time to run all over town.

MAN: I wouldn't of had to.

WOMAN: What?

MAN: There's this new service called Heart to Heart Express. I could have called em.

WOMAN: Oh but when would you have found time?

MAN: Well, with Heart to Heart you can call 24 hours a day for flowers.

WOMAN: 24 hours?

MAN: Sure. They make it easy. I don't know why I didn't do it.

WOMAN: Well...you had to look up the number.

MAN: No. It's really an easy number.

WOMAN: It is.

MAN: Yeah, flowers. You just dial flowers.

WOMAN: F-L-O-W-E-R-S?

MAN: Yeah. Clever idea huh? Heh heh. That's why they did it, so people don't have to look up the number. Just dial flowers.

WOMAN: Well...then you'd have to go pick them up.

MAN: Heart to Heart delivers to your door see.

WOMAN: To my door?

MAN: Yeah.

WOMAN: In other words, I could have gotten flowers delivered to my door?

MAN: Plants, fruit baskets, card, even balloons—I don't know why I didn't do it.

WOMAN: Beacuse you're a thoughtless cheap biscuit brain!

MAN: Say are you mad?

WOMAN: Get out of here!

MAN: You said you weren't mad.

WOMAN: (Screams) I'm not mad!

SFX: DOOR SLAMS.

MAN: Ya know I bet she's mad.

ANNCR: Heart to Heart Express is a service of Kroger. Just call flowers. Any Time.
Available only in the national metro area.

"PROMISES

ORIGINAL MUSICAL ACCOMPANIMENT (POST-SCORED)

ANNCR: Last New Year's you said—

WOMAN: "As soon as the holidays are over, I'm going to get in shape."

ANNCR: Winter ended. (MUSICAL FLOURISH. WIND DIES DOWN.) Spring came. (MUSICAL FLOURISH. BIRDS CHIRPING.) And went. (BIRDS STOP.) You said—

WOMAN: "I've got to go work out before summer comes or I'll look like a sausage in my bathing suit!"

ANNCR: So you did a little this. (EXERCYCLE) And a little that. (CLANK, CLANK) And it did a little good. (CLANK. SIGH.) For a little while. And the fall came. (MUSICAL FLOURISH) And you promised to turn over—a new leaf.

WOMAN: "Wait 'til you see me at Thanksgiving!"

ANNCR: So we waited.

WOMEN: "Okay, wait 'til Christmas!"

ANNCR: And then . . . (SFX: "HAPPY NEW YEAR!" HORNS, BELLS, CHEERS. MUSICAL FLOURISH.) Now it's January. Again. And you're about to say—

WOMEN: "Listen, I'm really broke from the holidays, but next month, I promise—"

ANNCR: (ALMOST CUTTING HER OFF) Don't make—any more empty promises. Okay? Do something. Now. At a health club that has everything it takes to get you the body you've been promising yourself. And everything you need to keep it that way. That a promise.

LIVE ANNCR. TAG: Join Holiday or Richard Simmons now, when you can still get 1986 rates. And don't worry if the holidays cleaned you out. You won't have to come up with a nickel for 30 days. Promise! Some restrictions apply.

"ELECTION UPDATE"

SFX: (HIGHWAY.)

RICH: Rich Hall here. On the road for Pizza Hut. You know, I'm having this election to find out what America's favorite Pizza Hut® pizza is. And someone said "Rich, I don't vote for presidents, why should I vote for a pizza?" Well, let me read you a letter I received from a small overseas child.

MUSIC: ("OH, BEAUTIFUL" MUSIC STARTS.)

RICH: Dear Mr. Rich, in the country from which I am to be writing at you, to find a Pizza Hut, no you wouldn't. So when it is I heard you on the short waves, I knew this might be my one life in chancetime to vote. Put me down for a bilini with thin crust. With great sincerely, name withheld. Well, as Americans, we can take a lesson from little name withheld. You should vote not only because voting is a sacred privilege, but because you could be one of the lucky people who wins a pizza a week for 52 weeks. Did democracy ever aspire to higher goals? I think not. This is Rich Hall, in America for Pizza Hut.

TAG ANNCR: No purchase necessary for sweepstakes entry. Full details and entry blanks availabe at participating Pizza Hut® restaurants through February 21, 1987. Void where prohibited.

ART DIRECTOR
Julie Markell

PRODUCER
Kaylyn Kramer

WRITER
Brandy French

CLIENT
Health & Tennis Corp.

AGENCY/STUDIO
J. Walter Thompson

RADIO

PRODUCER
David Prince

WRITER
Steve Kessler

CLIENT
Pizza Hut, Inc.

AGENCY/STUDIO
Chiat/Day Advertising

RADIO

PRODUCER
Ellen Israel

WRITERS
Jim Kochevar
Jeff Moore

CLIENT
Chi-Chi's Mexican
Restaurants

AGENCY/STUDIO
Young & Rubicam
Chicago

ART DIRECTOR
Jill Kohut

PRODUCER
Len Levy

WRITER
Wendi Knox

CLIENT
ARCO
LA Central Library

PRODUCTION COMPANY
Recording Place

AGENCY/STUDIO
Kresser, Craig/D.I.K.

"RENDEZVOUS"

MAN: I was at a gas station when this beautiful blonde drove up in a Jaguar. She was my favorite kind of woman…alone. So I walked over to make her acquaintance. I said hello. She said hello. To further this blossoming romance, I proposed a rendezvous. She suggested food. I knew we had a lot in common because I was feeling hungry, too. Then she said, "What do you feel like, handsome?" And that's when I peered into her baby blues, pursed my lips and said:

MAN SINGS MEXICAN MUSIC

ANNCR: Sometimes you feel a little Mexican, and when you feel a little Mexican, try Chi-Chi's Special Dinner. A zesty enchilada. Crunchy taco. Testy taquito in beef, and new chicken or seafood. And for a limited time, free sopaipillas for desert.

CHI-CHI'S. WHEN YOU FEEL A LITTLE MEXICAN.

"SAVE THE BOOKS"

ANNCR: Books can expand your mind…

MALE V/O #1: "I think, therefore I am."

ANNCR: and touch your heart.

FEMALE V/O #2: I'll just think about it tomorrow."

ANNCR: Books can keep you up at night…

MALE V/O #2: "Quoth the Raven nevermore."

ANNCR: and give you pleasant dreams.

FEMALE V/O #2: "Once upon a time there were three bears."

ANNCR: Books can make friends.

FEMALE V/O #3: "I've always depended upon the kindness of strangers."

ANNCR: Books can paint pictures.

MALE V/O #3: "Out! Out brief candle!"

ANNCR: Books can weave memories.

MALE V/O #4: "These are the times that try men's souls."

ANNCR: Unfortunately, books can also burn.

SFX: (SIRENS. FIRE ENGINES, ETC.)

ANNCR: The fire at the Central Library destroyed 400,000 books, but with your help, each and every one can be put back in its place. To make a donation, please call 486-BOOK. 486-BOOK. The next chapter is up to you.

"RATIO"

SFX: (ESTABLISH BAR SETTING. BEER BOTTLES OPENING THROUGHOUT.)

DONALD: As former Bud drinkers, we wanted to tell you that La Crosse, Wisconsin—home of Old Style beer—has one bar for every 248 people . . .

CURTIS: The second highest ratio in America.

DONALD: St. Louis, Missouri, home of Bud, has only one bar for every 1,379 people . . . which is an awful lot if you're waiting to use the restroom.

CURTIS: Or want another beer . . .

DONALD: The people of La Crosse could have built an arch, or had a symphony like those in St. Louis . . . but, with a beer as good as Old Style you need plenty of places for people to drink it . . .

CURTIS: And Old Style is so good, it now outsells Bud 3 to 1 in a lot of places . . .

DONALD: And about a thousand to one here in La Crosse . . .

DONALD: So maybe they don't have an arch here, or a symphony . . . but, almost every bar has a juke box that'll give you two plays for a quarter . . .

CURTIS: No symphony gives you two plays for a quarter . . .

DONALD: And you can get Old Style at those bars. America's best brewed premium beer . . . a beer so good they built an entire town on it.

ANNCR: G. Heileman Brewing Company, LaCrosse, Wisconsin

"HITS YOU IN ALL THE RIGHT PLACES"

SFX: (POP, SIP, GULP, AHHHH.)

BED & CHANT: Ha-wai-ian-Pun-ch Ha-wai-ian-Pun-ch

SFX: (CANS OPENING) (Click-click-click-click-click-click-click-click-click.)

VOCAL: Ow! It hits you in all the right places. Ahhhh.

BED & CHANT: Ha-wai-ian-Punch

SFX: (Sip-ahh-sip-ahh-sip-sip-sip-ahh.)

MALE SINGER: Hawaiian Punch.

FEMALE SINGER: It hits you in all the right

GROUP: Places.

SFX: (REWIND)

BED & CHANT: Hawaiian Punch

BED:

CHANT: Hawaiian Punch.

MUSIC & VOCALS: Hawaiian Punch. It hits you in all the right places. Hawaiian Punch. It hits you in all the right places.

SFX: (CANS OPENING AND AHHH'S)

AGENCY PRODUCER
Jan Collins
WRITER
Scott Burns
CLIENT
G. Heileman Brewing Co.
AGENCY/STUDIO
Young & Rubicam
Chicago

RADIO

PRODUCERS
Ken Fitzgerald
John Lee Wong
WRITER
Ken Fitzgerald
CLIENT
Hawaiian Punch
AGENCY/STUDIO
United Western Studios
PRODUCTION COMPANY
HLC

DESIGN

ANNUAL REPORT

ART DIRECTOR
Jim Berte

DESIGNER
Jim Berte

PRODUCER
Robert Miles Runyan
& Associates

DIRECTOR
Larry Watts

WRITER
Deborah Meyer

CLIENT
Caremark Inc.

AGENCY/STUDIO
Robert Miles Runyan
& Associates

PRODUCTION COMPANY
Robert Miles Runyan
& Associates

ART DIRECTOR
Robert Miles Runyan

DESIGNER
Douglas Joseph

PRODUCER
Robert Miles Runyan
& Associates

DIRECTOR
Robert Miles Runyan

WRITER
Client

ILLUSTRATOR
Guy Billout

CLIENT
Micom

AGENCY/STUDIO
Robert Miles Runyan
& Associates

PRODUCTION COMPANY
Robert Miles Runyan
& Associates

ART DIRECTOR
Tracey Shiffman

DESIGNER
Tracey Shiffman

EDITOR
Lisa Citron

PHOTOGRAPHER
Roland Young

*PHOTOGRAPHER
COVER*
Tracey Shiffman

*PHOTOGRAPHER
INSIDE*
Nancy Klobucar

CLIENT
Orthopaedic Hospitals

AGENCY/STUDIO
Tracey Shiffman
Roland Young
Design Group

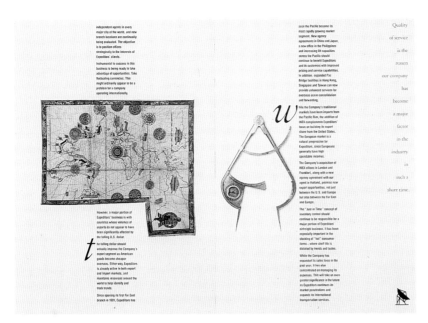

ANNUAL REPORT

ART DIRECTOR
John Van Dyke

DESIGNER
John Van Dyke

WRITER
Gary Fowler

PHOTOGRAPHER
Cliff Feiss

CLIENT
Expeditors International

AGENCY/STUDIO
Van Dyke Company

ART DIRECTOR
Bryan L. Peterson

DESIGNER
Bryan L. Peterson

WRITER
Gerald McGee

PHOTOGRAPHERS
Paul Talley
David Najjab

CLIENT
Southern Methodist
University

AGENCY/STUDIO
Peterson & Company

ART DIRECTOR
Mark Anderson

DESIGNER
Earl Gee

WRITER
James P. McNaul, PhD.

PHOTOGRAPHER
Henrik Kam

CLIENT
Datacopy Corporation

AGENCY/STUDIO
Mark Anderson Design

PRODUCTION COMPANY
AR Lithographers

DESIGN

ANNUAL REPORT

ART DIRECTOR
Peter Harrison

DESIGNER
Susan Hochbaum

WRITER
David Bither

PHOTOGRAPHER
Scott Morgan

CLIENT
Warner
Communications, Inc.

AGENCY/STUDIO
Pentagram Design

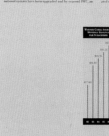

DESIGN DIRECTOR
Ivan Chermayeff

DESIGNER
Bill Anton

PHOTOGRAPHER
Alan Shortall

ILLUSTRATOR
Ivan Chermayeff

CLIENT
Hechinger Co.

AGENCY/STUDIO
Chermayeff & Geismar
Assoc.

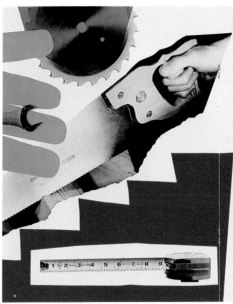

Last year, we also successfully premiered a more fashion-oriented insert, which has become a regular part of our advertising mix. In new markets, newspaper advertisements and our popular tabloid inserts are reinforced with television and radio commercials. Through our advertising, we work to make Hechinger a household word in all our markets.

To underscore our commitment to consumer education, we stage numerous consumer clinics throughout the year and frequently combine them into D-I-Y shows. These exciting productions build customer traffic and feature 50 to 60 concurrent "hands on" product demonstrations. Last year we held 13 D-I-Y shows and are planning a similar number for 1987.

Delivering the Goods
While our promotions, service and selection bring customers into our stores, our Central Distribution Center delivers many of the goods. Approximately 45% of sales move through our mammoth distribution center in Landover, Maryland.

Our computerized distribution system, developed in house, is the most sophisticated in the industry. Designed to ship to our stores no less than twice a week, it maximizes the amount shipped on each truck with the use of a computerized merchandise cubing support system. In addition to expediting delivery of advertised goods to our stores, our system of strong centralized distribution also allows us to handle seasonal and imported goods, as well as bulk quantities.

An additional 140,000 square feet of warehouse space is currently under construction in Landover, Maryland. When this space is completed, it will handle all products transported by flatbed. To further support our continued growth, we plan to open our first regional distribution center this year. This 310,000-square-foot facility will initially service 17 stores, with the capacity to ultimately service 30 stores. As the Company continues to cluster in the North and West, regional warehousing will be considered for those areas as well.

Putting Technology to Work
In addition to supporting the distribution center, our state-of-the-art management information systems play a crucial role in all of our operations. Last year we made several key improvements to the system, including a new credit authorization system that speeds up checkouts, an automated markdown system that eliminates the need for a physical count of sale merchandise before and after the sale, a computer-aided design system used by our real estate and store operations people, and an expansion of our data processing capacity through new hardware.

In 1987, we will take the most dramatic step in systems enhancement in the history of the Company—our revolutionary Integrated Retail Information System, IRIS for short, which will consolidate item movement, merchandising, advertising and accounting information into a powerful common data base. When implemented, IRIS will be a major contributor to further reducing our administrative costs and providing a new dimension in forecasting, evaluating and analyzing our business.

ART DIRECTOR
Kit Hinrichs

DESIGNERS
Kit Hinrichs
Karen Berndt

WRITER
Burson & Marsteller

PHOTOGRAPHERS
Terry Heffernan
Barry Robinson
Eric Meyer

ILLUSTRATOR
Doug Johnson (Cover)

CLIENT
MGM/UA
Communications

AGENCY/STUDIO
Pentagram Design

productivity and fully utilize hidden assets by reevaluating its structure and financial performance. They're working to align the interests of owners and managers by increasing equity values and investment returns. Their impact is evidenced in the increases in job formation, productivity and economic growth over the last five years.

Frequently, these financial entrepreneurs are substantial owners of the corporations they manage. In other cases, they may seek to acquire undervalued assets through a change in corporate control. In many cases, risk-taking managers are doing more innovative transactions, providing more attractive returns for shareholders. Like the early entrepreneurs of American history, they're not afraid of taking risks. But the risks they're taking are carefully calculated to increase corporate competitiveness and improve shareholder returns through restructuring. They are engaged in "creative destruction."

Who are these new entrepreneurs? They can be owners, managers, shareholders, financial partnerships or leveraged buyout organizations. They can be unsolicited bidders or dissenting shareholders seeking ways to maximize investment returns or increase their company's financial flexibility.

Restructuring to Stay Competitive

Restructuring is one important solution for many corporations preparing to compete in the global markets, and many of the new entrepreneurs have used it as their principal tool to maximize their companies' performance. Restructuring has also played an important role in the movement to realign the interests of owners and managers through going-private transactions. Since 1979, the annual number of going-private transactions has increased nearly fivefold from 16 to 76 per year. Over the same period, these transactions have grown from 6.4 percent to 19 percent of mergers and acquisitions.

Corporate leaders are taking a closer look at their existing assets. They are reassessing operating and performance ratios, as well as reevaluating liquidity and debt ratios using more realistic benchmarks and criteria. For in a period of tight competition and narrowing profit margins, corporations cannot afford to hold onto unproductive assets, let productivity falter or sit on unused cash reserves. The new entrepreneurs are streamlining the American corporation, increasing its financial efficiency and utilizing its full capacity. By divesting unproductive assets, they're freeing up capital for more productive uses. Conglomerates, many of which proved unable to manage their diverse business lines efficiently,

"All the conditions of doing business are always in the process of change."
Joseph A. Schumpeter

21

Drexel Burnham Lambert

ANNUAL REPORT

ART DIRECTOR
Colin Forbes

DESIGNER
Michael Gericke

PHOTOGRAPHER
Neil Selkirk

ILLUSTRATORS
Paul Keith
Irene Von Treskow
Su Huntley and
Donna Muir
Simon Stern
Ian Beck
George Hardie
Jonathan Field
Dan Fern
Matthew Bell
Ward Schumaker

CLIENT
Drexel Burnham
Lambert

AGENCY/STUDIO
Pentagram Design

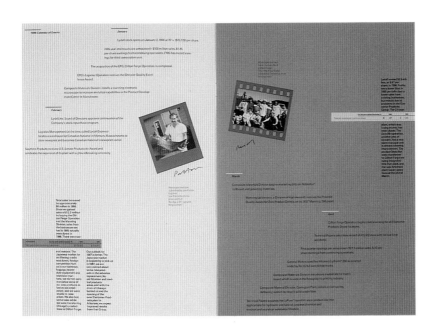

ART DIRECTOR
Robert Appleton

DESIGNER
Robert Appleton

WRITER
Carole F. Butenas

CLIENT
Lydall, Inc.

AGENCY/STUDIO
Appleton Design Inc.

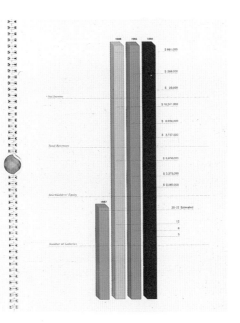

ART DIRECTORS
Brian Gormley
Koji Takei

DESIGNER
Dennis Michael Dimos

WRITER
Brian Gormley

CLIENT
Martin Lawrence
Limited Editions

AGENCY/STUDIO
Gormley/Takei, Inc.

ANNUAL REPORT

ART DIRECTOR
John Van Dyke

DESIGNER
John Van Dyke

WRITER
Bill Hays

PHOTOGRAPHERS
Terry Heffernan
Cliff Fiess

CLIENT
Weyerhaeuser
Paper Company

AGENCY/STUDIO
Van Dyke Company

ART DIRECTORS
Robert Meyer
Jean Page

DESIGNER
Jean Page

WRITER
Theodore Holmgren

PHOTOGRAPHER
Major: Joseph Chiu

CLIENT
Curtice-Burns, Inc.

AGENCY/STUDIO
Robert Meyer Design, Inc.

ART DIRECTOR
Greg Samata

DESIGNER
Greg Samata

DIRECTOR
Greg Samata

WRITER
Anne A. Sharp

PHOTOGRAPHER
Bob Tolchin

CLIENT
Kemper Reinsurance

AGENCY/STUDIO
Samata Associates

PRODUCTION COMPANY
Rohner Printing
Company

Book, Magazine
and Other Publishing

Consider: Lawyers provided with the latest intelligence on medical-malpractice issues. Health-care professionals receiving the most recent information on heart dysrhythmias. This is all part of the information explosion we've heard about. But nowhere is it more apparent than in Times Mirror's professional- and consumer-publishing operations.

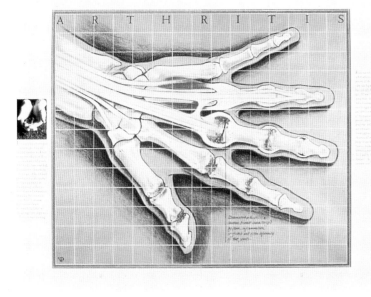

ANNUAL REPORT

ART DIRECTOR
Jim Berte

DESIGNER
Jim Berte

PRODUCER
Robert Miles Runyan
& Associates

DIRECTOR
Robert Miles Runyan

WRITER
Client

PHOTOGRAPHER
Scott Morgan

CLIENT
Times Mirror Company

AGENCY/STUDIO
Robert Miles Runyan
& Associates

PRODUCTION COMPANY
Robert Miles Runyan
& Associates

ART DIRECTOR
Kit Hinrichs

DESIGNERS
Kit Hinrichs
Belle How

PHOTOGRAPHER
Steve Firebaugh

ILLUSTRATOR
Vincent Perez

CLIENT
Immunex Corporation

AGENCY/STUDIO
Pentagram

ART DIRECTOR
Robert Miles Runyan

DESIGNER
Thomas Devine

PRODUCER
Robert Miles Runyan
& Associates

DIRECTOR
Robert Miles Runyan

WRITER
Client

PHOTOGRAPHER
Jim Sims

CLIENT
Fox Photo

AGENCY/STUDIO
Robert Miles Runyan
& Associates

PRODUCTION COMPANY
Robert Miles Runyan
& Associates

BROCHURE, FOLDER

ART DIRECTOR
John Cleveland

DESIGNER
John Cleveland

WRITER
Rose Deneve

PHOTOGRAPHER
Peter Darley Miller

CLIENT
S.D. Warren Company

AGENCY/STUDIO
John Cleveland, Inc.

ART DIRECTOR
Jim Cross
Michael Skjei

DESIGNER
Michael Skjei

PHOTOGRAPHER
Doug Manchee

CLIENT
Simpson Paper Co.

AGENCY/STUDIO
Cross Associates

▲

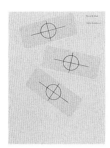

ART DIRECTOR
Leslie Smolan

DESIGNERS
Leslie Smolan
Eric Pike

WRITER
Rita Jacobs

PHOTOGRAPHERS
Barbara Bordnick
Dana Gluckstein
Steve Krongard
John Maramus
John Olson
Jerry Valente

CLIENT
Merrill Lynch

AGENCY/STUDIO
Carbone Smolan
Associates

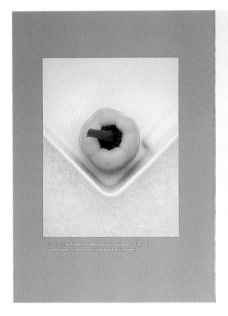

► A MARKET FOR FRESHNESS

Fresh, refrigerated salads
are shipped daily from our
plants in Los Angeles and
Atlanta. Retail and food
service markets are served
by a national network of
sales representatives and
food brokers. Turnaround
is critical, and we pride
ourselves on quick service.
Quality Control monitors
our products' life-cycles
beyond final delivery,
insuring that our cus-
tomers' consumers receive
the freshest salads possible.

BROCHURE, FOLDER

ART DIRECTOR
Kimberly Baer
DESIGNER
Barbara Cooper
WRITER
Fleishman-Hillard
PHOTOGRAPHERS
Color: George Monserrat
B/W: Jeff Corwin
CLIENT
Alex Brands
AGENCY/STUDIO
Kimberly Baer Design
Assoc.

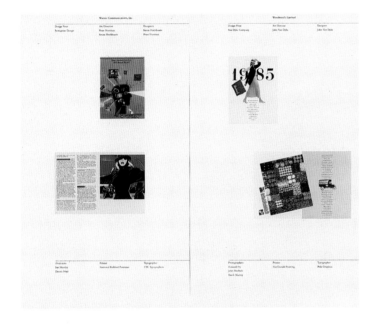

ART DIRECTOR
Jim Berte
DESIGNER
Jim Berte
PRODUCER
Robert Miles Runyan
& Associates
DIRECTOR
Robert Miles Runyan
WRITER
Client
PHOTOGRAPHERS
Peter Kane
Cynthia Moore
CLIENT
Mead Paper
AGENCY/STUDIO
Robert Miles Runyan
& Associates
PRODUCTION COMPANY
Robert Miles Runyan

ART DIRECTOR
Michael Patrick Cronan
DESIGNERS
Michael Patrick Cronan
Linda Lawler
PHOTOGRAPHER
Thomas Heinser
ILLUSTRATOR
Michael Cronan
CLIENT
Simpson Paper Co.
AGENCY/STUDIO
Cronan Design

DESIGN

BROCHURE, FOLDER

ART DIRECTOR
Leslie Smolan

DESIGNERS
Leslie Smolan
Alyssa Adkins

WRITER
Smith Barney

ILLUSTRATORS
Jack Goldstein
Mark Dean
Jean-Charles Blais
Roger Brown
Keith Haring
Mike Howard
Mark Kostabi
Walter Robinson
Andrew Stevovich
Karl Wirsum

CLIENT
Smith Barney

AGENCY/STUDIO
Carbone Smolan
Associates

ART DIRECTOR
Moshe Elimelech

DESIGNER
Moshe Elimelech

CLIENT
Dataproducts

AGENCY/STUDIO
ME Graphics

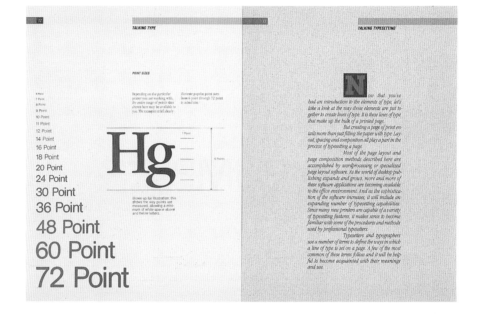

ART DIRECTOR
John Van Dyke

DESIGNER
John Van Dyke

WRITER
Peter Maloney

PHOTOGRAPHER
Terry Heffernan

CLIENT
Mead Paper Company

AGENCY/STUDIO
Van Dyke Company

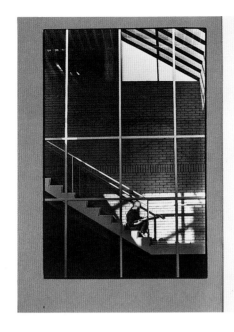

What will you find at MCAD that you won't find at a liberal arts college or university? A community of people whose lives are dedicated to creativity. MCAD's faculty, students, and staff are committed to exploring new ways of expressing ideas visually. People here experiment continually, often working on projects late into the night. And they find some mighty unusual places to exhibit their art—in the bathroom, in the stairwells, on the windows, from the ceiling, in the trees, even coming out of the ground! It's both exciting and challenging to attend college in such a stimulating, ever-changing environment.

What differentiates the Minneapolis College of Art and Design from other art and design colleges? An emphasis on problem solving, which lies at the core of all creative endeavor in our studio classes. At the heart, too, of MCAD's educational philosophy rests the conviction that the artist and designer play a powerful and responsible role in society.

The College's academic programs encourage students to cross boundaries between disciplines, to think in interdisciplinary terms, and to express their ideas through a variety of media. To enable these explorations, MCAD provides some of the finest equipment and facilities available to art and design students in the United States. Our photography, film, and video facilities are among the very best. We have a fully-equipped 3D Shop and print-making studio. And our computer graphics laboratory offers sophisticated, state-of-the-art computer equipment.

One of the greatest benefits of being a student at MCAD is that you are only 100 feet away from the Minneapolis Institute of Art. An encyclopedic art museum, the Institute has an impressive permanent collection of more than 80,000 objects, including important European and American paintings and sculpture, period rooms, and Oriental, African, Oceanic, Native American, and PreColumbian art, dating from 22,000 BC to the present. Admission to the Institute is free to all MCAD students.

The Minneapolis College of Art and Design is located in the heart of Minneapolis, just blocks away from a beautiful chain of lakes and parks and minutes from bustling downtown streets. We're only a short bus ride from Walker Art Center and from a growing number of small, independent galleries that show contemporary art in the city's warehouse district. Minneapolis and St. Paul are also known nationally for producing some of the hottest, most innovative creative talent in advertising and design. In short, if you're interested in the visual arts, then the Twin Cities are an ideal place to study and to work.

OUR STRENGTHS

A Commitment to Creativity

A Focus on Creative Problem Solving and Social Responsibility

Technical Facilities and Equipment

Minneapolis Institute of Art

Minneapolis/St. Paul

BROCHURE, FOLDER

DESIGN DIRECTOR
Ivan Chermayeff

DESIGNER
Bill Anton

WRITER
Liz Spring

CLIENT
Minneapolis Arts

AGENCY/STUDIO
Chermayeff & Geismar Assoc.

ART DIRECTOR
Mitchell Mauk

DESIGNER
Mitchell Mauk

WRITERS
Mitchell Mauk
Damien Martin
Raymond Burnham Jr.

CLIENT
Entertainment Technologies

AGENCY/STUDIO
Mauk Design

development center for the contemporary arts. In the course of an average year, Real Art Ways presents over a hundred events from major American artists to emerging regional artists. These programs reflect cutting edge experimental art in all its forms, meeting a need unfilled by most museums, symphonies and traditional arts institutions. The quality and thoughtfulness of these presentations have achieved regional, national and international critical acclaim. As a result, Real Art Ways has found itself, both by focused effort and by example, functioning as a catalyst for the strengthening and

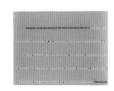

ART DIRECTOR
Robert Appleton

DESIGNER
Robert Appleton

WRITER
Ellie MacDougall

PHOTOGRAPHER
Various

CLIENT
Real Art Ways

AGENCY/STUDIO
Appleton Design Inc.

▲

BROCHURE, FOLDER

ART DIRECTOR
Kevin B. Kuester
DESIGNER
Kevin B. Kuester
COPY
Dick Cinquina
PHOTOGRAPHER
Terry Heffernan
CLIENT
Potlatch Corporation,
Northwest Division
AGENCY/STUDIO
Madsen and Kuester, Inc.

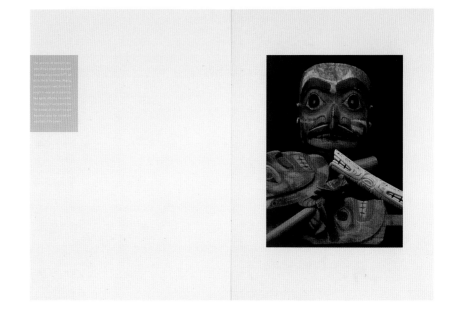

ART DIRECTOR
James Cross
DESIGNER
Yee-Ping Cho
WRITER
Maxwell Arnold
PHOTOGRAPHER
Various
ILLUSTRATOR
Various
CLIENT
Simpson Paper Co.
AGENCY/STUDIO
Cross Associates
▲

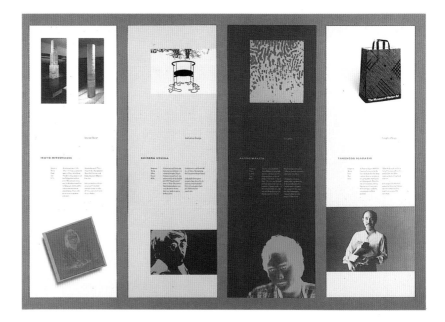

ART DIRECTOR
Byron Jacobs
DESIGNER
Byron Jacobs
CLIENT
Newport Harbor Art
Museum
AGENCY/STUDIO
Byron Jacobs Design

BROCHURE, FOLDER

ART DIRECTOR
Gwyn Smith

DESIGNERS
Kit Hinrichs
Niel Shakery

WRITER
John Dreyfuss
ACCD Development

PHOTOGRAPHERS
Jim Blackley
Steven A. Heller

CLIENT
Art Center College
of Design

AGENCY/STUDIO
Pentagram
▲

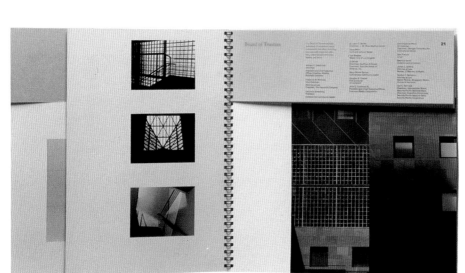

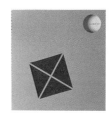

ART DIRECTORS
Tracey Shiffman
Roland Young

DESIGNER
Tracey Shiffman

PRODUCER
Kerry Buckley,
Director of Development,
MOCA

WRITER
Tom Pope

PHOTOGRAPHERS
R. Young
G. Mudford
D. Parker
D. Keeley
Squidds & Nunns

CLIENT
The Museum of
Contemporary Art

AGENCY/STUDIO
Tracey Shiffman
Roland Young Design
Group

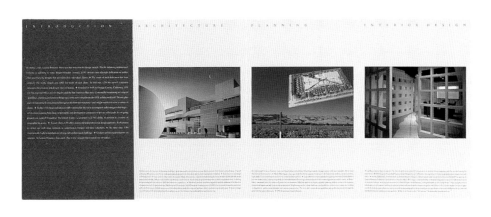

ART DIRECTOR
Michael Manwaring

DESIGNER
Michael Manwaring

CLIENT
Leason Pomeroy
Associates

AGENCY/STUDIO
The Office of
Michael Manwaring

BROCHURE, FOLDER

ART DIRECTOR
Jennifer Morla

DESIGNER
Jennifer Morla

WRITER
Jennifer Morla

PHOTOGRAPHER
Jeffrey Newbury

CLIENT
Levi Strauss & Co.

AGENCY/STUDIO
Morla Design, Inc.

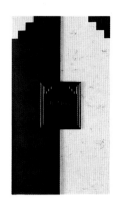

ART DIRECTORS
David Edelstein
Nancy Edelstein
Lanny French

DESIGNERS
David Edelstein
Nancy Edelstein
Lanny French
Carol Davidson

PRODUCER
D. Thom Bissett

WRITERS
Jeremy Wolff
Nancy Edelstein

PHOTOGRAPHER
Lara Rossignol

CLIENT
Generra Sportswear

AGENCY/STUDIO
Edelstein Associates
Advertising Inc.

ART DIRECTOR
Neal Zimmerman

DESIGNERS
Michael Cronan
Linda Lawler

PHOTOGRAPHER
Charles Kemper

ILLUSTRATORS
Michael Cronan
Linda Lawler
Sharon Fukatome

CLIENT
Levi Strauss & Co.

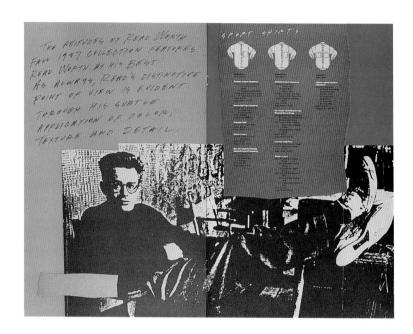

BROCHURE, FOLDER

ART DIRECTOR
John Bielenberg

DESIGNERS
John Bielenberg
Allen Ashton

CLIENT
Attitudes of Read Worth

AGENCY/STUDIO
The Marks Group

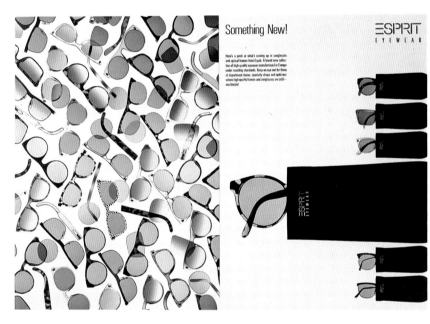

ART DIRECTOR
Tamotsu Yagi

DESIGNERS
Tamotsu Yagi
Hiroshi Serizawa

PHOTOGRAPHERS
Oliviero Toscani
Roberto Carra

CLIENT
Esprit de Corp

AGENCY/STUDIO
Esprit Graphic Design
Studio

PRODUCTION COMPANY
Graphic Arts Center

ART DIRECTOR
John Coy

DESIGNERS
John Coy
Kevin Consales

WRITER
Charles Labiner

PHOTOGRAPHER
COY, Los Angeles
& Richard Noble

ILLUSTRATOR
Scott Baldwin

CLIENT
Georgia Pacific Paper
Company

AGENCY/STUDIO
COY, Los Angeles

DESIGN

BROCHURE, FOLDER

ART DIRECTOR
James Sebastian

DESIGNERS
James Sebastian
Rose Biondi

INTERIOR DESIGNER
William Walter

PHOTOGRAPHER
Bruce Wolf

CLIENT
Martex / West Point
Pepperell

AGENCY/STUDIO
Designframe, Inc.

▲

ART DIRECTOR
Cheryl Heller

DESIGNER
Cheryl Heller

PHOTOGRAPHER
Helmut Newton

CLIENT
S.D. Warren

AGENCY/STUDIO
Heller Breene

MISSION STATEMENT
The Minneapolis College of Art and Design is an independent, private, specialized institution offering a professionally oriented education for artists and designers. The degree program integrates the liberal arts into studio-based curricula in Design, Fine Arts, and Media Arts. The Extension program offers introductory, advanced, and specialized learning opportunities for degree candidates, graduates, and the community at large.

The College is a regional resource, but the primary scope of its programs are universal. The College provides a personalized opportunity for students:
- to realize their aptitudes and interests;
- to acquire skills and techniques of visual and verbal expression;
- to develop creative, critical, responsible, and productive attitudes; and
- to reinforce the lifelong fulfillment of their personal potentials.

The teaching program employs professionally active faculty who use contemporary technology and historical perspective to encourage students to develop a skilled, contextual awareness and informed, discriminating opinions.

The College is committed to the fundamental principles of academic freedom and human rights. As an equal opportunity/affirmative action institution, MCAD provides the greatest possible access to those qualified to benefit from its programs.

THE BACHELOR OF FINE ARTS DEGREE
The Minneapolis College of Art and Design offers a four-year program leading to the Bachelor of Fine Arts (BFA) degree, with majors in Design, Fine Arts, Media Arts, and Interdisciplinary Studies.

New students enter the Visual Studies of the first year program which introduces them to a variety of media, a range of technique, and the process of creative problem solving. Liberal Arts courses, taken throughout the four years, familiarize students with historical, social, theoretical, literary, and anthropological contexts for the aesthetic problems they will research. By the end of their first year, most students choose a major based on their particular talents and interests in the work of the fine artist, the designer, or the media artist.

Credit Requirements
To graduate from MCAD, students must complete 135 credits to earn their Bachelor of Fine Arts degrees. The following chart outlines how many credits the typical student takes each year, in each of the College's divisions, to earn the BFA degree:

Division	1st Year	2nd Year	3rd Year	4th Year	Total
Visual Studies	18	–	–	–	18
Design/Fine Arts/or Media Arts	–	24	24	24	72
Liberal Arts	12	12	12	9	45
	30	36	36	33	135

To find out which classes you must take to earn the 135 credits needed for the BFA degree, consult each division's chapter in this catalog. During their first year, MCAD students must take 18 credits in Visual Studies; courses which satisfy this requirement are listed on page 3. Every student must complete 45 credits of Liberal Arts classes; see page 16 to find out which classes to take each of the four years you attend the College. Then, depending on which major you've chosen, consult the Design chapter on page 8, the Fine Arts chapter on page 10, the Media Arts chapter on page 15, or the Interdisciplinary Studies explanation on page 24, to discover how you complete 72 credits in your major to earn the Bachelor of Fine Arts degree.

Accreditation
Founded in 1886, the Minneapolis College of Art and Design is accredited by the North Central Association of Colleges and Schools and the National Association of Schools of Art and Design. MCAD is a member of the Minnesota Private College Council, the Association of Minnesota Colleges, and the Alliance of Independent Colleges of Art.

VISUAL STUDIES
The Division of Visual Studies seeks to broaden new students' perceptions of art and design, enhance their creativity, and develop their self-discipline. Instructors take students' skills as they are when they enter the College and build on them, strengthening and increasing them. Students have the opportunity to work on many projects and to investigate a variety of materials. Through this process, they acquire the basic understanding of art and design concepts and the basic technical skills needed to complete Design, Fine Arts, and Media Arts courses.

First-year faculty have a broad background in art and design that enables them to teach new students an interdisciplinary approach to the visual arts.

Visual Studies:
BFA Degree Requirements
To receive a BFA degree, students must earn 18 credits of Visual Studies, 9 each semester of their first year at MCAD as follows:

BROCHURE, FOLDER

DESIGN DIRECTOR
Ivan Chermayeff

DESIGNER
Bill Anton

WRITER
Liz Spring

PHOTOGRAPHER
Judy Olavsen

CLIENT
Minneapolis Arts

AGENCY/STUDIO
Chermayeff & Geismar Assoc.

STANFORD CONFERENCE ON DESIGN JULY 23-25 1987

ART DIRECTOR
Michael Patrick Cronan

DESIGNER
Michael Patrick Cronan

CLIENT
Stanford Design Conference

AGENCY/STUDIO
Cronan Design

▲

DESIGN

BROCHURE, FOLDER

ART DIRECTORS
Vance Studley
Stephen Levit
Lynn Easley
Suzanne Haddon
Trina Carter
Scott Allen
Ginny Egan
Jill Jacobson
Stacy Miereanu
Wendy Chism
Teal Rocco
Sean Ehringer
Jeff Hopfer
Sheri Myers Olmon
Nora Piibe
Charbel Bousraitt

DESIGNER
Vance Studley

WRITER
Edgar Allan Poe

CLIENT
Art Center College
of Design

AGENCY/STUDIO
ACCD Typography Class

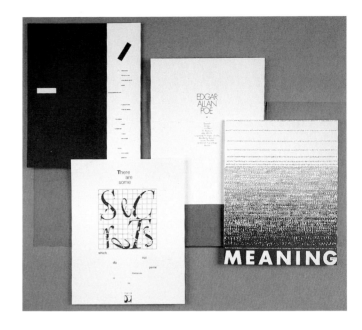

ART DIRECTORS
Brent L. Marmo
Elizabeth Rotter

DESIGNER
Elizabeth Rotter

PHOTOGRAPHER
Lou Goodman

CLIENT
Marcovici Designs

AGENCY/STUDIO
The Brownstone
Group, Inc.

ART DIRECTOR
Michael Patrick Cronan

DESIGNER
Michael Cronan

PHOTOGRAPHER
Thomas Heinser

CLIENT
Levi Strauss & Co.

AGENCY/STUDIO
Cronan Design

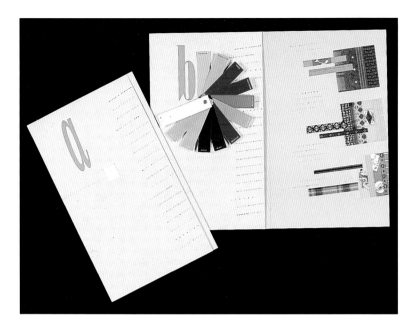

BROCHURE, FOLDER

ART DIRECTORS
David Edelstein
Nancy Edelstein
Lanny French

DESIGNERS
David Edelstein
Nancy Edelstein
Lanny French
Carol Davidson

PRODUCER
D. Thom Bissett

WRITERS
Kathy Cain
Nancy Edelstein

PHOTOGRAPHERS
Jim Cummins
Karl Bischoff

CLIENT
Generra Sportswear

AGENCY/STUDIO
Edelstein Associates
Advertising Inc.

▲

ART DIRECTORS
David Edelstein
Nancy Edelstein
Lanny French

DESIGNERS
David Edelstein
Nancy Edelstein
Lanny French
Carol Davidson
D. Thom Bissett

PRODUCER
D. Thom Bissett

WRITERS
Kathy Cain
Nancy Edelstein

PHOTOGRAPHERS
Jim Cummins
Karl Bischoff

CLIENT
Generra Sportswear

AGENCY/STUDIO
Edelstein Associates
Advertising Inc.

DESIGN

3-D PACKAGING

ART DIRECTOR
Hal Silverman

DESIGNER
Ko Starkweather Eann

PHOTOGRAPHER
Ed Ouellette

CLIENT
Hickory Farms

AGENCY/STUDIO
Silverman Advertising
Design

ART DIRECTOR
Jack Anderson

DESIGNERS
Jack Anderson
Mary Hermes
Cheri Huber
Julie Tanagi

ILLUSTRATOR
Jani Drewfs

CLIENT
Tradewell

AGENCY/STUDIO
Hornall Anderson
Design Works

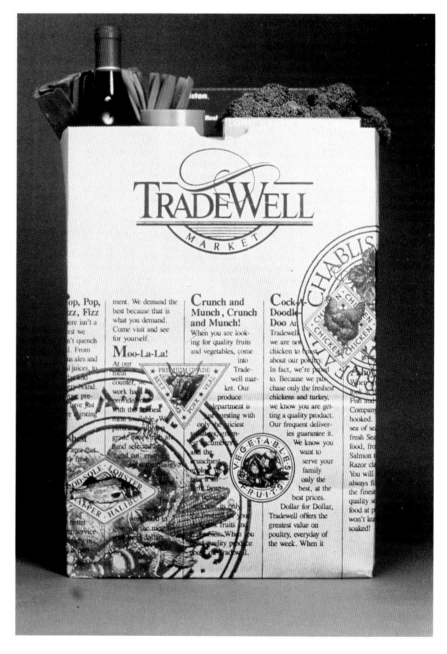

3-D PACKAGING

ART DIRECTORS
Hal Riney
Jerry Andelin
DESIGNERS
Primo Angeli
Ray Honda
ILLUSTRATOR
Mark Jones
CLIENT
Hal Riney & Partners
AGENCY/STUDIO
Primo Angeli, Inc.

ART DIRECTOR
Primo Angeli
DESIGNERS
Primo Angeli
Ray Honda
PHOTOGRAPHER
Ming Louie
CLIENT
Cambridge Nutrition
Canada Ltd.
AGENCY/STUDIO
Primo Angeli, Inc.

3-D PACKAGING

ART DIRECTOR
Mary Scott

DESIGNER
Tom Campbell

PRODUCER
Maddocks & Company

DIRECTOR
Frank Maddocks

CLIENT
Speedo

AGENCY/STUDIO
Tom Campbell +
Associates, Inc.

PRODUCTION COMPANY
Maddocks & Company

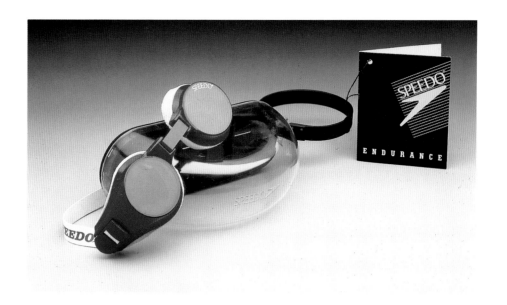

ART DIRECTORS
Rik Besser
Douglas Joseph

DESIGNER
Rik Besser

CLIENT
Vuarnet-France

STUDIO
Besser Joseph Partners

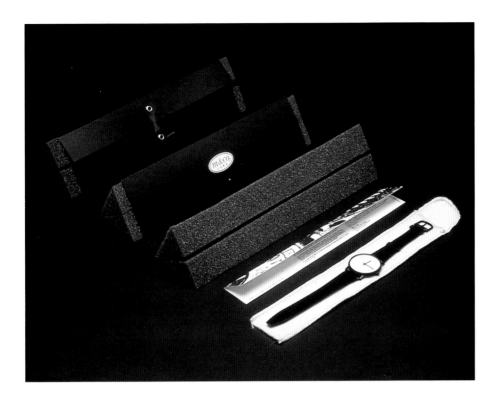

3-D PACKAGING

DESIGNERS
Tibor Kalman
Timothy Horn
CLIENT
M&Co. Labs
AGENCY/STUDIO
M&Co.

DESIGNERS
Tibor Kalman
Alexander Isley
CLIENT
M&Co. Lab
AGENCY/STUDIO
M&Co.

DESIGN

3-D PACKAGING

ART DIRECTOR
Tamotsu Yagi

DESIGNER
Tamotsu Yagi

CLIENT
Esprit de Corp

AGENCY/STUDIO
Esprit Graphic
Design Studio

PRODUCTION COMPANY
Georgia Pacific

ART DIRECTOR
Tamotsu Yagi

DESIGNER
Tamotsu Yagi

CLIENT
Esprit de Corp

AGENCY/STUDIO
Esprit Graphic Design
Studio

PRODUCTION COMPANY
Nissha Printing Co., Ltd.

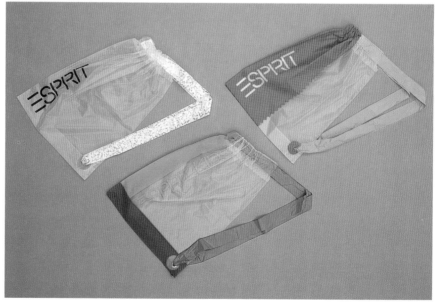

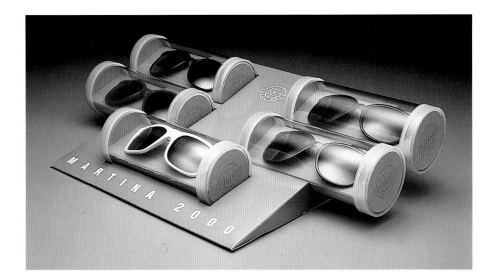

POINT OF PURCHASE,
DISPLAY

ART DIRECTORS
Rik Besser
Douglas Joseph
DESIGNER
Rik Besser
CLIENT
Vuarnet-France
STUDIO
Besser Joseph Partners

CAN WE ENLARGE SOMETHING FOR YOU?
We'd be more than happy to make 5x7, 8x10 or 11x14 enlargements of your favorite prints.

ART DIRECTOR
Yvonne Smith
DESIGNER
Yvonne Smith
WRITER
Marc Deschenes
PHOTOGRAPHER
Lamb & Hall Photography
CLIENT
Noritsu America
Corporation
AGENCY/STUDIO
(213) 827-9695 and
Associates
PRODUCTION COMPANY
The Production
Company

DESIGN

HOUSE ORGAN,
NEWSLETTER

ART DIRECTORS
Andy Molnar
Martha Schiebald

DESIGNER
George Watson

WRITER
Bruce Felton

PHOTOGRAPHERS
Robert Jackson
Sally Sanders
Nelson Greer
Berney Knox
Peter Young

ILLUSTRATORS
Larry Woznick
Stephen Schudlich
Lynn Boyer Pennington

CLIENT
DMB&B

AGENCY/STUDIO
Intergroup Marketing &
Promotions

**HOUSE ORGAN,
NEWSLETTER**

ART DIRECTOR
Lee Heidel

DESIGNERS
Lee Heidel
Jim Sanders

WRITER
Jennie Storey

ILLUSTRATOR
Karen Caldwell

CLIENT
Provident Companies

AGENCY/STUDIO
Provident Companies

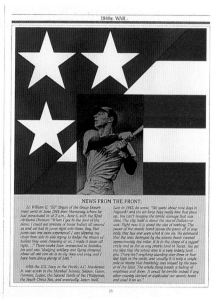

ART DIRECTOR
Richard Poulin

DESIGNERS
Richard Poulin
Kirsten Steinorth
Ran Van Koten

CLIENT
Heckscher Museum

AGENCY/STUDIO
de Harak & Poulin
Associates

ART DIRECTOR
Robert Appleton

DESIGNERS
Robert Appleton
Christopher Passehill

CLIENT
Real Art Ways

AGENCY/STUDIO
Appleton Design Inc.

▲

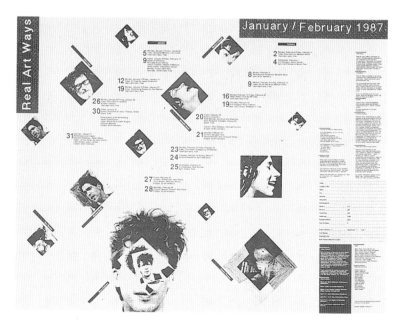

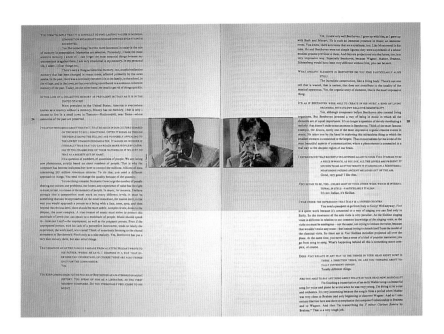

HOUSE ORGAN,
NEWSLETTER

DESIGNERS
Renee Cossutta
Judith Lausten

PHOTOGRAPHER
Steve Gunther

CLIENT
California Institute of
the Arts

AGENCY/STUDIO
Lausten/Cossutta Design

ART DIRECTOR
Kit Hinrichs

DESIGNERS
Kit Hinrichs
Lenore Bartz

WRITER
Susan Hoffman

PHOTOGRAPHERS
Steven A. Heller
Henrick Kam

ILLUSTRATORS
Gerald Huerta
Steven A. Heller

CLIENT
Art Center College
of Design

AGENCY/STUDIO
Pentagram, San Francisco

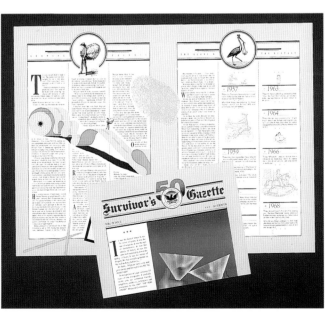

ART DIRECTOR
Tom Antista

DESIGNER
Thomas Fairclough

WRITER
Mickey Bower

ILLUSTRATOR
Thomas Fairclough

CLIENT
Western Direct
Marketing

AGENCY/STUDIO
Antista Design

PRODUCTION COMPANY
Printer: Ralphs Printing

POSTER
ART DIRECTOR
Craig Fuller
DESIGNER
Craig Fuller
PHOTOGRAPHER
Marshall Harrington
CLIENT
La Jolla Museum of
Contemporary Art
AGENCY/STUDIO
Crouch+Fuller, Inc.
PRODUCTION ARTIST
Nancy Mancuso
▲

ART DIRECTOR
Michael Patrick Cronan
DESIGNER
Michael Patrick Cronan
ILLUSTRATOR
Michael Patrick Cronan
CLIENT
Simpson Paper Company
AGENCY/STUDIO
Cronan Design

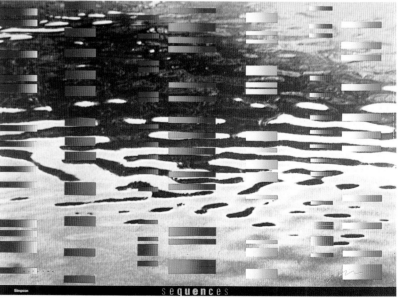

POSTER

ART DIRECTOR
Tom Antista

DESIGNER
Tom Antista

ILLUSTRATOR
Tom Antista

CLIENT
Bob Wellen
Ulano

AGENCY/STUDIO
Antista Design

ART DIRECTOR
Tom Antista

DESIGNER
Tom Antista

ILLUSTRATOR
Tom Antista

CLIENT
Chris Hopson
Tower Records

AGENCY/STUDIO
Antista Design
▲

POSTER

ART DIRECTOR Mike Hicks	*ART DIRECTOR* Tom Antista
DESIGNER Mike Hicks	*DESIGNER* Tom Antista
ILLUSTRATOR Michael Schwab	*ILLUSTRATOR* Tom Antista
CLIENT Seton Medical Center	*CLIENT* Chez Helene
AGENCY / STUDIO HIXO, Inc.	*AGENCY / STUDIO* Antista Design

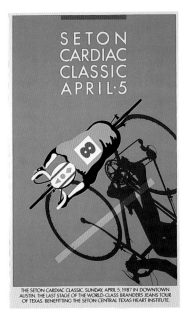

ART DIRECTOR
Steff Geissbuhler

DESIGNER
Steff Geissbuhler

PHOTOGRAPHER
Alan Shortall

CLIENT
AIGA / New York

AGENCY / STUDIO
Chermayeff & Geismar
Assoc.

POSTER

ART DIRECTOR
John Van Dyke

DESIGNER
John Van Dyke

PHOTOGRAPHER
Howard Petrella

AGENCY/STUDIO
Van Dyke Company

Connecticut   Volunteers
Special Olympics make the difference

ART DIRECTOR
Robert Appleton

DESIGNER
Robert Appleton

CLIENT
United Technologies
Corporation

AGENCY/STUDIO
Appleton Design, Inc.

ART DIRECTOR
Robert Appleton

DESIGNER
Robert Appleton

CLIENT
Pratt & Whitney Aircraft

AGENCY/STUDIO
Appleton Design, Inc.

DESIGN

POSTER

ART DIRECTOR
William Wondriska

DESIGNER
William Wondriska

PRODUCER
William Wondriska

DIRECTOR
William Wondriska

ILLUSTRATOR
William Wondriska

CLIENT
Boston Symphony
Orchestra

PRINTER
Allied Printing Services

AGENCY/STUDIO
Wondriska Associates
Inc.

▲

ART DIRECTOR
Ronald Kovach

DESIGNERS
Kwok Chan
Ronald Kovach

CLIENT
Mobium

AGENCY/STUDIO
Mobium

ART DIRECTOR
April Greiman

DESIGNER
April Greiman

CLIENT
(di-zin), Akbar
Alijamshid

AGENCY/STUDIO
April Greiman, Inc.

▲

ART DIRECTOR
Katherine Lorenzetti

DESIGNER
Katherine Lorenzetti

DIRECTOR
Katherine Lorenzetti

CLIENT
The New City YMCA

AGENCY/STUDIO
Burson-Marsteller

PRODUCTION COMPANY
Proto-Grafix Limited

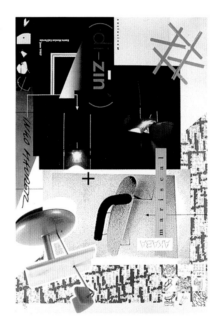

ART DIRECTOR
April Greiman

DESIGNER
April Greiman

PRODUCER
April Greiman

WRITER
April Greiman

PHOTOGRAPHER
Computer Graphic:
April Greiman

ILLUSTRATOR
Videographer:
April Greiman

CLIENT
Walker Art Center

AGENCY/STUDIO
April Greiman, Inc.

▲

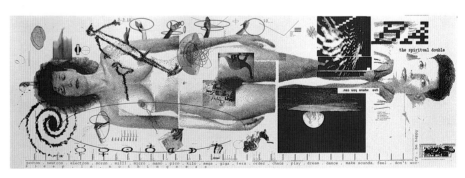

POSTER

ART DIRECTOR
Bryan L. Peterson
DESIGNER
Bryan L. Peterson
WRITER
Al Younts
ILLUSTRATOR
Bryan L. Peterson
CLIENT
Council for Advancement
& Support of Education
AGENCY/STUDIO
Peterson & Company

DESIGN DIRECTOR
Ivan Chermayeff
DESIGNER
Bill Anton
CLIENT
New York International
Festival of the Arts, Inc.

POSTER

ART DIRECTOR
Pearl Beach

DESIGNER
Pearl Beach

ILLUSTRATOR
Pearl Beach

CLIENT
Oingo Boingo

AGENCY/STUDIO
Walter/Johnsen

▲

ART DIRECTOR
William Wondriska

DESIGNER
William Wondriska

PRODUCER
William Wondriska

DIRECTOR
William Wondriska

WRITER
Lis Ingoldsby
United Technologies

PHOTOGRAPHER
J.R. Freiman

CLIENT
Wadsworth Atheneum

PRINTER
Allied Printing Services

AGENCY/STUDIO
Wondriska Associates
Inc.

▲

ART DIRECTOR
Primo Angeli

DESIGNER
Primo Angeli

ILLUSTRATORS
Ian McLean
Mark Jones

CLIENT
Friends of the Golden
Gate Bridge

AGENCY/STUDIO
Primo Angeli, Inc.

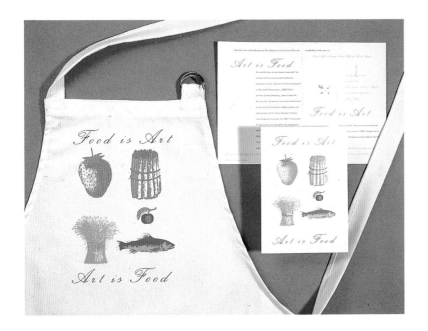

MENU, CALENDAR,
ANNOUNCEMENT

ART DIRECTOR
Deborah Sussman
DESIGNER
Gigi McGee
CLIENT
Womans Building, L.A.
AGENCY/STUDIO
Sussman/Prejza & Co.,
Inc.

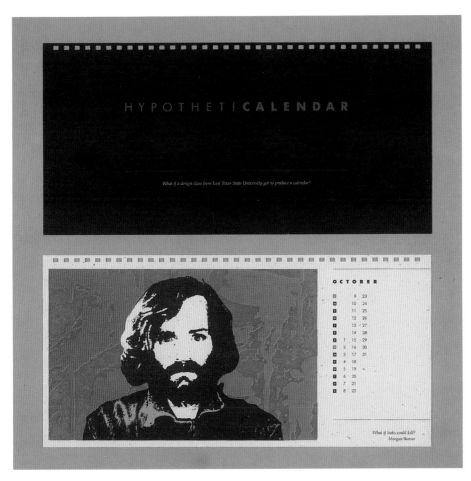

ART DIRECTOR
David Beck
DESIGNER
David Beck
PHOTOGRAPHERS
Jim Olvera
Larry Schultz
Rocky Powell
Bill Evans
ILLUSTRATORS
Allen Weaver
Linda Martin
Cary Trout
David Beck
John Peterson
Bruce Wynne-Jones
Brad Sims
Mark Smith
Robert Shniderson
Ellen Alva Hales
Paul Munsterman
David Lerch
Tad Griffin
Morgan Bomar
Haesun Kim
John Norman
Karla Compalans
CLIENT
East Texas State
University
AGENCY/STUDIO
David Beck

MENU, CALENDAR,
ANNOUNCEMENT

ART DIRECTOR
Kit Hinrichs

DESIGNERS
Kit Hinrichs
Gwyn Smith

WRITER
Peterson & Dodge

PHOTOGRAPHER
Terry Heffernan

CLIENT
American President Lines

AGENCY/STUDIO
Pentagram Design

ART DIRECTOR
Margi Denton

DESIGNER
Margi Denton

ILLUSTRATOR
Catherine Lorenz

CLIENT
Denton Design
Associates

AGENCY/STUDIO
Denton Design
Associates

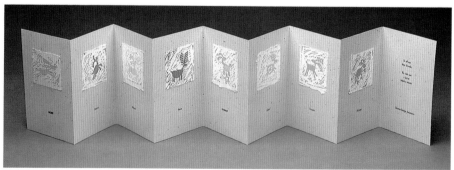

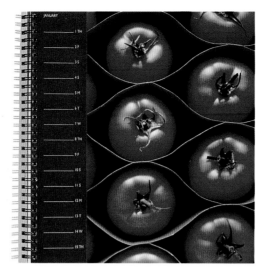

MENU, CALENDAR,
ANNOUNCEMENT

ART DIRECTOR
Carole Bouchard
DESIGNER
Carole Bouchard
WRITER
Peter Caroline
PHOTOGRAPHER
Various
CLIENT
General Electric Plastics
AGENCY/STUDIO
Heller Breene

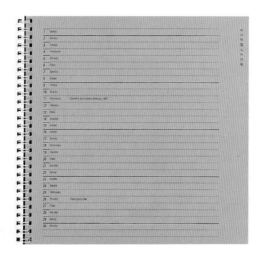

ART DIRECTOR
James Cross
DESIGNERS
Michael Mescal
Joseph Jacquez
PHOTOGRAPHER
Charles Imstepf
CLIENT
Simpson Paper Company
AGENCY/STUDIO
Cross Associates

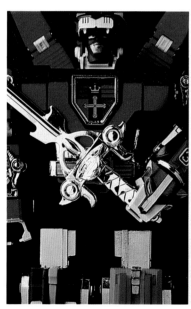

ART DIRECTOR
Kit Hinrichs
DESIGNERS
Kit Hinrichs
Gwyn Smith
WRITER
Peterson & Dodge
PHOTOGRAPHER
Terry Heffernan
CLIENT
American President
Companies
AGENCY/STUDIO
Pentagram Design

DESIGN

MENU, CALENDAR, ANNOUNCEMENT

ART DIRECTOR
Michael Carabetta

DESIGNER
Jenny Leibundgut

CLIENT
San Francisco Museum of Modern Art

AGENCY/STUDIO
Landor Associates

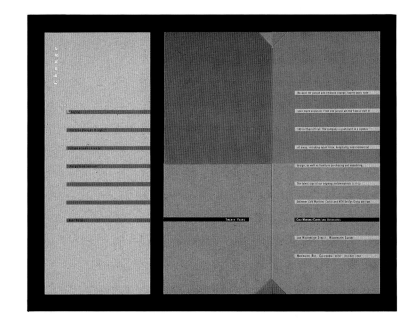

ART DIRECTOR
Ken White

DESIGNER
Lisa Levin

WRITER
Aileen Farnan

CLIENT
Cole Martinez Curtis

AGENCY/STUDIO
White & Associates

ART DIRECTOR
Rex Peteet

DESIGNER
Rex Peteet

WRITER
Rex Peteet

ILLUSTRATORS
Rex Peteet
Judy Dolim

CLIENT
International Paper Company

AGENCY/STUDIO
Sibley/Peteet Design, Inc.

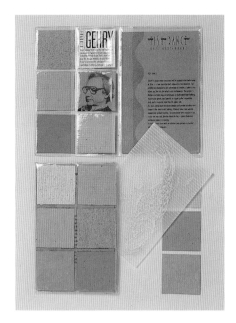

MENU, CALENDAR,
ANNOUNCEMENT

ART DIRECTOR
Tamotsu Yagi
DESIGNER
Tamotsu Yagi
CLIENT
Esprit de Corp.
AGENCY/STUDIO
Esprit Graphic Design
Studio
PRODUCTION COMPANY
Menu:
Charles Douglas
Printing, diecutting
shape:
Golden State Embossing
Company, Inc.

ART DIRECTOR
Tamotsu Yagi
DESIGNER
Tamotsu Yagi
ILLUSTRATOR
Frank O. Gehry
CLIENT
World Company, Ltd.
AGENCY/STUDIO
Nissha Printing
Company, Ltd.
▲

ART DIRECTORS
John Evans
Laura Malan Evans
DESIGNERS
John Evans
Laura Malan Evans
WRITERS
John Evans
Laura Malan Evans
ILLUSTRATOR
John Evans
CLIENT
John Evans
Laura Malan Evans
AGENCY/STUDIO
Sibley/Peteet
Design, Inc.

SELF PROMOTION

ART DIRECTOR
Tom Antista

DESIGNER
Tom Antista

ILLUSTRATORS
Tom Antista
Tom Fairclough

CLIENT
Les Sechler, Fashion
Institute of Design and
Merchandising

AGENCY/STUDIO
Antista Design

ART DIRECTOR
Michael Manwaring

DESIGNER
Michael Manwaring

CLIENT
New Mexico
Communicating Artists

AGENCY/STUDIO
The Office of
Michael Manwaring

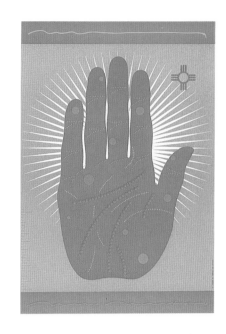

ART DIRECTOR
Tamotsu Yagi

DESIGNER
Tamotsu Yagi

PHOTOGRAPHERS
Robert Carra
Oliviero Toscani

CLIENT
Esprit Graphic Design
Studio

AGENCY/STUDIO
Esprit Graphic Design
Studio

PRODUCTION COMPANY
Nissha Printing
Company, Ltd.
▲

Best of Show

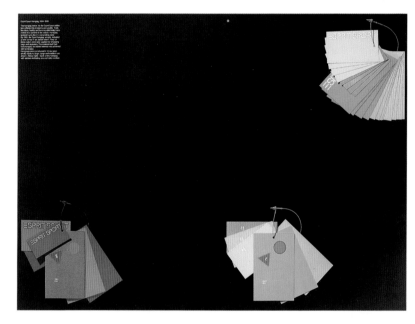

ART DIRECTOR
Kit Hinrichs

DESIGNER
Kit Hinrichs

WRITER
Delphine Hirasuna

PHOTOGRAPHER
Barry Robinson

ILLUSTRATOR
Various Historical

CLIENT
Pentagram Design

AGENCY/STUDIO
Pentagram Design

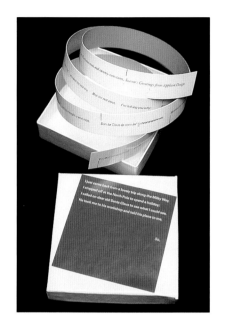

SELF PROMOTION

ART DIRECTOR
Robert Appleton

DESIGNER
Robert Appleton

CLIENT
Appleton Design, Inc.

AGENCY/STUDIO
Appleton Design Inc.

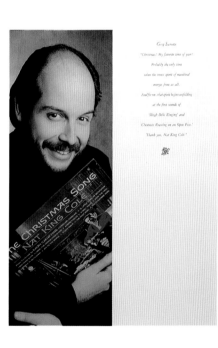

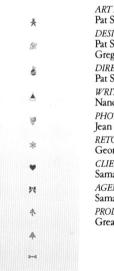

ART DIRECTOR
Pat Samata

DESIGNERS
Pat Samata
Greg Samata

DIRECTOR
Pat Samata

WRITER
Nancy Bishop

PHOTOGRAPHER
Jean Moss

RETOUCHER
George Sawa

CLIENT
Samata Associates

AGENCY/STUDIO
Samata Associates

PRODUCTION COMPANY
Great Northern Design

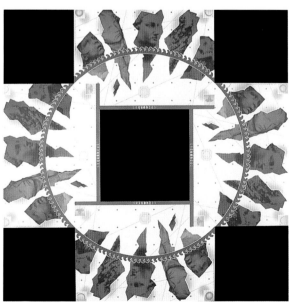

ART DIRECTOR
Michael Manwaring

DESIGNER
Michael Manwaring

CLIENT
Simpson Paper Company

AGENCY/STUDIO
The Office of
Michael Manwaring

ART DIRECTOR
Roberto Barazzuol
DESIGNER
Roberto Barazzuol
PRODUCER
Esprit
CLIENT
Esprit
AGENCY/STUDIO
Esprit
PRODUCTION COMPANY
Esprit

ART DIRECTOR
Roberto Barazzuol
DESIGNER
Roberto Barazzuol
PRODUCER
Esprit
CLIENT
Esprit
AGENCY/STUDIO
Esprit
PRODUCTION COMPANY
Esprit
▲

ART DIRECTOR
Scott Ray
DESIGNER
Scott Ray
CLIENT
Phillip Cooke
AGENCY/STUDIO
Peterson & Company

ART DIRECTORS
Tom Suiter
Jerry Kuyper
DESIGNER
Jenny Leibundgut
CLIENT
World Wildlife
Fund (WWF)
AGENCY/STUDIO
Landor Associates

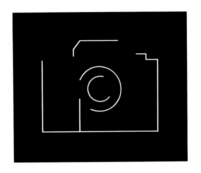

ART DIRECTOR
Moshe Elimelech
DESIGNER
Moshe Elimelech
CLIENT
Dataproducts
AGENCY/STUDIO
ME Graphics

ART DIRECTOR
Julia Tam
DESIGNER
Julia Tam
ILLUSTRATOR
John Lanuza
CLIENT
Laise Adzer
AGENCY/STUDIO
Rabuck & Fox

ARCHITECTURAL
FOUNDATION
O F   L O S   A N G E L E S

ART DIRECTOR
Wayne Hunt
DESIGNER
Brian Deputy
CLIENT
Architectural Foundation
of Los Angeles
AGENCY/STUDIO
Wayne Hunt Design, Inc.

Channeling Children's Anger

ART DIRECTORS
Terri Bogaards
Ellen Shapiro
DESIGNER
Terri Bogaards
ILLUSTRATOR
Terri Bogaards
CLIENT
Institute for Mental
Health Initiatives
AGENCY/STUDIO
Shapiro Design
Associates, Inc.
PRINTER
Metropolitan

ART DIRECTORS
Anthony Fedele
David Wesko
DESIGNER
David Wesko
ILLUSTRATOR
David Wesko
CLIENT
Partners National
Health Plans
AGENCY/STUDIO
Point Design/Point
Communications

ART DIRECTOR
Tamotsu Yagi
DESIGNER
Tamotsu Yagi
CLIENT
World Company, Ltd.
AGENCY/STUDIO
Sunao Ishii

DESIGN

VISUAL IDENTITY

ART DIRECTOR
Paul Ison

DESIGNER
Paul Ison

ILLUSTRATOR
Paul Ison

CLIENT
Paul Ison Design

AGENCY/STUDIO
Paul Ison Design

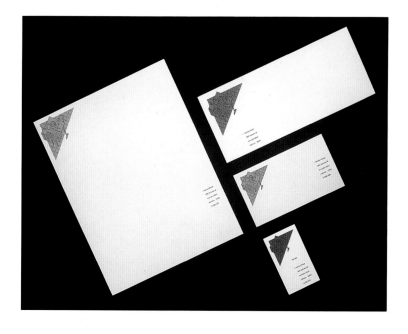

ART DIRECTOR
Mark Anderson

DESIGNER
Earl Gee

ILLUSTRATOR
Earl Gee

CLIENT
AR Lithographers

AGENCY/STUDIO
Mark Anderson Design

PRINTER
AR Lithographers

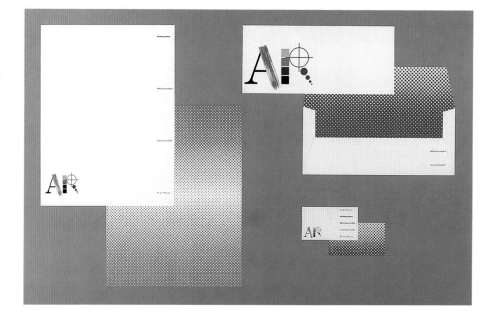

ART DIRECTOR
John Coy

DESIGNER
Laurie Handler

PHOTOGRAPHER
Timothy Bradley

CLIENT
San Diego Design Center

AGENCY/STUDIO
COY, Los Angeles

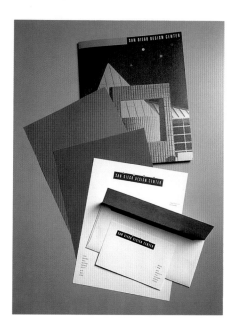

VISUAL IDENTITY

ART DIRECTOR
John Swieter

DESIGNER
John Swieter

ILLUSTRATOR
John Swieter

CLIENT
Winger Muscle Therapy

AGENCY/STUDIO
Swieter Design

PRODUCTION COMPANY
Premier Printing

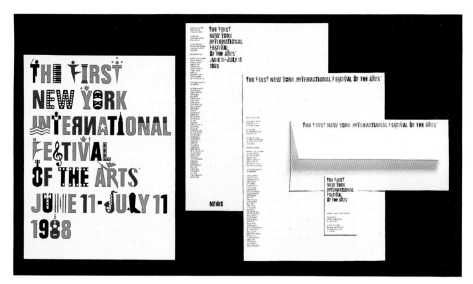

DESIGN DIRECTOR
Ivan Chermayeff

DESIGNER
Bill Anton

CLIENT
New York International
Festival of the Arts, Inc.

AGENCY/STUDIO
Chermayeff & Geismar
Assoc.

ART DIRECTOR
James A. Stygar

DESIGNER
James A. Stygar

CLIENT
Saxon Medical, Inc.

AGENCY/STUDIO
Folio2, Inc.

DESIGN

VISUAL IDENTITY

ART DIRECTOR
Robert Valentine

DESIGNER
Robert Valentine

ILLUSTRATOR
Robert Valentine

CLIENT
Sonia Kashuk Hair
& Makeup

AGENCY/STUDIO
Robert Valentine, Inc.

ART DIRECTORS
John Reeder
Tom Binnion

CLIENT
Manhattan
Confectioners, Inc.

AGENCY/STUDIO
Thomas Binnion

ART DIRECTOR
John Van Dyke

DESIGNER
John Van Dyke

CLIENT
Stuart Clugston

AGENCY/STUDIO
Van Dyke Company

▲

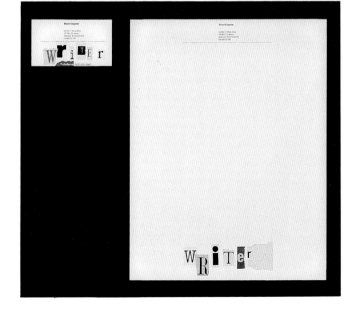

VISUAL IDENTITY

ART DIRECTOR
John Swieter
DESIGNER
John Swieter
ILLUSTRATOR
John Swieter
CLIENT
Watters & Watters
AGENCY/STUDIO
Sweiter Design
PRODUCTION COMPANY
Premier Printing

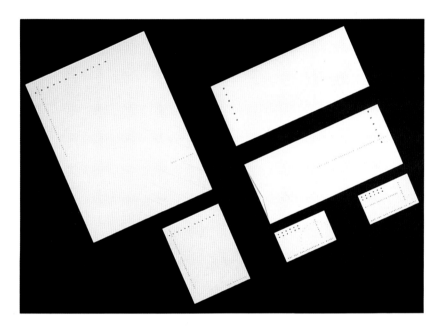

ART DIRECTOR
Michael Patrick Cronan
DESIGNERS
Michael Cronan
Linda Lawler
CLIENT
Cronan Design
AGENCY/STUDIO
Cronan Design

▲

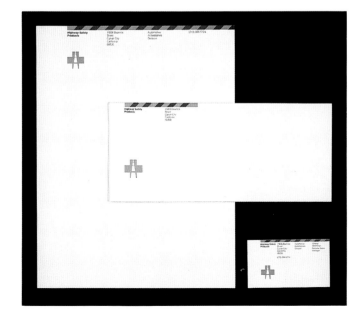

ART DIRECTOR
Arthur Nagano
DESIGNER
Arthur Nagano
CLIENT
Highway Safety Products
AGENCY/STUDIO
Works of Art

VISUAL IDENTITY

ART DIRECTOR
Butler Kosh Brooks
DESIGNER
Larry Brooks
AGENCY/STUDIO
Butler Kosh Brooks

VISUAL IDENTITY

DESIGN DIRECTOR
Ivan Chermayeff
DESIGNER
Bill Anton
WRITERS
Bill Anton
Mary McBride
CLIENT
New York International
Festival of the Arts, Inc.
AGENCY/STUDIO
Chermayeff & Geismar
Assoc.

The left spread shows a brand manual for "THE FIRST NEW YORK INTERNATIONAL FESTIVAL OF THE ARTS" — MUSIC, DANCE, THEATRE, OPERA, AND FILM OF THE 20TH CENTURY, with festival colors, the festival alphabet (ABCDEFGHIJKLMNOPQRSTUVWXYZ&$.,'-:;!? 1234567890), and special characters.

ART DIRECTOR
Primo Angeli
DESIGNERS
Primo Angeli
John Lodge
ILLUSTRATOR
Mark Jones
CLIENT
Lucca Delicatessen, Inc.
AGENCY/STUDIO
Primo Angeli, Inc.

VISUAL IDENTITY

ART DIRECTORS
Jack Anderson
Luann Bice

DESIGNERS
Jack Anderson
Luann Bice
Julie Tanagi
Cheri Huber
Jani Drewfs

CLIENT
Tradewell

AGENCY/STUDIO
Hornall Anderson
Design Works

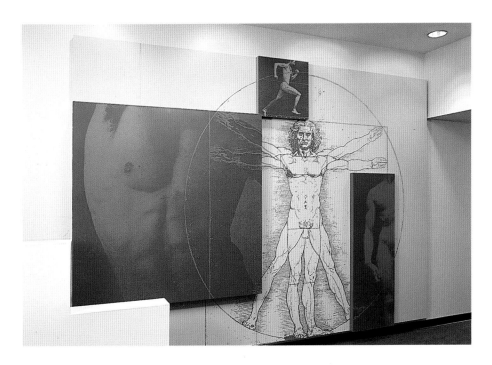

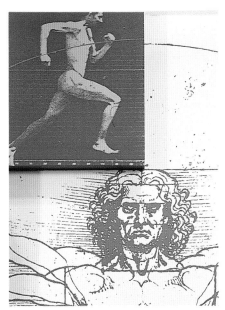

ENVIRONMENTAL
GRAPHICS

ART DIRECTOR
Richard Poulin
DESIGNER
Richard Poulin
Kirsten Steinorth
PHOTOGRAPHER
Ken Haak
CLIENT
Paragon Group
AGENCY/STUDIO
de Harak & Poulin
Associates
PRODUCTION COMPANY
HW Exhibits, Inc.

DESIGN

ENVIRONMENTAL GRAPHICS

ART DIRECTOR
Richard Foy

DESIGNERS
Michael Gerike
Bryan Gough
Chi-ming Kan
Susan Kinzig
Mark Tweed

PROJECT MANAGER
Gary Kushner

CLIENT
The Rouse Company

AGENCY/STUDIO
Communications Arts
Incorporated

PROJECT DIRECTORS
Richard Kung-
Environmental;
Creighton Dinsmore-
Graphics

DESIGNER
Creighton Dinsmore

CLIENT
ANEW (Way of
Wellness)

AGENCY/STUDIO
Landor Associates

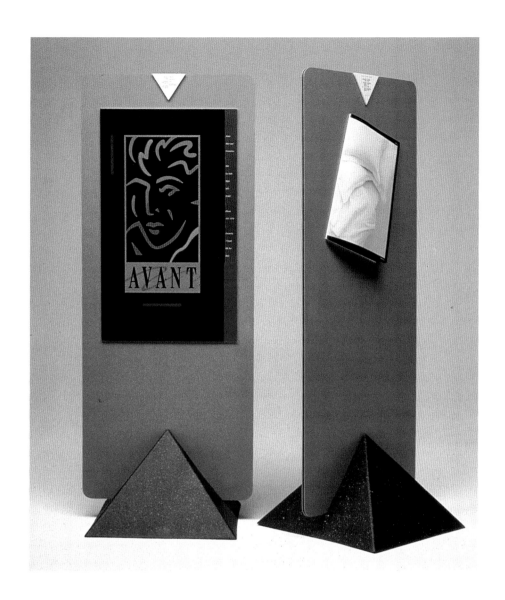

ENVIRONMENTAL GRAPHICS

ART DIRECTOR
Wayne Hunt

DESIGNERS
Wayne Hunt
Brian Deputy

CLIENT
Simpson Paper Co.

AGENCY/STUDIO
Wayne Hunt Design, Inc.

EDITORIAL

EDITORIAL

BOOK DESIGN
COVER

ART DIRECTOR
Tommy Steele

DESIGNER
Tommy Steele

WRITER
Tommy Steele

PHOTOGRAPHERS
Tommy Steele
Dennis Keeley

CLIENT
Abbeville Press, Inc.

AGENCY/STUDIO
SteeleWorks Design, Inc.

Best of Show

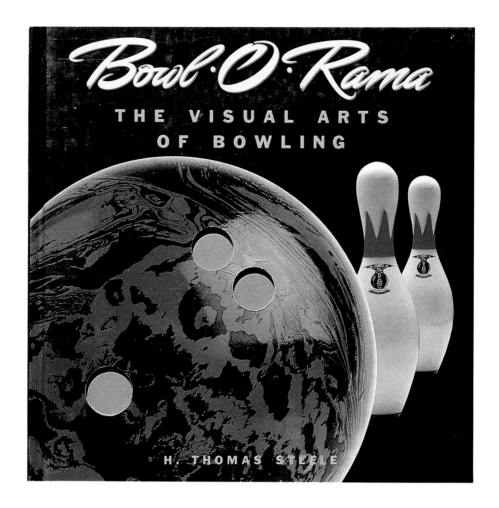

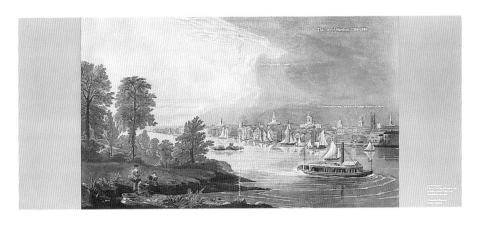

BOOK DESIGN
COVER

ART DIRECTOR
William Wondriska

DESIGNER
Ann O'Brien

PRODUCER
Ann O'Brien

DIRECTOR
William Wondriska

PHOTOGRAPHER
Robert Hawell

CLIENT
Society for Savings /
Connecticut Historical
Society

PRINTER
Mark-Burton

AGENCY/STUDIO
Wondriska Associates
Inc.

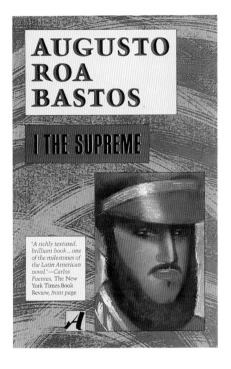

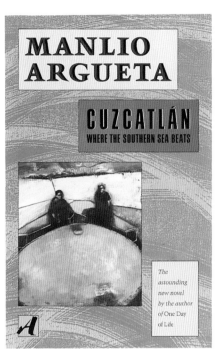

ART DIRECTOR
Keith Sheridan

DESIGNERS
Marie Barab
Craig Warner

ILLUSTRATOR
Vivienne Flesher

CLIENT
Random House, Inc.

▲

ART DIRECTOR
Keith Sheridan

DESIGNERS
Marie Barab
Craig Warner

ILLUSTRATOR
Vivienne Flesher

CLIENT
Random House, Inc.

AGENCY/STUDIO
Keith Sheridan Assoc.,
Inc.

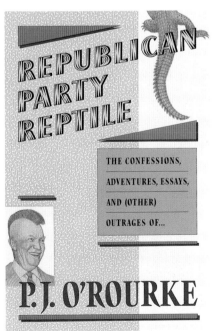

ART DIRECTOR
Robin Schiff

DESIGNERS
Keith Sheridan
Marie Barab
Craig Warner

ILLUSTRATOR
Kevin Sprouls

CLIENT
Atlantic Monthly Press

AGENCY/STUDIO
Keith Sheridan
Assoc., Inc.

EDITORIAL

BOOK DESIGN
COVER

ART DIRECTOR
Rod Dyer
DESIGNER
Harriett Baba
WRITER
Tommy Steele
PHOTOGRAPHERS
Tommy Steele
Jim Heimann
CLIENT
Abbeville Press, Inc.
AGENCY/STUDIO
Dyer/Kahn, Inc.

BOOK DESIGN

ART DIRECTORS
Tom Poth
Mike Hicks
DESIGNERS
Tom Poth
Mike Hicks
PHOTOGRAPHER
Robert Latorre
ILLUSTRATOR
Mike Hicks
CLIENT
Texas Monthly Press
AGENCY/STUDIO
HIXO, Inc.

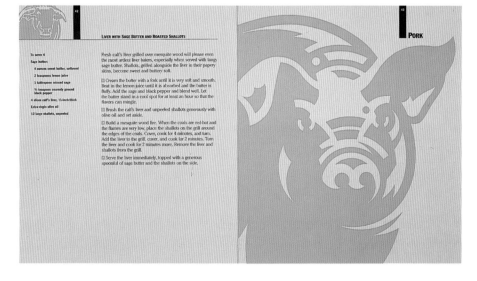

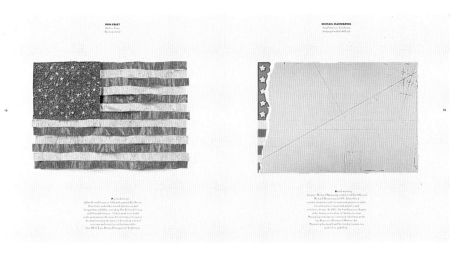

BOOK DESIGN

BOOK DESIGN

ART DIRECTOR
Kit Hinrichs

DESIGNER
Kit Hinrichs

WRITERS
Delphine Hirasuna
Steve Heller

PHOTOGRAPHERS
Michele Clement
Terry Heffernan
Barry Robinson

CLIENT
American Institute of
Graphic Arts

AGENCY/STUDIO
Pentagram Design

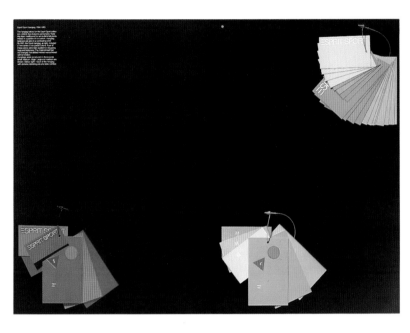

ART DIRECTOR
Tamotsu Yagi

DESIGNER
Tamotsu Yagi

PHOTOGRAPHERS
Robert Carra
Oliviero Toscani

CLIENT
Esprit De Corp.

AGENCY/STUDIO
Esprit Graphic Design
Studio

PRODUCTION COMPANY
Nissha Printing Co., Ltd.

▲

ART DIRECTORS
Terence Mitchell
Yee-Ping Cho

DESIGNER
Yee-Ping Cho

WRITER
Various

PHOTOGRAPHERS
Jay Venezia
Chris Morland

CLIENT
Community
Redevelopment Agency

AGENCY/STUDIO
In-house

two hundred twenty three

BOOK DESIGN

ART DIRECTOR
Leslie Smolan

DESIGNERS
Leslie Smolan
Thomas Walker

PRODUCER
A Day in the Life, Inc.

WRITER
Rita Jacobs

PHOTOGRAPHER
200 various
photographers

CLIENT
Collins Publishers

AGENCY/STUDIO
Carbone Smolan
Associates

ART DIRECTOR
Patrick Dooley

DESIGNER
Patrick Dooley

WRITER
Mike Weaver

PHOTOGRAPHER
Julia Margaret Cameron

CLIENT
The J. Paul Getty
Museum

AGENCY/STUDIO
The J. Paul Getty
Museum Publications

ART DIRECTOR
Don Weller

DESIGNER
Don Weller

WRITER
Nan Chalat

PHOTOGRAPHERS
Michael Schoenfeld
Don Weller

CLIENT
The Weller Institute for
the Cure of Design, Inc.

AGENCY/STUDIO
The Weller Institute for
the Cure of Design, Inc.

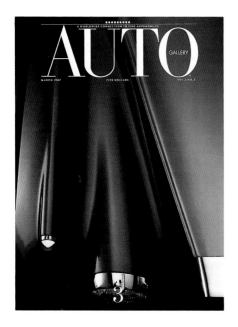

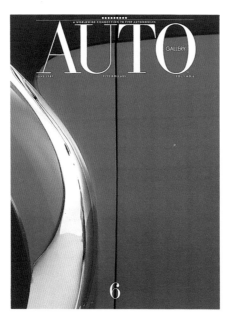

MAGAZINE DESIGN
COVER

ART DIRECTOR
Michael Brock
DESIGNERS
Michael Brock
Al Esguerra
PHOTOGRAPHER
Tim Hargrove
CLIENT
Auto Gallery
Publishing Co.
AGENCY/STUDIO
Michael Brock Design

ART DIRECTOR
Michael Brock
DESIGNER
Michael Brock
PHOTOGRAPHER
Cindy Lewis
CLIENT
Auto Gallery
Publishing Co.
AGENCY/STUDIO
Michael Brock Design

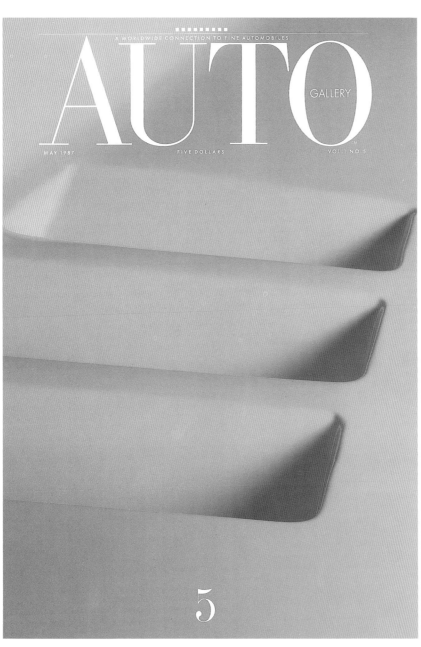

ART DIRECTOR
Michael Brock
DESIGNERS
Michael Brock
Al Esguerra
PHOTOGRAPHER
Glenn McCallister
CLIENT
Auto Gallery
Publishing Co.
AGENCY/STUDIO
Michael Brock Design

MAGAZINE DESIGN
COVER

ART DIRECTOR
Matthew Drace
WRITER
Matthew Drace
ILLUSTRATOR
Anita Kunz
AGENCY/STUDIO
San Francisco Focus

ART DIRECTOR
Janice Fudyma
DESIGNER
Ron Shankweiler
ILLUSTRATOR
Tim Girvin
CLIENT
Maxwell House
AGENCY/STUDIO
Bernhardt Fudyma
Design Group

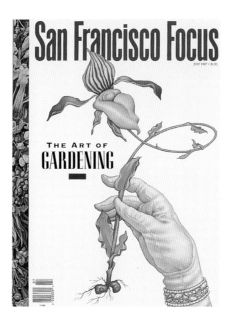
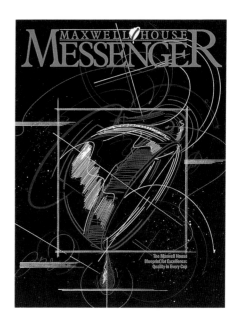

ART DIRECTOR
Janice Fudyma
DESIGNER
Iris Brown
ILLUSTRATOR
Brian Ajhar
CLIENT
Maxwell House
AGENCY/STUDIO
Bernhardt Fudyma
Design Group

ART DIRECTORS
Saul Bass
Art Goodman
DESIGNER
Saul Bass
PHOTOGRAPHER
George Arakaki
CLIENT
UCLA
AGENCY/STUDIO
Bass/Yager & Assoc.

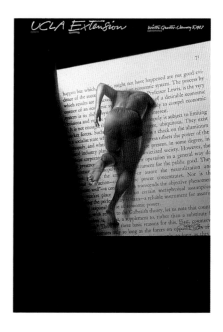

MAGAZINE DESIGN

ART DIRECTOR
Michael Brock

DESIGNER
Michael Brock

WRITER
Dean Batchelor

PHOTOGRAPHER
Mickey McGuire

CLIENT
Auto Gallery
Publishing Company

AGENCY/STUDIO
Michael Brock Design

THE 1967 FERRARI 275 GTB 4

"I covered, in complete safety and the greatest comfort… the 75 kilometers which separate the Porte d'Orleans from Nemours in a little less than 23

minutes… an average of 195 km/h (121 mph), which is remarkable enough without noting that I had to stop for the toll gates."

Jean Pierre Beltoise

By Dean Batchelor

Photographs By Mickey McGuire

EDITORIAL

MAGAZINE DESIGN

ART DIRECTOR
Bryan L. Peterson
DESIGNER
Bryan L. Peterson
WRITER
James W. Pennebaker
ILLUSTRATOR
Tom Dolphens
CLIENT
Southern Methodist
University
AGENCY/STUDIO
Peterson & Company

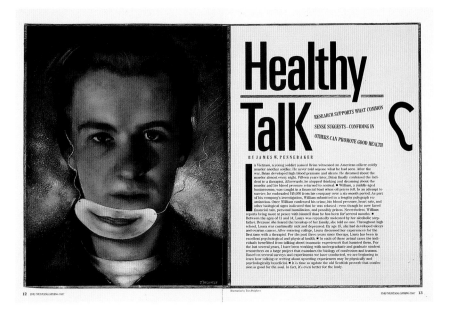

ART DIRECTOR
Tom Staebler
DESIGNER
Kerig Pope
ILLUSTRATOR
Blair Drawson
CLIENT
Playboy Enterprises, Inc.
AGENCY/STUDIO
Playboy Magazine

ART DIRECTOR
David Carson
DESIGNER
David Carson
WRITER
Garry Davis
PHOTOGRAPHER
Todd Swank
CLIENT
Skateboarding Mag
AGENCY/STUDIO
Carson Design

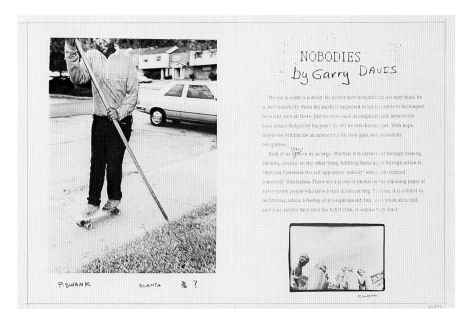

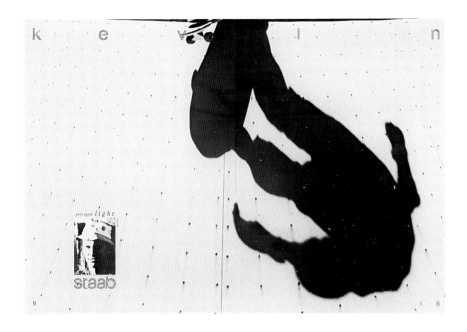

k e v i n

pro spot light

staab

MAGAZINE DESIGN

ART DIRECTOR
David Carson
DESIGNER
David Carson
PHOTOGRAPHER
Grant Brittain
CLIENT
Skateboarding Mag
AGENCY/STUDIO
Carson Design

paul heisterling/annis

I I 9

jeff grosse/brittain

jeff legger/temmermand

I I I 8

ART DIRECTOR
David Carson
DESIGNER
David Carson
PRODUCER
David Carson
PHOTOGRAPHERS
Zemnick
Temmermand
Brittain
CLIENT
Skateboarding Mag
AGENCY/STUDIO
Carson Design

SURF
OHIO

There is a skate shop in Dayton called Surf Ohio. It stands in an older part of town, being pretty aged itself, next to one of the many drive-thru beer marts in the area. In the rear of this establishment, behind the well-stocked pro shop, sits a five-foot tall halfpipe. This small fun-ramp, equipped with metal coping and roll-out decks, is sessioned often during the winter months by a hearty clan of local kids, plus the Squids, and Jimmy George, the manager of Surf Ohio.

Amateur Street Contest/Pro Session,
February 22, 1987. Hard-core.

Sam Cunningham and Rich Windsor relax
at the bar during the band performances.

Jesse Martinez, giving the Buckeye State
a small dose of Santa Monica.

ART DIRECTOR
David Carson
DESIGNER
David Carson
PRODUCER
David Carson
WRITER
Garry Davis
PHOTOGRAPHER
Todd Swank
CLIENT
Skateboarding Mag
AGENCY/STUDIO
Carson Design

MAGAZINE DESIGN

DESIGNER
Phil Waters

EDITOR
Kathleen Baxley

PHOTOGRAPHER
Various

ILLUSTRATOR
Patrick SooHoo

CLIENT
California Magazine

AGENCY/STUDIO
Phil Waters Design

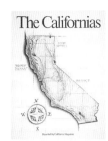

ART DIRECTOR
Michael Pardo

DIRECTOR
Lowell C. Paddock
(Mag. Editor)

WRITER
Lowell C. Paddock

PHOTOGRAPHER
Herbert W. Hesselmann

CLIENT
Automobile
Quarterly Mag.

AGENCY/STUDIO
Diamandis
Communications, Inc.

PRODUCTION COMPANY
Automobile
Quarterly Pub.

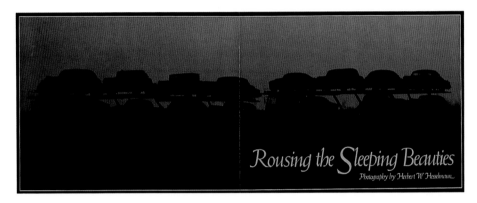

ART DIRECTOR
April Greiman

DESIGNER
April Greiman

PRODUCER
April Greiman

WRITER
April Greiman

VIDEOGRAPHER
April Greiman

CLIENT
Walker Art Center

AGENCY/STUDIO
April Greiman Inc.

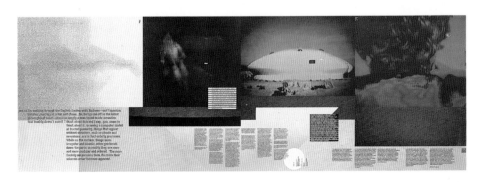

MAGAZINE DESIGN

ART DIRECTOR
Bryan L. Peterson

DESIGNERS
Bryan L. Peterson
Scott Ray
Paul Marince
Mary Asplund

WRITER
Various

PHOTOGRAPHER
Various

ILLUSTRATOR
Various

CLIENT
Arts Illustrated

AGENCY/STUDIO
Peterson & Company

ART DIRECTOR
Richard M. Baron

DESIGNER
Richard M. Baron

PHOTOGRAPHER
John Lamm

CLIENT
Road & Track Specials
DCI Magazines

AGENCY/STUDIO
Road & Track Specials

ART DIRECTOR
Tom Antista

DESIGNER
Tom Antista

WRITER
Jonathan Roberts

PHOTOGRAPHER
Barbara Owen

CLIENT
Main Magazine

AGENCY/STUDIO
Antista Design

ENTERTAINMENT

MOTION PICTURE—PRINT

ART DIRECTORS
Lucinda Cowell
Ron Michaelson

DESIGNER
Jeffrey Spear

ILLUSTRATOR
Jeffrey Spear

CLIENT
Concept Arts

AGENCY/STUDIO
Jeffrey Spear Graphic
Design

ART DIRECTOR
Tony Seiniger

DESIGNERS
Olga Kaljakin
Dan Chapman

PHOTOGRAPHER
Richard Noble

CLIENT
Paramount Pictures

AGENCY/STUDIO
Seiniger Advertising

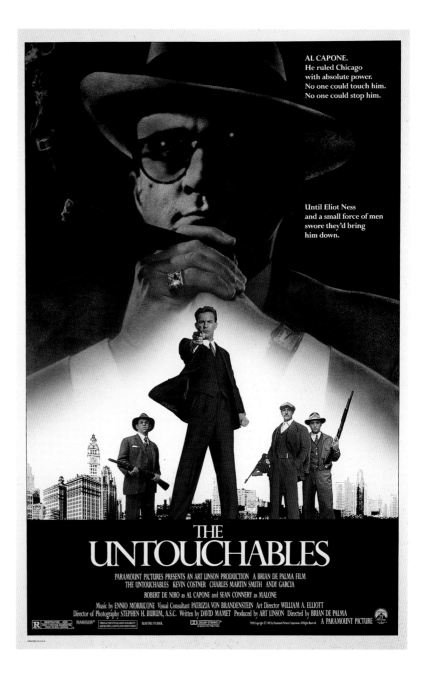

MOTION PICTURE—PRINT

ART DIRECTOR
Tony Lane-Roberts

DESIGNER
Tony Lane-Roberts

ILLUSTRATOR
Kazuhiko Sano

CLIENT
Cineplex Odeon Films

AGENCY/STUDIO
TL-R & Associates

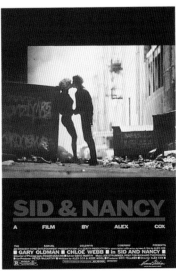

ART DIRECTOR
Ron Michaelson

DESIGNERS
Lucinda Cowell
Gunther Stotz

WRITER
Ron Michaelson

CLIENT
Island Pictures

AGENCY/STUDIO
Concept Arts

PRODUCTION COMPANY
Hemdale/Island

ART DIRECTORS
Cliff Hauser
Dan Gelfand

DESIGNERS
Tracy Weston
Kathie Broyles

RETOUCHING
Kasinger Mastel

CLIENT
The Samuel Goldwyn
Company

AGENCY/STUDIO
Broyles/Garamella,
Kavanaugh & Associates

▲

ENTERTAINMENT

MOTION PICTURE—PRINT

ART DIRECTOR
Lucinda Cowell

ART DIRECTOR
Cheryl Pellegrino

DESIGNER
Lucinda Cowell

DESIGNER
Cheryl Pellegrino

WRITER
Ron Michaelson

PHOTOGRAPHER
Lynn Goldsmith/LGI

PHOTOGRAPHER
Annie Leibovitz

RETOUCHER
Wild Studios

CLIENT
Warner Bros.

PRINTERS
Anderson Printing
Tom Andre

AGENCY/STUDIO
Concept Arts

AGENCY/STUDIO
Skouras Pictures

PRODUCTION COMPANY
Pressman Film Corp.
Warner Bros.
▲

▲

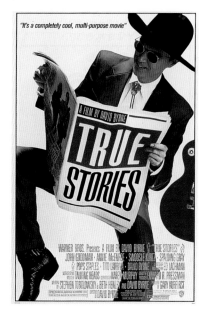

ART DIRECTOR
Brian D. Fox

ART DIRECTOR
Lucinda Cowell

DESIGNER
Robert Biro

DESIGNER
Ron Michaelson

WRITER
Marshall Drazen

WRITER
Ron Michaelson

PHOTOGRAPHER
Don Smetzer

ILLUSTRATOR
Lucinda Cowell

ILLUSTRATOR
Mike Bryan

CLIENT
Island Pictures

CLIENT
Orion Picture Corp.

AGENCY/STUDIO
Concept Arts

AGENCY/STUDIO
B.D. Fox & Friends
Advertising, Inc.

PRODUCTION COMPANY
Island Pictures

ART DIRECTOR
Tony Sella

PRODUCER
Art Hekker

CREATIVE DIRECTOR
Robert Jahn

ILLUSTRATOR
Paul Wenzel

CLIENT
The Walt Disney Studios

AGENCY/STUDIO
Creative Services
Department
The Walt Disney Studios

PRODUCTION COMPANY
Continental Graphics

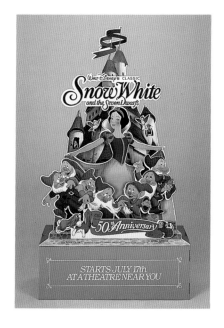

MOTION PICTURE—PRINT

ART DIRECTOR
Doug Smith
DESIGNERS
Doug Smith
Janet Johnson
ILLUSTRATOR
Doug Smith
CLIENT
Karson-Higgins-Shaw
Communications, Inc.
American Film
Marketing Association
AGENCY/STUDIO
Doug Smith & Associates

PRODUCER
Craig Murray
DIRECTOR
Robert Jahn
AGENCY/STUDIO
Walt Disney Studio

VO EDDIE: "He's got . . ."

Vince looking straight toward camera.

VO EDDIE: ". . . the eyes, . . ."

Vince makes a shot on pool table; camera pans to left along cue stick as cue ball hits other racked balls.

VO EDDIE: ". . . he's got the stroke, . . ."

Vince holding cue stick up and kissing it.

VO EDDIE: ". . . he's got the flake."

Vince kissing Carmen.

CARMEN: "This is the best."

Up angle Carmen and Vince as he takes his cue stick and mimics a Ninja warrior in battle then making the "kill."

Vince looking toward camera.

VO EDDIE: "You gotta . . ."

Vince's cue stick case; camera pans up to reveal Vince's face; he turns.

VO EDDIE: ". . . resource here, . . .*
a thoroughbred, . . ."

Reverse angle; Carmen and Eddie.

EDDIE: ". . . you make him feel good, I teach . . ."

Reverse angle; Eddie and Carmen.

EDDIE: ". . . him how to run."

Low angle as Vince breaks a rack of balls on the pool table.

Down angle; Eddie about to break rack of balls; camera zooms in on cluster.

Eddie hitting cue ball.

Vince and Eddie at pool table as cue ball hits racked balls.

VO MAN: "Let's see some Eddie legend action."

Carmen and Eddie.

EDDIE: "I want his best game."

Vince.

VINCE: "You want my game? You couldn't deal with my game Jack, you're out manned."

Carmen and Eddie.

EDDIE: "I'm gonna beat him you know."

Vince looking down.

VINCE: "What makes you so sure."

Eddie at pool table; he rises to face Vince.

Cue stick hitting cue ball in slow-motion.

Nine ball as camera zooms in on it.

Vince, Carmen and Eddie.

EDDIE: "Do you smell what I smell?"

VINCE: "Smoke?"

CARMEN: "Money."

Red title animates over black b.g.

"PLATOON"

PICTURE: B&W photo of Oliver Stone with members of his platoon in Vietnam slowly zooms back against black, then jungle canopy with rays of sunlight dissolves in. Montage of the men of Platoon *in battle and behind the lines follows— set to "Tracks of My Tears."*

AUDIO: In 1967, Oliver Stone was a combat infantry man in Vietnam. During his tour he received a bronze star for gallantry. Ten years later in Hollywood he was picking up an Oscar for the screenplay of MIDNIGHT EXPRESS.

Now he has another story to tell, a movie that grew out of his own experience.

Stone has come a long way from Vietnam, but he has not left it behind.

SONG: "Tracks of My Tears."

The first real casualty of war is innocence. The first real movie about the war in Vietnam is *PLATOON.*

CREATIVE DIRECTORS
Charles O. Glenn
Michael Kaiser
ART DIRECTORS
Tony Silver
Larry Lurin
Sam Alexander
WRITERS
Tony Silver
Michael Kaiser
Charles O. Glenn
PRODUCERS
Barbara Glazer
Linda Habib
DIRECTOR
Tony Silver
EDITOR
Barbara Glazer
STUDIO/PRODUCTION COMPANY
Tony Silver Films, Inc.
CLIENT
Orion Pictures
Corporation

PRODUCERS
Brian Leonard
Craig Murray
DIRECTOR
Robert Jahn
AGENCY/STUDIO
Walt Disney Studio

"RUTHLESS COUPLES"

NARRATOR: Tarzan and Jane . . .
. . . Frankenstein and his bride . . .
. . . Beauty and the Beast . . .
. . . and now, Barbara and Sam . . .
. . . the wildest couple of all.

SAM: "You inhuman slime!"

BARBARA: "You low life!"

SAM: "Screetchy little witch! . . ."

BARBARA: (Bette YELLS! as she throws a lamp
across the room.)

SAM: " . . . Pasty face troll!"

NARRATOR: From Touchstone Films comes a
movie for the ruthless romantic . . . in all of us.

RUTHLESS PEOPLE.

See it with someone you love.

"DANCE"

OPPONENT: "What you got in there?"

VINCENT: "Doom."

At this point TOM CRUISE dances, lip syncs, and shoots his usual great game of 9 Ball to Warren Zevon's hit song 'WEREWOLVES OF LONDON.' This has almost become a TOM CRUISE trademark and tradition, having done similar music sequences in some of his previous motion pictures, such as RISKY BUSINESS and TOP GUN. These scenes have a very special quality about them, as does the highly talented star performing them.

NARRATOR: Paul Newman, Tom Cruise in a Martin Scorsese picture *THE COLOR OF MONEY.*

PRODUCER
Craig Murray
DIRECTOR
Robert Jahn
AGENCY/STUDIO
Walt Disney Studio

CREATIVE DIRECTORS
Charles O. Glenn
Michael Kaiser

ART DIRECTORS
Tony Silver
Larry Lurin
Sam Alexander

WRITERS
Tony Silver
Michael Kaiser
Charles O. Glenn

PRODUCERS
Barbara Glazer
Linda Habib

DIRECTOR
Tony Silver

EDITOR
Barbara Glazer

*STUDIO/PRODUCTION
COMPANY*
Tony Silver Films, Inc.

CLIENT
Orion Pictures
Corporation

"PLATOON—OLIVER TV SPOT"

VIDEO: PLATOON *logo superimposed over light streaming through jungle canopy. Montage of soldiers in battle and behind the lines.*

AUDIO: In 1967, Oliver Stone was a soldier in Vietnam. Ten years later his screenplay for MIDNIGHT EXPRESS won an academy award. Stone has come a long way from Vietnam, but he has not left it behind. Tom Berenger, Willem Dafoe, Charlie Sheen.

The first real casualty of war is innocence. The first real movie about the war in Vietnam is *PLATOON*.

THE TWO MRS. GRENVILLES

TELEVISION—PRINT

ART DIRECTOR
Jack Halpern
DESIGNER
Jack Halpern
TITLE TREATMENT
Jack Halpern
CREATIVE DIRECTOR
Melanie Paykos
CLIENT
NBC-TV
AGENCY/STUDIO
AC&R/DHB & BESS

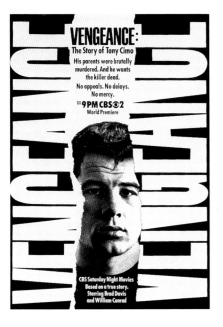

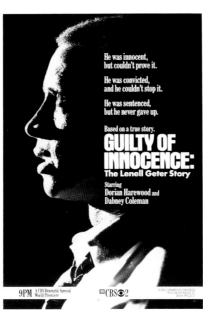

ART DIRECTOR
Jay Rothman
DESIGNER
Bill Collins
WRITER
Richard Posalski
CLIENT
CBS Entertainment
AGENCY/STUDIO
CBS Entertainment

ART DIRECTOR
Jay Rothman
DESIGNER
Susan Roskens
WRITER
David Spetner
PHOTOGRAPHER
Dick Zimmerman
CLIENT
CBS Entertainment
AGENCY/STUDIO
CBS Entertainment

ART DIRECTOR
Vahé Fattal
DESIGNER
Vahé Fattal
WRITERS
Oren Aviv
David Ames
*PHOTO
COMPOSITIONS*
Mike Koehler
RETOUCHING
Tom Slately
CLIENT
Capital Cities
ABC
AGENCY/STUDIO
Gem/F&C

ENTERTAINMENT

TELEVISION—PRINT

ART DIRECTORS
Marsha Takeda
Vince Manze

DESIGNER
Kim Zimmerman

WRITERS
Vince Manze
Marty Iker

PHOTOGRAPHER
David Jacobson

CLIENT
KNBC-TV

AGENCY/STUDIO
Marsha Takeda Designs

ART DIRECTOR
Randy Hipke

DESIGNERS
Randy Hipke
Brad Jansen
Keith Kaminski

CLIENT
Paramount Network
Television

AGENCY/STUDIO
5 Penguins Design, Inc.

PRINTER
A&L Graphico

ART DIRECTOR
Alan Sekuler

DESIGNER
Alan Sekuler

WRITER
Eliot Sekuler

ILLUSTRATOR
Rhonda Burns

CLIENT
The Entertainment
Network

AGENCY/STUDIO
Alan Sekuler &
Associates

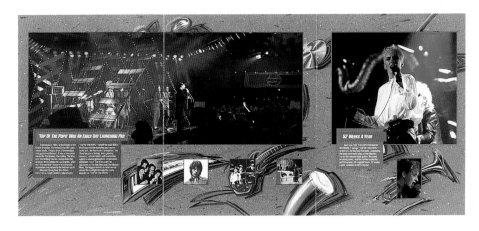

"DOG"

Open on beautiful park at dusk. Dog is lying in center.
Close-up of dog.
Slow move in as dog begins to dig a hole.
Dog digging deeper. Move in continues.
Dog no longer visible.
We see book in tunnel.
Move in tight on book as it closes.
NBC logo.
ANNCR: Discover the Wonder.
Monday nights on *NBC.*

ART DIRECTOR
Rick Boyko
PRODUCER
Richard O'Neill
DIRECTOR
Ken Davis
WRITER
Jaime Seltzer
CLIENT
Amblin Entertainment
PRODUCTION COMPANY
RSA Films
AGENCY/STUDIO
Chiat/Day Advertising

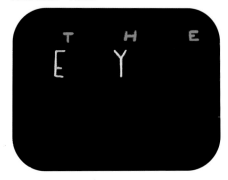

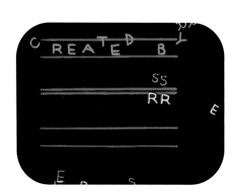

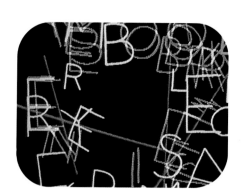

ART DIRECTOR
Gabor Csupo

DESIGNER
Jeffrey Townsend

PRODUCER
Margot Pipkin

DIRECTOR
Gabor Csupo

MUSIC
George Clinton

ANIMATION
Bill Hedge

ANIMATORS
David Blum
Gabor Csupo

CLIENT
Fox Broadcasting

AGENCY/STUDIO
Gracie Films

PRODUCTION COMPANY
Klasky Csupo, Inc.

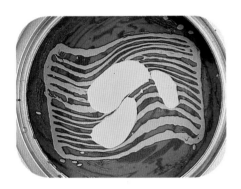
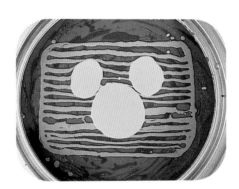

ART DIRECTORS
Michael Nichols
Carl Willat

DESIGNERS
Michael Nichols
Carl Willat
Heather Selick

PRODUCER
Chris Whitney

DIRECTORS
Carl Willat
Heather Selick

PHOTOGRAPHERS
Melissa Mullin
John Gazdik

CLIENT
The Disney Channel

AGENCY/STUDIO
Direct

PRODUCTION COMPANY
Colossal Pictures

Best of Show

RECORDS

ART DIRECTOR
Jeff Ayeroff
DESIGNER
Margo Chase
CLIENT
Virgin Records America,
Inc.
AGENCY/STUDIO
Margo Chase Design

ART DIRECTORS
Mick Haggerty
DESIGNER
Mick Haggerty
ILLUSTRATOR
Mick Haggerty
CLIENT
OMD
AGENCY/STUDIO
A&M Records, Inc.

ART DIRECTOR
Norman Moore
DESIGNER
Norman Moore
ILLUSTRATOR
Norman Moore
CLIENT
Capitol Records
Trudy Green
AGENCY/STUDIO
Design/Art, Inc.

ART DIRECTOR
Kenneth Jan Leonard
DESIGNER
Kenneth Jan Leonard
PHOTOGRAPHER
Nancy Ketelsen
VOICE TALENT
Jack Roth
AGENCY/STUDIO
Calico

RECORDS

ART DIRECTORS
Tony Lane
Nancy Donald
DESIGNERS
Tony Lane
Nancy Donald
PHOTOGRAPHER
Dominick
CLIENT
Epic
AGENCY/STUDIO
CBS Records

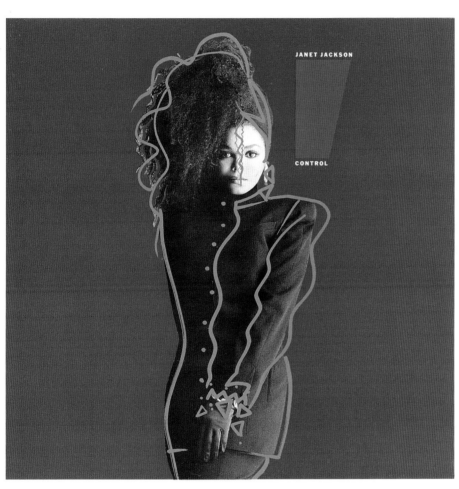

ART DIRECTORS
Chuck Beeson
Melanie Nissen
PHOTOGRAPHER
Tony Viramontes
CLIENT
A&M Records, Inc.
AGENCY/STUDIO
A&M Records, Inc.

RECORDS
ART DIRECTOR
Carol Bobolts
DESIGNER
Carol Bobolts
PHOTOGRAPHER
Robin Nedboy
CLIENT
Atlantic Records
AGENCY/STUDIO
Atlantic In-House

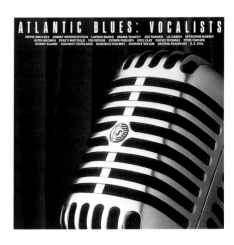

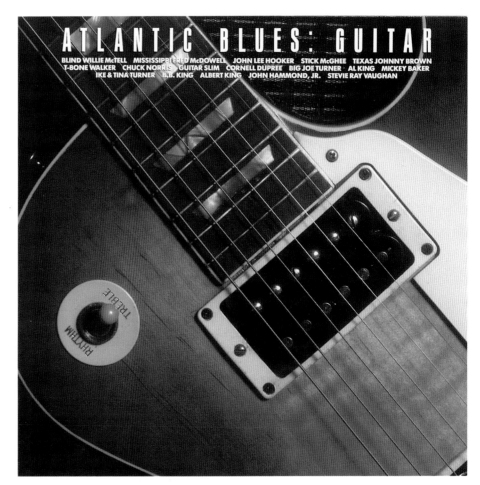

ART DIRECTOR
Norman Moore

DESIGNER
Norman Moore

ILLUSTRATOR
Norman Moore

CLIENT
Ria Lenerke / RCA

AGENCY / STUDIO
Design / Art, Inc.

ART DIRECTOR
Jeri McManus Heiden

DESIGNER
Jeri McManus Heiden

PHOTOGRAPHER
Knut Bry

CLIENT
a-ha

AGENCY / STUDIO
Warner Bros. Records

ART DIRECTORS
Jeff Adamoff
Tommy Steele

DESIGNER
Tommy Steele

ILLUSTRATOR
Todd Schorr

CLIENT
MCA Records, Inc.

AGENCY / STUDIO
SteeleWorks Design, Inc.

RECORDS

ART DIRECTOR
Laura LiPuma

DESIGNER
Laura LiPuma

ILLUSTRATOR
Lindsey Loch

CLIENT
Bonnie Raitt

AGENCY/STUDIO
Warner Bros. Records

ART DIRECTORS
Chuck Beeson
Melanie Nissen

DESIGNER
Melanie Nissen

PHOTOGRAPHER
Chris Callis

ILLUSTRATOR
Melanie Nissen

CLIENT
A&M Records, Inc.

AGENCY/STUDIO
A&M Records, Inc.

RECORDS
PROMOTIONAL MATERIAL

ART DIRECTOR
Norman Moore
DESIGNER
Norman Moore
PHOTOGRAPHER
Phillip Dixon
CLIENT
Trudy Green
AGENCY/STUDIO
Design/Art, Inc.

ART DIRECTOR
Chuck Beeson
DESIGNER
Melanie Nissen
CREATIVE DIRECTOR
Jeff Gold
PHOTOGRAPHER
Chris Callis
ILLUSTRATOR
Melanie Nissen
CLIENT
A&M Records, Inc.
AGENCY/STUDIO
A&M Records, Inc.

ART DIRECTOR
Chuck Beeson
DESIGNER
Melanie Nissen
PHOTOGRAPHER
Veronica Sim
ILLUSTRATOR
Melanie Nissen
CLIENT
A&M Records, Inc.
AGENCY/STUDIO
A&M Records, Inc.

ENTERTAINMENT

HOME VIDEO

ART DIRECTOR
Scott A. Mednick

DESIGNERS
Scott A. Mednick
Scott MacPhee
Phil Krahn

CLIENT
Hi-Tops Video

AGENCY/STUDIO
Scott Mednick &
Associates

ART DIRECTOR
Scott A. Mednick

DESIGNERS
Scott A. Mednick
Scott MacPhee

ILLUSTRATOR
Greg Martin

CLIENT
Hi-Tops Video

AGENCY/STUDIO
Scott Mednick &
Associates

ART DIRECTORS
Scott Mednick
Sharon Streger

DESIGNERS:
Scott A. Mednick
Cheryl Rehman
Tom LeClerc

PHOTOGRAPHER
Various

CLIENT
Vestron Video

AGENCY/STUDIO
Scott Mednick &
Associates

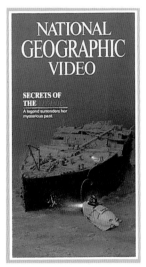

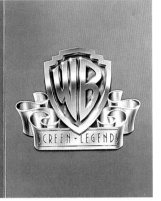

HOME VIDEO

ART DIRECTOR
Brian D. Fox

DESIGNER
Georgia Young

WRITER
Client

PHOTOGRAPHER
David Sessions

ILLUSTRATOR
Chris Delorco

CLIENT
Warner Home Video/
Danielle Beatty

AGENCY/STUDIO
B.D. Fox & Friends, Inc.

HIS INSANE HUMOR UNHINGED LATE NIGHT TV FOR GOOD.

ART DIRECTOR
Scott A. Mednick

DESIGNERS
Scott A. Mednick
Scott MacPhee
Mike Armijo

ILLUSTRATOR
Greg Martin

CLIENT
Hi-Tops Video

AGENCY/STUDIO
Scott Mednick &
Associates

ART DIRECTOR
Jorge Alonso

DESIGNER
Jorge Alonso

WRITER
Farida Fotouhi

AGENCY/STUDIO
Fotouhi Alonso

INDEX

DESIGN/CREATIVE DIRECTOR
ART DIRECTOR

Adamoff, Jeff   251
Alonso, Jorge   255
Andelin, Jerry   183
Anderson, Jack   100, 182, 214
Anderson, Mark   165, 208
Angeli, Primo   32, 183, 198, 213
Antista, Tom   191, 193, 194, 204, 231
Appleton, Robert   167, 173, 188, 190, 195, 205
Arola, Michael   103
Ayeroff, Jeff   248
Baer, Kimberly   171
Barazzuol, Roberto   206
Baron, Richard M.   231
Bartels, David   61, 102
Bass, Saul   226
Bazzel, Tom   33, 99
Beach, Pearl   198
Beaumont, Steve   71
Beck, David   199
Beeson, Chuck   86, 249, 252, 253
Berte, Jim   26, 164, 169, 171
Bess, Rich   36, 72, 74, 77, 90
Besser, Rik   184, 187
Bice, Luann   214
Bielenberg, John   177
Binnion, Tom   210
Blain, Ian   114, 123, 124, 125
Bobolts, Carol   250
Bogaards, Terri   188, 207
Bojorgez, Roberto   118
Bouchard, Carole   201
Boyko, Rick   41, 48, 49, 50, 75, 76, 82, 107, 120, 129, 130, 131, 138, 245
Brock, Michael   225, 227
Brooks, Butler Kosh   212
Campbell, Mike   143
Caraballo, Richard   92
Carabetta, Michael   202
Carson, David   228, 229
Chermeyeff, Ivan   166, 173, 179, 197, 209, 213
Cho, Yee-Ping   30, 223
Church, Jann   96
Cleveland, John   170
Cohen, Peter   39, 111, 112

Condit, Jim   95
Cordner, Tom   135
Coutroulis, Peter   91
Coverdale, Jac   60, 66, 154
Cowell, Lucinda   234, 236
Cox, Jim   140
Coy, John   29, 177, 208
Crispo, Richard   68, 92
Cronan, Michael Patrick   171, 179, 180, 192, 211
Cross, James   170, 174, 201
Csupo, Gabor   246
Cunningham, Pam   64
Dalthorp, James   73, 79
Davis, Lon   110
Dayton III, Glen O.   93
Della Sala, Laura   48, 49, 50, 64, 120, 129, 130, 131
Denton, Margi   200
Dijak, Andy   61, 75, 105, 108
Donald, Nancy   249
Dooley, Patrick   224
Drace, Matthew   226
Dusenberry, Phil   44, 137
Dyer, Rod   36, 222
Edelstein, David   176, 181
Edelstein, Nancy   176, 181
Elimelech, Moshe   172, 206
Erbe, Maureen   100
Evans, John   203
Evans, Laura Malan   203
Fattal, Vahe   243
Fedele, Anthony   207
Fittipaldi, Jim   91
Forbes, Colin   167
Fox, Brian D.   255
Fox, David   60, 236
Foy, Richard   216
French, Lanny   176, 181
Fudyma, Janice   226
Fuller, Craig   100, 192
Geissbuhler, Steff   194
Gelfand, Dan   235
Gentile, Jerry   64
Glazer, Barbara   239, 242
Gold, Jeff   86
Goodman, Art   226

Gormley, Brian   167
Greiman, April   31, 196, 230
Grubb, Kathy   62
Haggerty, Mick   248
Halpern, Jack   243
Harrison, Greg   61, 62, 65
Harrison, Peter   166
Hauser, Cliff   235
Hecht, Arthur   70
Heidel, Lee   190
Heiden, Jeri McManus   251
Heise, David   70
Heller, Cheryl   31, 70, 87, 96, 97, 102, 103, 178
Hensley, Randall   33, 99
Herz, Rony   70
Hicks, Mike   194, 222
Hinrichs, Kit   28, 29, 30, 166, 169, 191, 200, 201, 204, 223
Hipke, Randy   33, 244
Holland, Prueit   71, 73
Horvath, Ivan   63
Huberty, Deidre   106
Hunt, Wayne   207, 217
Ison, Paul   208
Jacobs, Byron   174
Johnston, Gary   126, 127, 128
Joseph, Douglas   184, 187
Kanipe, Melinda   36, 72, 74, 77, 90
Kelly, Mike   103
Kettering, Chip   60
Kohut, Jill   70, 160
Kovach, Ronald   196
Kuester, Kevin B.   174
Küng, Richard   216
Kuperman, Bob   36, 72, 74, 77, 90, 157
Kuyper, Jerry   206
Lamonte, Tony   42, 119, 144
Lane, Keith   51, 52, 53, 145, 146, 147
Lane, Tony   249
Lane-Roberts, Tony   234

Leinh, Parker   117
Lennon, Dan   33, 99
Leonard, Kenneth Jan   249
Lim, Dennis   92
LiPuma, Laura   252
Lorenzetti, Katherine   196
Low, Gary   90
MacIntosh, Robert E.   81
Maier, Gunther   38, 78, 85
Manwaring, Michael   175, 204, 205
Manze, Vince   244
Markell, Julie   159
Marmo, Brent L.   180
Mauk, Mitchell   27, 173
Mayhew, Marce   80
McConnell, Beth   62
McVey, Todd   88
Mednick, Scott A.   254, 255
Mendelsohn, Jordin   43, 45, 63, 132, 136
Mendez, Carlos   121
Meyer, Robert   168
Michaelson, Dennis   63
Michaelson, Ron   234, 235
Mitchell, Terence   30, 223
Molnar, Andy   189
Montgomery, Scott   157
Moore, Norman   248, 251, 253
Morla, Jennifer   176
Nagano, Arthur   211
Nichols, Michael   57, 247
Nissen, Melanie   249, 252
Norton, Tery   156
O'Brien, John   69
Orvides, Ken   63
Page, Jean   168
Pardo, Michael   230
Patterson, Doug   84
Pellegrino, Cheryl   236
Peteet, Rex   202
Peterson, Bryan L.   165, 197, 228, 231
Petruccio, Joe   139
Pitzer, Michael   74
Poth, Tom   222
Poulin, Richard   190, 215

Price, Ralph   133, 155
Prins, Robert   61, 62, 65
Pruneau, Paul   32, 97, 99, 188
Raphan, Neil   83
Ray, Scott   206
Reeder, Jon   210
Reger, John C.   30, 101
Reinschmiedt, Larry   104
Rhodes, Anne   89, 93
Riney, Hal   183
Risch, Monique   134, 148, 149, 150
Robaire, Jean   40, 115, 116
Roll, Jeff   75, 105, 108, 113
Rosenfield, Tom   71
Rothman, Jay   243
Rotter, Elizabeth   180
Runyan, Robert Miles   164, 169
Ryoshima, David   92
Sakoda, Ken   109, 157
Samata, Greg   168
Samata, Pat   205
Schiebald, Martha   189
Schiff, Robin   35, 221
Schubeck, Barbara   126, 127, 128
Scott, Mary   184
Sebastian, James   28, 178
Seiniger, Tony   234
Sekuler, Alan   244
Sella, Tony   236
Shapiro, Ellen   188, 207
Sheridan, Keith   221
Shiffman, Tracey   27, 164, 175
Shortlidge, Tom   63, 117
Sibley, Don   101
Silverman, Hal   182
Sjogren, Kathy   69, 90
Skjei, Michael   170
Small, Terri   94
Smith, Doug   237
Smith, Gwyn   27, 175
Smith, Yvonne   37, 63, 67, 71, 73, 98, 103, 187
Smolan, Leslie   170, 172, 224
Staebler, Tom   228
Steele, Tommy   35, 220, 251
Stepner, Chuck   142
Strand, Rick   46, 47, 122, 141, 151, 152, 153

Streger, Sharon   254
Studley, Vance   32, 180
Stygar, James A.   209
Suiter, Tom   206
Sussman, Deborah   199
Sutton, Liz   97
Swieter, John   209, 211
Takeda, Marsha   244
Takei, Koji   167
Tam, Julia   206
Taylor, Terri   63
Tonnis, Marten   72
Turpin, Miles   138
Valentine, Robert   101, 210
Van Dyke, John   26, 165, 168, 172, 195, 210
Van Noy, Jim   96, 98
Vitro, John   61, 62, 74
Vogel, Tyler   148, 149, 150
Weller, Don   224
Wesko, David   207
White, Ken   26, 202
Willat, Carl   57, 247
Wondriska, William   196, 198, 221
Wong, John Lee   91
Wong, Tracy   72
Yagi, Tamotsu   28, 34, 35, 177, 186, 203, 204, 207, 223
Yearsley, Larry   110
Young, Roland   27, 175
Zelinsky, Ed   156
Zimmerman, Neal   176

Adkins, Alyssa   172
Alonso, Jorge   255
Anderson, Jack   100, 182, 214
Angeli, Primo   32, 183, 198, 213
Antista, Tom   193, 194, 204, 231
Anton, Bill   166, 173, 179, 197, 209, 213
Appleton, Robert   167, 173, 188, 190, 195, 205
Armijo, Mike   255
Ashton, Allen   177
Asplund, Mary   231
Baba, Harriett   36, 222
Barab, Marie   35, 221
Barazzuol, Roberto   206
Baron, Richard M.   231
Bartz, Lenore   191
Bass, Saul   226
Bazzel, Tom   33, 99
Beach, Pearl   198
Beck, David   199
Beeson, Sam   96
Berndt, Karen   166
Berte, Jim   26, 164, 169, 171
Bess, Rich   36, 72, 74, 77
Besser, Rik   184, 187
Bice, Luann   214
Bielenberg, John   177
Biondi, Rose   28, 178
Biro, Robert   236
Bissett, D. Thom   181
Bobolts, Carol   250
Bogaards, Terri   188, 207
Bouchard, Carole   201
Brock, Michael   225, 227
Brooks, Larry   212
Brown, Iris   226
Broyles, Kathie   235
Campbell, Tom   184
Carson, David   228, 229
Chadwick, G.   32, 99

Chan, Kwok   196
Chapman, Dan   234
Chase, Margo   248
Cho, Yee-Ping   30, 174, 223
Church, Jann   96
Cleveland, John   170
Cohen, Jeff   70
Cohen, Peter   39, 111, 112
Collins, Bill   243
Consales, Kevin   29, 177
Cooper, Barbara   171
Cordner, Tom   135
Cossutta, Renee   191
Cowell, Lucinda   235, 236
Coy, John   29, 177
Cronan, Michael   171, 176, 179, 180, 192, 211
Davidson, Carol   176, 180
DeLucia, Diana   33, 99
Denton, Margi   200
Deputy, Brian   207, 217
Devine, Thomas   169
Dimos, Dennis Michael   167
Dinsmore, Creighton   216
Donald, Nancy   249
Dooley, Patrick   224
Drewfs, Jani   214
Eann, Ko Starkweather   182
Edelstein, David   176, 181
Edelstein, Nancy   176, 181
Einfrank, Rob   114, 123, 124, 125
Elimelech, Moshe   172, 206
Erbe, Maureen   100
Esguerra, Al   225
Evans, John   203
Evans, Laura Malan   203
Fairclough, Thomas   191
Fattal, Vahe   243
Fittipaldi, Jim   91
French, Lanny   176, 181
Fuller, Craig   100, 192
Gee, Earl   165, 208
Geissbuhler, Steff   194
Gerike, Michael   167, 216

Gough, Bryan   216
Gregg, Mutsumi   98
Greiman, April   31, 196, 230
Grubb, Kathy   62
Haggerty, Mick   248
Halpern, Jack   243
Handler, Laurie   208
Hart, Chuck   61
Hatlestad, Heidi   100
Heidel, Lee   190
Heiden, Jeri McManus   251
Heise, David   70
Heller, Cheryl   31, 70, 87, 96, 97, 102, 103, 178
Hensley, Randall   33, 99
Hermes, Mary   182
Herz, Rony   70
Hicks, Mike   194, 222
Hinrichs, Kit   27, 28, 29, 30, 166, 169, 175, 191, 200, 201, 204, 223
Hipke, Randy   33, 244
Hochbaum, Susan   166
Holland, Preuit   71, 73
Honda, Ray   183
Horn, Timothy   185
How, Belle   169
Huber, Cheri   182, 214
Hunt, Wayne   217
Isley, Alexander   185
Ison, Paul   208
Ivester, Devin   188
Jacobs, Byron   174
Jacquez, Joseph   201
Jansen, Brad   33, 244
Johnson, Janet   237

Joseph, Douglas   164
Kaldenbaugh, Nick   103
Kaljakin, Olga   234
Kalman, Tibor   185
Kaminski, Keith   33, 244
Kan, Chi-Ming   216
Kanipe, Melinda   36, 72, 74, 77
Kinzig, Susan   216
Kovach, Ronald   196
Krahn, Phil   254
Krieger, Donald   86
Kuester, Kevin B.   174
Kuperman, Bob   36, 72, 74, 77
Kurtz, Bob   134, 148, 149, 150
Lane, Tony   249
Lane-Roberts, Tony   234
Lausten, Judith   191
Lawler, Linda   171, 176, 211
LeClerc, Tom   254
Leibundgut, Jenny   202, 206
Lennon, Dan   33, 99
Leonard, Kenneth Jan   249
Levin, Lisa   26, 202
LiPuma, Laura   252
Lodge, John   32, 213
Lorenzetti, Katherine   196
Lurin, Larry   239, 242
MacIntosh, Robert E.   81
MacPhee, Scott   254, 255
Maier, Gunter   38, 78, 85
Manwaring, Michael   175, 204, 205
Marince, Paul   231
Mauk, Mitchell   27, 173
Mayhew, Marce   80
McGee, Gigi   199
McVey, Todd   88
Mednick, Scott A.   254, 255
Mescal, Michael   201
Michaelson, Ron   236

Molina, Luis   118
Moore, Norman   248, 251, 253
Morla, Jennifer   176
Nagano, Arthur   211
Nichols, Michael   57, 247
Nissen, Melanie   249, 252, 253
Norton, Gina   63, 71, 73
O'Brien, Ann   221
O'Brien, John   69
Olson, Dan   30, 101
Page, Jean   168
Passehl, Christopher   188, 190
Pellegrino, Cheryl   236
Peteet, Rex   202
Peterson, Bryan L.   165, 197, 228, 231
Pike, Eric   170
Pope, Kerig   228
Poth, Tom   222
Poulin, Richard   190, 215
Price, Ralph   133, 155
Raphan, Neil   83
Ray, Scott   206, 231
Rehman, Cheryl   254
Rosenfield, Tom   71
Roskens, Susan   243
Rotter, Elizabeth   180
Samata, Greg   168, 205
Samata, Pat   205
Sanders, Jim   190
Sann, Ted   44, 137
Sebastian, James   28, 178
Segura, Ed   61, 62, 65
Sekuler, Alan   244
Selick, Heather   57, 247
Serizawa, Hiroshi   177
Shakery, Niel   27, 175
Shankweiler, Ron   226
Sheridan, Keith   35, 221
Shiffman, Tracey   27, 164, 175
Sibley, Don   101
Silver, Tony   239, 242
Skjei, Michael   170
Smith, Buck   102
Smith, Doug   237

Smith, Gwyn   29, 200, 201
Smith, Yvonne   37, 67, 71, 98, 103, 187
Smolan, Leslie   170, 172, 224
Spear, Jeffrey   234
Steele, Tommy   35, 220, 251
Steinorth, Kirsten   190, 215
Stotz, Gunther   235
Stratton, Trish   93
Studley, Vance   32, 180
Stygar, James A.   209
Sutton, Liz   32, 97, 99
Swieter, John   209, 211
Switz-Harger, Lauren   98
Tam, Julia   206
Tanagi, Julie   182, 214
Townsend, Jeffrey   56, 246
Tweed, Mark   216
Valentine, Robert   101, 210
Van Dyke, John   26, 165, 168, 172, 195, 210
VanKoten, Ran   190
Vaughn, R.   32, 99
Voltaggio, Joe   33, 99
Walker, Thomas   224
Warner, Craig   35, 221
Waters, Phil   230
Watson, George   189
Weller, Don   224
Wesko, David   207
Weston, Tracy   235
Willat, Carl   57, 247
Wondriska, William   196, 198
Wong, John Lee   191
Wong, Tracy   72
Yagi, Tamotsu   28, 34, 35, 177, 186, 203, 204, 207, 223
Young, Georgia   255
Zimmerman, Kim   244

(213) 827-9695 and Associates   71, 73, 98, 103, 187
5 Penguins Design, Inc.   33, 244
A&M Records, Inc.   86, 248, 249, 252, 253
AC&R/DHB & BESS   243
ACCD Typography Class   32, 180
Anderson Design, Mark   165, 208
Angeli, Inc., Primo   32, 183, 198, 213
Antista Design   191, 193, 194, 204, 231
Apple Creative Services   32, 97, 99, 188
Appleton Design Inc.   167, 173, 188, 190, 195, 205
Atlantic Records   250
B.D. Fox & Friends Advertising, Inc.   236, 255
Baer Design, Kimberly   171
Bartles & Carstens   61, 102
Bass/Yager & Assoc.   226
BBDO   37, 42, 44, 46, 47, 63, 67, 71, 73, 74, 119, 122, 141, 143, 144, 151, 152, 153
Beck, David   199
Bernhardt Fudyma Design Group   226
Besser Joseph Partners   184, 187
Binnion, Thomas   210
Brock Design, Michael   225, 227
Browand & Associates, Lewis   148, 149, 150
Brownstone Group, Inc., The   180
Broyles/Garamella, Kavanaugh & Assoc.   235
Burson-Marsteller   196
Butler Kosh Brooks   212
Calico   249
Campbell + Associates, Inc., Tom   184
Campbell Mithun—Chicago   158
Capitol Records, Inc.   69
Carbone Smolan Associates   170, 172, 224
Carson Design   228, 229
CBS Entertainment   243
CBS Records   249
Chase Design, Margo   248
Chermayeff & Geismar Assoc.   166, 173, 179, 194, 197, 209, 213
Chiat/Day Advertising   41, 48, 49, 50, 61, 62, 64, 71, 72, 74, 75, 76, 82, 105, 107, 108, 113, 120, 129, 130, 131, 138, 159, 245
Church, Jann   96
Clarity Coverdale Rueff   60, 66, 154
Cleveland, Inc., John   170

Cochrane Chase, Livingston   103
Cole Henderson Drake, Inc.   95
Communications Arts Inc.   216
Concept Arts   235, 236
COY, Los Angeles   29, 177, 208
Cronan Design   171, 176, 179, 180, 192, 211
Cross Associates   170, 174, 201
Crouch+Fuller, Inc.   100, 192
Dayton Associates   93
DDB Needham Worldwide   83
DDB Needham Worldwide—Los Angeles   36, 40, 64, 72, 74, 77, 90, 115, 116, 157
de Harak & Poulin Associates   190, 215
Denton Design Associates   200
Design/Art, Inc.   248, 251, 253
Design Center   30, 101
Designframe, Inc.   28, 178
Diamandis Communications Inc.   230
Direct   57, 247
Disney Studio, Walt   54, 238, 240, 241
Disney Studios, Walt/Creative Services Department   236
DJMC, Inc.   69, 90, 91
DMB&B   139
Doyle Dane Bernbach   71
Dyer/Kahn, Inc.   36, 222
DYR   91
Edelstein Associates Advertising Inc.   176, 181
Elen & Associates, Robert   61, 62, 65
Emerson Lane Fortuna   51, 52, 53, 145, 146, 147
Erbe Design, Maureen   100
Esprit   206
Esprit Graphic Design Studio   28, 34, 35, 177, 186, 203, 204, 223
Fittipaldi Design, Jim   91
Folio2, Inc.   209
Foote, Cone & Belding   133, 155
Fotouhi Alonso   255
Geer DuBois   80
Gem/F&C   243
AC&R/DHB & BESS   114, 123, 124, 125
Getty Museum Publication, The J. Paul   224
Gormley/Takei, Inc.   167
Gracie Films   56, 246
Greiman, Inc., April   31, 196, 230
Grey Advertisng, Inc./Orange County   110
Gruen Creative Services, Gabby   158
Heller Breene   31, 70, 87, 96, 97, 102, 103, 178, 201
HIXO, Inc.   194, 222
Hornall Anderson Design Works   100, 182, 214

Hunt Design, Inc., Wayne   207, 217
Intergroup Marketing & Promotions   189
Ishii, Sunao   207
Ison Design, Paul   208
J. Walter Thompson   60, 159
Jacobs Design, Byron   174
Ketchum Advertising   68, 84, 92
Knoth & Meads   140
Kresser, Craig/D.I.K.   70, 160
Kurtz & Friends   134
Landor Associates   202, 206, 216
Lausten/Cossutta Design   191
Lennon and Associates   33, 99
Levine, Huntley, Schmidt & Beaver, Inc.   39, 88, 111, 112
Lord, Geller, Federico, Einstein, Inc.   70, 126, 127, 128
M&Co.   185
MacIntosh Communications, Inc., Rob   81
Madsen and Kuester, Inc.   174
Manwaring, The Office of Michael   175, 204, 205
Marks Group, The   177
Mauk Design   27, 173
McCaffrey and McCall   38, 78, 85
McCann-Erickson, Inc.   106
McCann Erickson, P.R.   121
McNaney, Pat   117
ME Graphics   172, 206
Mednick & Associates, Scott   254, 255
Megaphone   156
Mendelsohn/Zien Advertising   43, 45, 63, 132, 136
Mendoza Dillon & Associados   118
Meyer Design, Inc., Robert   168
Mobium   196
Morla Design, Inc.   176
Muir Cornelius Moore, Inc.   33, 99
NBC Advertising & Promotion   70, 142
Ogilvy & Mather   72
Ogilvy & Mather Direct   92
Ogilvy & Mather—Los Angeles   135
Patterson, George Advertising/Melbourne—AC&R/DHB & BESS   114, 123, 124, 125
Pentagram   27, 169, 175
Pentagram Design   28, 29, 30, 166, 167, 200, 201, 204, 223
Pentagram, San Francisco   191
Peterson & Company   165, 197, 206, 228, 231
Playboy Magazine   228
Point Design/Point Communications   207

Provident Companies   190
Rabuck & Fox   206
Reyes Art Works   109, 157
Road & Track Specials   231
Runyan & Associates, Robert Miles   26, 164,
169, 171
Samata Associates   168, 205
San Francisco Focus   226
Seiniger Advertising   234
Sekuler & Associates, Alan   244
Shapiro Design Associates, Inc.   188, 207
Sheridan Assoc. Inc., Keith   35, 221
Sibley/Peteet Design, Inc.   101, 202, 203
Silver Films, Inc., Tony   55, 239, 242
Silverman Advertising Design   182
Skouras Pictures   236
Smith & Associates, Doug   237
Spear Graphic Design, Jeffrey   234
SteeleWorks Design, Inc.   35, 220, 251
Sundown Studios   62
Sussman/Prejza & Co.   199
Swieter Design   209, 211
Syfred, Elgin   89, 93, 94
Takeda Designs, Marsha   244
TL-R & Associates   234
Tracey Shiffman Roland Young Design
Group   27, 164, 175
Tracy-Locke   73, 79, 104
United Western Studios   161
Valentine, Inc., Robert   101, 210
Van Dyke Company   26, 165, 168, 172, 195,
210
Van Noy Group, The   96, 98
Walter/Johnsen   198
Warner Bros. Records   251, 252
Waters Design, Phil   230
Weller Institute for the Cure of Design,
Inc., The   224
White + Associates   26, 202
Wondriska Associates, Inc.   196, 198, 221
Works of Art   211
Young & Rubicam, Chicago   63, 160, 161

A&M Records, Inc.   86, 249, 252, 253
a-ha   251
Abbeville Press, Inc.   35, 36, 220, 222
AIGA / New York   194
Alex Brands   171
Amblin Entertainment   41, 245
American Express   92
American Honda Motor Co., Inc.   68, 84
American Institute of Graphic Arts   30, 223
American President Companies   29, 201
American President Lines   200
AMI   133
ANEW (Way of Wellness)   216
Apple   37, 67
Apple Computer, Inc.   32, 42, 44, 46, 47, 63,
71, 73 74, 97, 99, 119, 122, 137, 141, 143, 144, 151,
152, 153, 188
Appleton Design, Inc.   205
AR Lithographers   208
Architectural Foundation
of Los Angeles   207
ARCO   70
ARCO / LA Central Library   70, 160
Art Center College of Design   27, 32, 175,
180, 191
Arts Illustrated   231
Atlanta Ad Club   95
Atlantic Monthly Press   35, 221
Atlantic Records   250
Attitudes of Read Worth   177
Auto Gallery Publishing Company   225, 227
Automobile Quarterly Magazine   230
Bartels & Carstens   61
Ben Hogan Co.   73, 79
Big Brothers of Greater Los Angeles   69
Blue Cross of Washington and Alaska   93, 94
Boardwalk & Baseball   157
Bob Wellen, Ulano   193
Bonnie Raitt   252
Borden   83
Boston Symphony Orchestra   196
Business Week   30, 101
California Institute of the Arts   191
California Magazine   230
Cambridge Nutrition Canada Ltd.   183
Capitol Cities / ABC   243
Capitol Records, Trudy Green   248
Capitol Records, Inc.   69
CBS Entertainment   243

Chez Helene   194
Chi-Chi's Mexican Restaurants   160
Chris Hopson, Tower Records   193
Cigna Healthplan   64
Cineplex Odeon Films   234
Citizen Watches   88
Cole Martinez Curtis   26, 202
Collins Publishers   224
Community Redevelopment Agency   30, 223
Computerland   148, 149, 150
Concept Arts   234
Council for Advancement & Support
of Education   197
Cronan Design   211
Curtice-Burns, Inc.   168
Datacopy Corporation   165
Dataproducts   172, 206
Denton Design Associates   200
Disney Channel, The   57, 247
Disney Studios, Walt   236
(di-zin), Akbar Alijamshid   196
DMB&B   189
Drexel Burnham Lambert   167
Drug Free America   36, 72, 74, 77
East Texas State University   199
Entertainment Network, The   244
Entertainment Technologies   27, 173
Epic   249
Esprit   206
Esprit De Corp.   28, 34, 35, 177, 186, 203,
204, 223
ESRI   96
Expeditors International   165
Factory Fashion Works, The   158
Foster Farms   48, 49, 50, 62, 82, 107, 120, 129,
130, 131
Foster's Lager   114, 123, 124, 125
Fox Broadcasting   56, 64, 246
Fox Photo   169
Friends of the Golden Gate Bridge   198
G. Heileman Brewing Co.   63, 161
General Dynamics   140
General Electric Plastics   201
Generra Sportswear   176, 181
Georgia Pacific Paper Company   29, 177
Getty Museum, The J. Paul   224
Gillette   121
Gray Baumgarten Layport, Inc.   62
Hal Riney & Partners   183
Hawaiian Punch   161
Health & Tennis Corporation   159

Hechinger Company   166
Heckscher Museum   190
Hi-Tops Video   254, 255
Hickory Farms   182
Highway Safety Products   211
Home Savings of America   138
IBM Corporation   70
IBM Entry Systems Division / P. Armstrong /
L.D. Green / M. Psaras   33, 99
IBM PS / 2   126, 127, 128
Immunex Corporation   169
Infinity Broadcasting / KROQ Radio   91
Institute for Mental Health
Initiatives   188, 207
Interleaf Inc.   188
International Missing Children's
Foundation   93
International Paper Company   202
Island Pictures   235, 236
Jack Roth   249
Jaguar   80
JanSport   89
John and Laura Evans   203
Karson-Higgins-Shaw Communications, Inc.
and American Film Marketing
Association   237
Kemper Reinsurance   168
Kentucky Fried Chicken—Southern California
Co-Op   91
KNBC-TV   244
Knott's Berry Farm   90
Kroger Stores   158
La Jolla Museum of Contemporary Art   192
Lackawanna   33, 99
Laise Adzer   206
Le Menu Frozen Foods   72
Leason Pomeroy Associates   175
Les Sechler, Fashion Institute of Design and
Merchandising   204
Levi Strauss & Co.   176, 180
Lewis Browand   134
Lincoln Savings   157
Los Angeles Herald Examiner   92
Los Angeles Mitsubishi Dealer Advertising
Association   110
Lucca Delicatessan Inc.   32, 213
Lydall, Inc.   167

M & Co. Labs   185
Mac B Sports   100
Main Magazine   231
Maine Teenage Males Preventing
Pregnancy   156
Manhattan Confectioners, Inc.   210
Marcovici Designs   180
MarineWorld   91
Martex/West Point Pepperell   28, 178
Martin Lawrence Limited Editions   167
Maxwell House   226
MCA Records, Inc.   251
McGuire-Nicholas Manufacturing
Company   98
McIlhenny Company, The   104
Mead Paper Company   26, 171, 172
Mercedes-Benz of North America   38, 78, 85
Merrill Lynch   170
Mexicana   60
MGM/UA Communications   166
Micom   164
Miller Brewing Company   118
Minneapolis Arts   173, 179
Mitsubishi Electric Sales America   72, 75, 76
Mobium   196
Monadnock Paper Mills, Inc.   81
Museum of Contemporary Art, The   27, 175
National Dairy Board   106
NBC Corporate Relations   70
NBC Entertainment   142
NBC-TV   243
New City YMCA, The   196
New Mexico Communicating Artists   204
New York International Festival
of Arts, Inc.   197, 209, 213
Newport Harbor Art Museum   174
Noritsu America Corporation   71, 73, 98, 103, 187
North Memorial Medical Center   60
Oingo Boingo   198
OMD   248
Orion Pictures Corporation   236, 239, 242
Orthopaedic Hospital   164
Pamper's   139
Paragon Group   215
Paramount Network Television   33, 244
Paramount Pictures   234
Partners National Health Plans   207

Paul Ison Design   208
Penguin's Frozen Yogurt   43, 45, 132, 136
Pentagram Design   28, 204
Phillip Cooke   206
Pirelli Tire Corporation   103
Pizza Hut, Inc.   159
Playboy Enterprises, Inc.   228
Porsche Cars North America   61, 75, 105, 108, 113
Potlatch Corporation, Northwest
Division   174
Pratt & Whitney Aircraft   195
Provident Companies   190
Random House, Inc.   221
Real Art Ways   173, 190
Reebok   31, 70, 87, 102
Ria Lenerke/RCA   251
Road & Track Specials/DCI Magazines   231
Rouse Company, The   216
S.D. Warren Company   31, 96, 97, 170, 178
S.W. Bell Telephone   102
Samata Associates   205
Samuel Goldwyn Company, The   235
San Diego Design Center   208
San Francisco Museum of Modern Art   202
Saxon Medical, Inc.   209
Scandiline Furniture Corporation   100
Sea World Orlando   90
Sea World San Diego   116
Sea World Ohio   40, 115
Seagrams   71
Seton Medical Center   194
Silver Reed   135
Simpson Paper Company   170, 171, 174, 192, 201, 205, 217
Skateboarding Mag   228, 229
Smith Barney   172
Southern California Honda Dealers
Association   61, 62, 65
Society for Savings/Connecticut Historical
Society   221
Sonia Kashuk Hair & Makeup   210
Southern California Acura Dealers
Association   63
Southern Methodist University   165, 228
Speedo   184
Stanford Design Conference   179
Stuart Clugston   210
Texas Monthly Press   222
Times Mirror Company   169

Tradewell   182, 214
Trammell Crow Company   101
Trudy Green   253
Tupperware Home Parties   117
U.S. Forest Service   155
U.S. Grant Hotel   100
UCLA   226
United Technologies Corporation   195
Vestron Video   254
Virgin Records America, Inc.   248
Vuarnet-France   184, 187
Wadsworth Atheneum   198
Walker Art Center   31, 196, 230
Walker Art Center Book Shop   101
Warner Bros.   236
Warner Communications, Inc.   166
Warner Home Video/Danielle Beatty   255
Watters & Watters   211
Webster Industries—Good Sense   39, 111, 112
Weller Institute for the Cure
of Design, Inc., The   224
Western Direct Maketing   191
Western States Advertising Agencies
Association   96
Weyerhaeuser Paper Company   26, 168
Winger Muscle Therapy   209
WMJX FM Radio   51, 52, 53, 145, 146, 147
Woman's Building, Los Angeles   199
World Company, LTD.   203, 207
World Wildlife Fund (WWF)   206
Xavier Hair Salon   103
Yamaha International   109
Yamaha Motor Corporation, USA   62, 71, 74
YMCA—Metro   60, 66
YMCA   154

DESIGN/CREATIVE DIRECTOR
ART DIRECTOR/DESIGNER

Antista, Tom   193
Appleton, Robert   173, 190
Barab, Marie   221
Barazzuol, Roberto   206
Beach, Pearl   198
Biondi, Rose   28, 178
Broyles, Kathie   235
Cho, Yee-Ping   174
Cowell, Lucinda   236
Cronan, Michael Patrick   179, 211
Cross, James   170, 174
Davidson, Carol   181
Edelstein, David   181
Edelstein, Nancy   181
French, Lanny   181
Fuller, Craig   192
Gelfand, Dan   235
Greiman, April   31, 196
Hauser, Cliff   235
Hinrichs, Kit   27, 175
Lawler, Linda   211
Passehill, Christopher   190
Pellegrino, Cheryl   236
Sebastian, James   28, 178
Shakery, Niel   27, 175
Sheridan, Keith   221
Skjei, Michael   170
Smith, Gwyn   27, 175
Van Dyke, John   210
Wondriska, William   198
Yagi, Tamotsu   28, 203, 205, 223

AGENCY/STUDIO

Antista Design   193
Appleton Design Inc.   173, 190
Concept Arts   236
Cronan Design   179, 211
Cross Associates   170, 174
Crouch + Fuller   192
Designframe, Inc.   28, 178
Edelstein Associates Advertising Inc.   181
Esprit   206
Esprit Graphic Design Studio   28, 205, 223
Greiman, Inc., April   31, 196
Pentagram   27, 175
Sheridan Associates, Inc., Keith   221
Skouras Pictures   236
Van Dyke Company   210
Walter/Johnson   198

CLIENT

Art Center College of Design   27, 175
Chris Hopson/Tower Records   193
Clugston, Stuart   210
(di-zin), Akbar Alijamshid   196
Esprit   206
Esprit de Corp.   223
Esprit Graphic Design Studio   28, 205
Generra Sportswear   181
La Jolla Museum of Contemporary Art   192
Martex/West Point Pepperell   28, 178
Oingo Boingo   198
Random House, Inc.   221
Real Art Ways   170, 190
Samuel Goldwyn Company, The   235
Simpson Paper Company   170, 174
Stanford Design Conference   179
Wadsworth Atheneum   198
Walker Art Center   31, 196
Warner Bros.   236
World Company, Ltd.   203

REAL CHARACTERS

Andresen Typographics

LA Melrose: **213** 464-4106
LA 6th Street: **213** 384-2525
LA West: **213** 452-5521
Orange County: **714** 250-4450
San Francisco: **415** 421-2900
Phoenix: **602** 254-1710
Tucson: **602** 623-5435

TYPOGRAPHERS

There's no finer freedom than
the freedom to choose top quality and
terrific turnaround. Every time. In characters
classic and contemporary.

ALPHAGRAPHIX

213 / 388 • 0401

Andresen Typographics

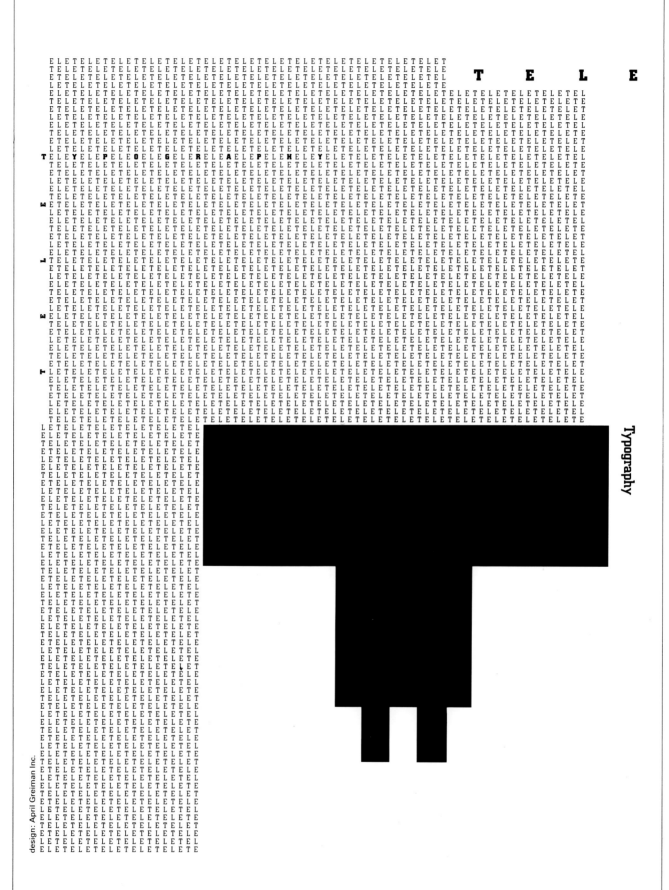

T E L E

Typography

design: April Greiman Inc.